WITHDRAWN

TURKEY'S FOREIGN POLICY
IN TRANSITION
1950-1974

SOCIAL, ECONOMIC AND POLITICAL
STUDIES OF THE MIDDLE EAST
ÉTUDES SOCIALES, ÉCONOMIQUES ET
POLITIQUES DU MOYEN ORIENT

VOLUME XVII

KEMAL H. KARPAT
and Contributors

TURKEY'S FOREIGN POLICY
IN TRANSITION
1950-1974

LEIDEN
E.J. BRILL
1975

TURKEY'S FOREIGN POLICY IN TRANSITION

1950–1974

BY

KEMAL H. KARPAT
and Contributors

LEIDEN
E.J. BRILL
1975

Comité de rédaction — Editorial committee

F. Barth (University of Bergen), E. Gellner (London School of Economics), C. Issawi (Columbia University), S. Khalaf (American University of Beirut), M. F. al-Khatib (Cairo University), P. Marthelot (École Pratique des Hautes Études, Paris), S. H. Nasr (Arya-Mehr University of Technology, Tehran), M. Soysal (Ankara University), M. Zghal (Université de Tunis).

Rédacteur — Editor

C. A. O. van Nieuwenhuijze

Le but de la collection est de faciliter la communication entre le grand public international et les spécialistes des sciences sociales étudiant le Moyen-Orient, et notamment ceux qui y résident. Les ouvrages sélectionnés porteront sur les phénomènes et problèmes contemporains: sociaux, culturels, économiques et administratifs. Leurs principales orientations relèveront de la théorie générale, de problèmatiques plus précises, et de la politologie: aménagement des institutions et administration des affaires publiques.

The series is designed to serve as a link between the international reading public and social scientists studying the contemporary Middle East, notably those living in the area. Works to be included will be characterized by their relevance to actual phenomena and problems: whether social, cultural, economic, political or administrative. They will be theory-oriented, problem-oriented or policy-oriented.

ISBN 90 04 04323 3

Copyright 1975 by E. J. Brill, Leiden, Netherlands

All rights reserved. No part of this book may be reproduced or translated in any form, by print, photoprint, microfilm, microfiche or any other means without written permission from the publisher

PRINTED IN THE NETHERLANDS

TABLE OF CONTENTS

Introduction	1
MEHMET GONLUBOL, NATO and Turkey	13
GEORGE S. HARRIS, Turkey and the United States	51
KEMAL H. KARPAT, Turkish Soviet Relations	73
KEMAL H. KARPAT, Turkish and Arab-Israeli Relations	108
SUAT BILGE, The Cyprus Conflict and Turkey	135
KEMAL H. KARPAT, War on Cyprus: The Tragedy of Enosis	186
BARAN TUNCER, External Financing of the Turkish Economy and its Foreign Policy Implications	206
Presidents, Prime Ministers and Foreign Ministers of Turkey, 1938-1974	225
Selected Bibliography on Turkish Foreign Policy with Emphasis on the Period, 1950-1974	226
Index	232

INTRODUCTION

The purpose of this book is to study the foreign policy of Turkey after WW II, and especially after the 1960's, when the country began to improve its relations with the Soviet Union and the non-aligned bloc while maintaining its affiliation with NATO and other Western international organizations. The Turkish foreign policy, and especially the debates about it in 1960-74, reflect rather accurately the state of mind, the currents of thought which prevailed in the country at the time, and could forecast the possible direction of Turkey's domestic policies and international relations. One can state firmly from the very beginning that the foreign policy of Turkey after WW II had a profound effect upon the social and economic structure, the political regime and the cultural outlook of the country. It was partly as the consequence of this policy that Turkey underwent a period of development and structural transformation which manifested itself in the rise of expectations, dissatisfaction with the slow rate of economic development and search for a new social and political understanding and interpretation of the consequence of the association with the West. On the other hand, the foreign policy of Turkey after 1964, was to a large extent a consequence and reaction to her alliance with and expectations from the West.

In order to place the Turkish foreign policy in 1960-1974, in a proper perspective, it is necessary to review first, the major events which produced Turkey's alignment with the West, second, the objectives of her foreign policy, and third, the manner in which Turkey understood and implemented her pro-Western policy.

The Turkish foreign policy after World War II was a by-product and an extension of the Western policy towards the Soviet Union, and subsequently towards the Middle East and the third world in general. The full association of Turkey with the West occurred through the Truman Doctrine in 1947, admission to NATO in 1952, the Eisenhower Doctrine in 1957, as well as through membership at various dates in practically all major European regional organizations such as The Council of Europe, OECD and the Common Market. The identification of Turkey with the Western foreign policy was caused by the Soviet denunciation of the Treaty of Friendship of 1925, and its demands for territory in the northern part of the country and bases on the Straits. Both, the Soviet demands and the Western opposition to them, the latter materialized in the form of strong support for the Turkish decision to resist the Soviets,—stemmed from the global policies of USSR and USA respectively, and their assessment of the strategic and military potential of Turkey in promoting their own foreign policy or in containing the ambition of the other. The cold war highlighted the importance of Turkey because of her control over the Straits which linked the Black Sea to the Mediterranean, and over the high plateau of Anatolia which commanded the entire Fertile Crescent down to the Persian Gulf and Red Sea. The importance of Turkey for the Big Powers in the past, as in the present, has varied in relation to the intensity of their rivalry and the role attributed to the Straits and Turkey in the solution of their conflicts. The Soviet Union claimed that the defense of the Straits, hence the foreign policy of Turkey, was linked directly to her internal security, while the United States and NATO looked upon Turkey as a forward defensive, and in case of need as an offensive, outpost. As might be expected, neither bloc felt any direct moral urge to put Turkey's interests above its own. In fact each bloc assumed that Turkey's interests would be served best through a total acceptance of its own foreign policy line. Turkey had limited freedom of choice in the conflict of the big powers. The Soviet demands in 1946, coming on the heels of a period of friendship with Turkey and rejection of the old Czarist expansionist aims, proved that the Straits preserved their vital geopolitical importance for the Russians, even in the era of super power status achieved by the Soviet Union. It was the immensity of Soviet military power and her insatiable ambition for territorial and ideological expansion in 1946, which forced Turkey to seek full affiliation with the West almost at any price, and embark at the same time upon a policy of identification with the West in the economic, social political and cultural fields. Probably at no time in history was the Westernization of Turkey so intensive and one-sided as in the period after WW II, and this thanks to the pressure coming from the Soviet Union. The Soviets realized quickly that their policy towards Turkey had forced her to seek close identification with the West, and tried to correct this policy almost immediately after Stalin's death in 1953. However, the new approach did not bear fruit until 1964, when conditions compelled Turkey to re-evaluate the conduct of her foreign policy.

There has been considerable speculation lately whether Turkey wanted, and could have pursued, a somewhat neutralist policy immediately after WW II. It is difficult to understand how a small country such as Turkey, sandwiched between two giant blocs, and given the international circumstances prevailing in 1945-50, could have pursued a neutralist policy. In reality Republican Turkey conducted her foreign policy practically since her inception in the 1920ies, leaning upon and with the support of one of the Great Powers, although she avoided formal affiliation with any one of them until 1939. Indeed, until 1936-39, the Turkish foreign policy decisions likely to affect USSR were taken in consultation with the Soviet Union as the result of good neighborly policy initiated by Lenin and Ataturk, although Turkey maintained friendly relations with the West. Turkey realigned herself closely with the West through an alliance with England and France in 1939, due in part to the Soviet Union's rapprochement to Germany and search for spheres of influence in the south to the detriment of Turkey. Thus, one may say that Turkish foreign policy before WW II was based on friendship with one of the Big Powers but without being totally submerged in the policy of that Power or by remaining isolated from the rest of the world. This policy was undermined in 1938-39, after the Soviets began to pursue a policy designated to isolate Turkey and deprive her of Western support. It should be noted that the USSR advanced her territorial demands in 1945-46, during a period when Turkey was relatively isolated due to the displeasure of the West over her hesitation to engage in war against Germany in 1941-44. Consequently, it is impossible to substantiate the view that the Soviet Union advanced territorial claims because she feared that the Turkish foreign policy of alliance with the West posed a threat to her security and she wanted to reassure herself by acquiring territory and military bases on the Straits. The facts mentioned above and analyzed at some length in Chapter IV, indicated that it was the Soviet Union which upset the traditional friendly Turkish policy towards her.

The Turkish alignment with the West developed to a large

extent in 1946-59, in the form of Turkish-United States relations. The United States attached high importance to Turkey during this period, well above the actual military and economic potential of the country. This importance derived from the special role the United States expected Turkey to perform in the Middle East politics, from her unique position in the defense of eastern Mediterranean—as well as from a string of military bases and a sophisticated network of intelligence-gathering devices located near the Soviet border. During the early part of this period, Turkey was treated almost as though she were a Big Power. One enthusiastic American stated publicly that she really was. Obviously such compliments pleased enormously at that time some foreign ministry officials in Turkey, whose exaggerated Big Power complex inherited from the Ottoman times had not been trimmed to its realistic size yet.

The determining question was whether Turkey's national interests in the Western alliance were being served as well as the interests of the NATO itself. As long as Turkey believed that her alliance with the West served optimally her national interests, she pursued a policy of almost passive acquiescence to the decisions of NATO and the United States.

The basic aims of Turkish foreign policy have been the preservation of national independence, territorial integrity, and modernization. These are foreign policy objectives natural for any country. But for Turkey, those objectives acquired added significance. She had emerged as a national state after the final disintegration of the multi-national Ottoman state in 1918-20, through a desperate struggle for survival against the invading forces of Greece, England and France. Still struggling to build a viable unitary nation by overcoming regional and cultural differences, Turkey was overly sensitive to any outside threat likely to challenge her unity and nationhood. A policy of peace, as embodied in the principle "peace at home peace abroad" enunciated by Ataturk was deemed to serve best her long-range interests. Consequently, Turkey felt that close association with the West would secure her peace and assure her independence.

The Turkish drive for modernization and the keen desire to achieve it as rapidly as possible acquired a new meaning and a new direction after affiliation with the West in 1946/50. Modernization has been a fundamental state principle in Republican Turkey as its insertion in the Constitution in 1937, as *inkilapçılık* or reformism indicate it. Originally, modernism was understood as a dual movement towards acquiring the civilization (medeniyet) of the West, and towards developing a national culture based on the Turkish folklore, language and history. The dual aspects of modernization as civilization and national culture, whatever its merits, stemmed from the teachings of Ziya Gökalp, the ideologue of Turkish nationalism. However, after 1950, modernization came to be understood, much more in practice than in theory, almost as a total imitation of the West, and as a drive for achieving higher living standards or maximum material comfort. Probably the lifting of political restrictions, the dismissal of the state as the force guiding the drive for national culture, the abandonment of some of the early ideals of the Republic after the one-party rule ended in 1950, the participation of the economically powerful and of the conservative groups in politics facilitated if not accelerated this process of indiscriminate imitation and adoption of everything Western as being inherently good, just and superior. The reaction to this understanding of modernization which emerged after 1960 was to be equally strong and indiscriminate in rejecting almost everything Western.

Turkey developed immediately after WW II an economic dimension to her foreign policy which gave in turn a new meaning and direction to the idea of modernization. In fact, international economic aid came to play a vital part in determining the structural transformation of Turkey, and in cementing her foreign policy affiliation with the West. Originally in the 1920's, Turkey was adverse to borrowing abroad because of the bad memory left by Ottoman experience with such borrowings. However, heavy military expenditure in 1939-45, amounting to 40-60 per cent of the budget, drained Turkey's financial resources and produced economic hardship for the population. The idea of economic development which began to acquire importance in the early 1930's, emerged as a capital goal after WW II. Indeed economic development appeared as a key priority in the program of the ruling Republican Party, as early as 1945-46, when it approached the Export-Import Bank for a loan of 300 million dollars. Thus it was clear that Turkish economic development had to be financed in part, at least for some time, by capital from abroad. Thus, by the early 1950's economic development based on foreign assistance became a vital issue in Turkish domestic politics as parties traded economic promises for votes, and in the process mobilized the economic expectations of the masses. The West, notably the United States, provided initially rather generous military and economic assistance to Turkey in the hope of strengthening her resistance to the Soviet Union. Turkey received some five billion dollars until 1970, although only a limited amount of this sum was invested in projects of truly long range value. This aspect of foreign aid was going to be bitterly criticized after 1964.

Early in the 1950's the Democratic Party government of Adnan Menderes seemed to have decided that the West had an overwhelming military and strategic interest in Turkey and would finance its development plans, however extravagant and ill planned these might be. In turn, the government outdid itself in fulfilling its share of the bargain by meeting fully its military and political obligations as attested by numerous and very generous bilateral agreements signed with the United States. Some sentimental and historical factors also helped to strengthen the special political and economic relations which developed between Turkey and the United States. The American public greeted with undisguised admiration the bravery of the Turkish soldiers fighting in Korea in 1950-53, who had sailed on U.S. ships thousands of miles away from home to defend on the shores of Asia, freedom, democracy, and ultimately the civilization of the West. The irony in the situation was drummed up in the sixties after the Turkish involvement in Korea had played its part in foreign relations, and regardless whether one liked it or not, it acquired a place in the Turkish epic. The new role as partners of the West, and especially the uninhibited friendship of the United States, the defender of the Western civilization was in some Turkish eyes the proof that they were finally accepted and became part of the Western world. With an almost total dedication to a cause encountered only among new converts to a faith Turkey appeared to have become more Westernist than the West.

The economic aid coming amidst this favourable political and cultural atmosphere had far reaching impact not only in diversifying the social structure, but also in creating a series of attitudes and problems similar to the developed countries of the West. The far reaching social and political impact of the foreign aid may be attributed to at least four factors. One, Turkey had developed in

1923-50, the political, social and organizational infra structure necessary for economic development. Two, the introduction of a parliamentary democracy which accompanied the economic development placed emphasis on individual happiness thought to be achievable through increased consumption and material welfare. Three, the economic aid was coupled almost with unlimited Turkish access to technical assistance, training and education in USA and West-Europe, which in due time produced a small but highly capable group of economists, engineers, business administrators, etc. These people became instrumental in appraising more objectively Turkey's problems and in proposing solutions accordingly. Four, the security provided by the Western alliance against outside aggression gave Turkey a much needed period of peace necessary to consolidate her unity and to dedicate her efforts to internal reconstruction.

Finally, it must be mentioned that until the 1960's the Turkish foreign policy was made and carried out by a small group of foreign officials with a minimum of discussion either in the press or Parliament. The foreign service personnel represented a group of the best educated, the most Westernized, but also the most aristocratic and farthest removed from the country's realities among the civil service. Political parties, in turn, had adopted a common view on foreign policy and accepted government proposals with a minimum of debate or dissension. Thus, foreign policy was kept out of domestic politics. However, already by 1957, there were signs that the opposition Republican Party was critical of some government decisions and would eventually make foreign policy subject to public debate.

The changes in the Turkish foreign policy after 1960-64, consisted in large measure of a reevalution, reinterpretation and reaction to the foreign policy commitments made in the past two decades. All this was caused in turn by the detente in the relations between East and West, which decreased the strategic and military importance of Turkey, by the rise of new social forces in the country, as well as by the creation of political conditions conducive to public debate. The beginning of this movement towards foreign policy reappraisal may be traced first to the conditions created by the revolution of 1960. Thus, the Constitution of 1961 established extensive freedom of thought and discussion, and was consequently instrumental in subjecting foreign policy matters to public debate in the press and the Parliament. The Legislature, although still following closely the advice of the professionals within the Foreign Ministry became actively involved in making the foreign policy of Turkey. Meanwhile, a purge in the Foreign Ministry early in the 1960's led to the retirement of many old time diplomats and allowed a younger generation, trained better and atuned to the realities of the country, to assume key positions. Finally, a Marxist Labor Party established in 1961 gradually made foreign policy a major issue in its attacks on the government by accusing it of collusion with the West and its capitalist system.

The concrete causes leading to Turkish disenchantment with the West after 1960/4 appeared first in the form of dissatisfaction with the amount of economic aid, and especially with the strings attached as to its allocation and spending. The removal by the United States of the Jupiter missiles from Turkey in 1963, presumably in exchange for the removal of Soviet missiles from Cuba, without approval or consultation with the government created deep apprehension. This was considered a convincing proof that the United States used Turkish territory without much regard for national sovereignty. Already, in 1958, the use by USA of Turkish bases in landing troops in Lebanon, had given place to criticism; in fact it was the first overt dissension over foreign policy. It was apparent that when American interests demanded it, the United States would not hesitate to engage in deals with the USSR or other nations at the expense of Turkey. This was followed by the failure of the West to support Turkey in the Cyprus dispute, and the United States opposition to Turkish plans in 1964 and 1967 to land troops on this island as entitled by treaties. The Cyprus dispute produced an open clash between the national interest of Turkey and the interests of the United States and NATO, and forced Turkey to place her own national interest above her international commitments. The ensuing discussion about the bilateral agreements signed with the U.S. revealed that these had been enacted at random and had deprived Turkey of her sovereign rights over some areas used as military bases. Finally, Turkey became painfully aware during the Cyprus debates in the United Nations that she had been isolated from most of the countries in the world.

The basic Turkish reaction to all these adverse conditions was to strive to regain freedom of initiative in foreign affairs, to strengthen her bargaining position within and outside the Western alliance, to break out of isolation, and to lessen her economic dependence on the West. These were a series of new goals which called for Turkey to rely on her own resources, to build new communication with the Socialist bloc and Third World nations, while loosening at the same time her ties to the West. Turkey never contemplated a total revision of her foreign policy nor a complete severing of her ties to the West. Yet, the pitfalls in the situation were more than obvious since the rapprochement to the Socialist countries and the Third World called for a series of political, cultural and ideological adjustments and compromises which in some ways conflicted with the political and ideological course followed in the previous decades. The question for Turkey was how to carry out the new foreign policy and where to stop so as not to jeopardize the gains secured in the past and to compromise her long-range interests in the future. It was to be, as a Turkish statesman put it, a policy designated to "rely upon a balance between alliance with the West and friendship with the East." The success of the new policy depended on making the right decision but also on possessing the skill to make the proper move at the right time and use most effectively the available resources. For a small country the efficient use of diplomatic skill is far more vital than a big nation which can always use economic or military power to overcome its diplomatic blunders and inefficiency. Turkey could not afford to make a mistake in foreign affairs, consequently she had to move with utmost caution.

The Turkish foreign policy after 1964, aimed first at gathering international support for her Cyprus policy, which was incidentally a legitimate cover for achieving necessary adjustments in other spheres of foreign relations. The major move consisted of a rapprochement to the Soviet Union and the Socialist bloc, which was achieved through a series of visits by high officials. At the same time, Turkey began placing restrictions on U.S. and NATO in the use of military facilities located on her territory, while allowing the leftist groups to organize and spread relatively freely its own teaching. Parallel to the rapprochement to the USSR, Turkey improved considerably her relations with the

Arab countries and the Third World nations, while striving to maintain a neutral policy toward the Arab-Israeli dispute. She renegotiated with the U.S. the bilateral agreements—and gradually reduced the number of American personnel in the country. She also took possession of most of the NATO military bases and shared in the control of nuclear devices located on her soil.

These readjustments in foreign policy were accompanied by a vitriolic anti-American campaign, and a rejection of the West in every field launched mostly by leftist groups which strove earnestly to sever Turkey's ties with NATO and other European organizations. This campaign which created severe internal crises was fed by a resurgent nationalism, a sense of rejection and injustice stemming from the West's attitude in the Cyprus dispute, and especially by a sense of frustration caused by the slow rate of economic development and antagonism against the rich entrepreneurial groups which supposedly acted as ideological agents of the West and put their selfish interests above national welfare. The campaign did not end the Turkish alignment with the West in foreign policy, but eroded deeply the political and cultural influence of the West, and nearly liquidated the good will and admiration Turkey nurtured towards it. This was a crucial development which shall have some effect upon the future of Turkish foreign policy and her political regime. The military intervention on March 12, 1971, which led to the resignation of the Demirel government and the installment of a new cabinet under Nihat Erim, and to a series of drastic measures designated to restore order had its roots in the bitter disagreement between the radical left and the Establishment over the foreign policy and internal regime of Turkey. The two came to be seen as inseparable.

There are now several disquieting international problems which concern Turkey closely. It is obvious that the Soviet naval presence in the Mediterranean and her growing influence in the Arab world has increased the importance of the Turkish Straits. Yet, the Soviets have made no move to discuss the status of the Straits despite a lapse of nearly a quarter of a century since they indicated keen interest in revising the Montreaux Convention of 1936, which governs passage through the waterways. However meanwhile the USSR did its best to improve her relations with Turkey and increase her cultural and economic influence. Meanwhile, notwithstanding a series of difficult problems, the population of Turkey has increased to about 40 million. The standard of living and education has improved, the rate of political education, urbanization and industrialization has intensified and raised substantially the quality of Turkey's people. With a standing army of almost half a million people and a trained reserve of two million mobilizable in about 72 hours, Turkey has the potential to change drastically the balance of power and determine, through a shift of foreign policy the course of politics in the Middle East, the Balkans and beyond. Friends and enemies alike must consider properly not only the contribution or the deterrent represented by Turkey to their foreign policy, but also the new internal and external factors which may compel or persuade Turkey to change her policy in favor or against either side.

This situation was dramatized fully by the Turkish landing in Cyprus on July 20, 1974, as a response to Greek junta's effort to install their own man as President of the island and to declare Enosi's soon. The landing was done against the advice of the United States which feared a war between Greece and Turkey, and despite the fact that Turkey had a rather weak coalition government formed by the social democrats represented by the Republican Party and the conservative National Salvation Party. As it happened repeatedly in the past, Turkey took drastic action when her national security was threatened, and the opposition parties rallied to support unanimously the government's foreign policy. Shortly after the Cyprus events the coalition government disintegrated, not because of dissension on foreign policy but rather to pave the road for national elections and elect a strong government capable of conducting diplomatic negotiations with Greece from a position of strength.

There is no question that the Cyprus problem, discussed at length in two articles in this book, is a turning point in Turkey's foreign relations. The Soviet Union will attempt to capitalize on this event in order to undermine the NATO power in the Mediterranean and increase her influence in Cyprus, Turkey and Greece. Already the withdrawal of Greek armed forces from NATO, the freedom of activity granted to the Communist Party in Greece favor the Soviet Union. One may assume that the anti-American feeling in Greece and the possible Greek actions against the United States and NATO have reached their climax. Greece being so dependent on the United States and Europe for income and support, and in view of her limited options for a foreign policy totally independent from the West, cannot move further into the Soviet camp without undermining her security and the prevailing political regime.

The reaction of the American Congress to Turkish action in Cyprus and her decision to cut off military aid, despite opposition by President Ford and Secretary Kissinger, is an unprecedented action which will show sooner or later its impact in the form of anti-American and anti-NATO reaction and radicalism, especially if Turkey is forced to settle for an unfavorable solution in Cyprus. Consequently one may assume that the potential solution to the Cyprus issue and other potential role of the West in it, will have a powerful effect in charting Turkey's foreign policy. It goes without saying that a major shift in Turkish foreign policy towards non-alignment, or even towards the Soviets, will affect profoundly the position of the West in eastern Mediterranean and the Middle East as well as Arab-Israeli relations. Turkish foreign policy has reached a vital crossroads today and should be assessed accordingly since Turkey's decision, in view of her vital strategic position, will have determining impact upon Asian and African politics.

This book in essence analyzes the Turkish foreign policy developments outlined above by placing chief emphasis on the events occurring chiefly after 1960. It is divided into seven chapters, each one dealing with one major area of Turkish foreign policy, such as relations with NATO, the United States, the USSR, the Middle East, the Cyprus dispute, the war in Cyprus, and foreign aid. Each chapter has been prepared by an author possessing special insight and knowledge about Turkish politics and foreign relations. The book represents and reflects the state of mind prevailing in the country as well as an analysis, a critical justification and explanation of Turkey's foreign policy in the last decade.

December 1974
Madison

Kemal H. Karpat,
University of Wisconsin
Madison

NATO, USA AND TURKEY

MEHMET GONLUBOL

School of Political Science, Ankara

I

From the end of the Second World War until the 1970's, Turkey was confronted with two major foreign policy issues of direct relevance to her vital interests. First, immediately following the Second World War in 1945, the Soviet Union exerted pressure on Turkey for territory. The Soviet claims on Turkey disclosed during a series of meetings held among the Allies to reorganize the post-war world, or, in better terms, to divide war spoils, became eventually subject to an exchange of notes between Turkey on the one hand, and the Soviet Union, the United States and Great Britain on the other. As is well known, Soviet claims comprised a suggestion to revise the Montreux Convention of 1936, governing the right of passage through the Turkish Straits, in order to obtain bases on the Straits, as well as demands to annex some of the eastern provinces of Turkey, and ultimately to induce a change in the existing political regime of the country. This episode led Turkey to abandon overnight her policy of *de facto* neutrality maintained since the beginning of the Second World War, and to seek stronger and closer ties with the West, and particularly with the United States. The relations between Turkey and the USA, which originally took form of foreign aid extended under the Truman Doctrine and the Marshall Plan, eventually resulted in Turkey's membership in NATO in 1952.

The second most important foreign policy issue facing Turkey in the period mentioned was Cyprus. The problem of Cyprus was first posed as an international issue by Greece in 1954-55, in the United Nations. The three countries directly involved in the issue—Turkey, Greece and Great Britain—finally found a solution to the problem by granting conditional independence to Cyprus through the London and Zurich Agreements of 1959 and the Nicosia Treaties of 1960. Relative tranquillity dominated the Cyprus scene until December 1963. At that date President Makarios violated unilaterally and openly the provisions of the abovementioned agreements and treaties with the intention of changing the status of the Republic of Cyprus totally to the advantage of the Greek community. The action of Archbishop Makarios was reflected in turn in the relations between Turkey and Greece. These relations rapidly deteriorated, while new and serious conflicts unresolved to this day arose. The Cyprus issue which caused repeatedly armed conflicts in the interior of the island produced also some very important side-effects in Turkey proper. One of these, and probably the most important effect was the sudden expansion and intensification of a recent anti-Western feeling, which was followed soon by explicit demand on the part of certain circles that Turkey pursue a "neutral" foreign policy, to be proven by the withdrawal from NATO.

In short, while the Soviet demands in 1945/46, brought Turkey into NATO, the Cyprus issue created antagonism to Turkey's membership in NATO, and even resuscitated hostile attitudes in some circles toward the same organization.

The impact of the Soviet demands on Turkish public opinion in 1945-46 was so violent and continuous that even the reluctant admission of Turkey into NATO, in 1952, after prolonged, and at times seemingly hopeless endeavours and diplomatic manouvers, was acclaimed by the Government and the opposition as a great foreign policy victory. From the time marking Turkey's admission into NATO until the beginning of the 1960's, there was practically no reaction in the country against this organization. On the contrary, NATO was praised and exalted in Turkish political circles to such an extent that it was not deemed necessary or even possible to think of a Turkish defense policy outside of this alliance. Some circles in Turkey found the activities of the American information and propaganda agencies in Turkey aimed at "acquainting the Turkish public with NATO" as completely unnecessary on the ground that "these could cause harm rather than sympathy since there existed no anti-NATO feelings in Turkey."

This positive attitude towards NATO continued even after the National Unity Committee came to power through the military revolution of 1960. It remained in power one year and a half. Indeed, the revolutionary government, in one of its first public declarations, reaffirmed Turkey's allegiance to NATO and

CENTO. The reasons that prompted these declarations of fidelity cannot be explained solely in terms of Turkey's real and enthusiastic attachment to NATO. Among the underlying considerations that led the military to this declaration were the following: the persistence of a feeling of insecurity towards the Soviet Union as a result of the negative attitude of the Russians towards various foreign policy issues concerning Turkey, despite the time lapsed since the Soviet territorial demands in 1946 and the public renunciation by the new Soviet leaders of the same demands; a strong yearning towards Westernization, a yearning turned into tradition since the time of Ataturk. This yearning, especially prevalent among the military, was regarded often almost as synonymous with cooperation of any kind with the West. Furthermore, there was the conviction that a strong and disciplined army could be maintained best only through American aid. There was anxiety over the possibility of withdrawal of Western assistance in reaction to a negative Turkish stand on NATO. Such an action could have deteriorated further the economy which was expected to enter a period of stagnation as a consequence of the Revolution of 1960, and thus acerbate internal tensions. Finally the military government feared losing the confidence and support of the West as a result of an all-out attack on NATO and did not want to jeopardize its own survival from the very start. Nevertheless, criticism and objections concerning the Turkish foreign policy in general, and NATO in particular were first heard after 1961. The military government, remaining faithful to its original promise, produced a liberal constitution, and ultimately yielded its powers to a popularly elected civilian government in 1961. The liberal constitution of 1961 allowed leftist ideas which until then had never been expressed in complete freedom to circulate freely. Works by many socialist leaders and writers including those by Marx and Lenin, were translated, and the Turkish domestic and foreign policies were reinterpreted in light of these doctrines. The radical leftists, inspired by Lenin's ideas, used the terms "capitalism" and "imperialism" interchangeably and asserted that the capitalists would inevitably turn into imperialists. Eventually their foreign policy criticism zeroed in on American attitudes toward Turkey, and against NATO. In the opinion of these circles, NATO was the major instrument of American imperialism in the world. Consequently Turkey had no choice but to free herself from NATO, if she wanted to achieve real national independence, and join the nonaligned block made up of underdeveloped countries like herself.

However, until 1964, most people considered such criticism a leftist prejudice, since NATO had not until then, given rise to any "concrete" incidence harmful to Turkish foreign policy. So these ideas were tolerated since very few people paid attention to them.

Most astonishing was the fact that for the first time in the long history of Turkey the government could be criticised openly on its foreign policy, a subject which had been treated as taboo so far. It is true that the First Grand National Assembly of the Turkish Republic that convened during the War of National Independence, under Mustafa Kemal in 1920-22, discussed fully foreign policy issues and leveled criticism to the same.

But from then until the establishment of the multi-party system in 1945, the task of formulating and directing foreign policy lay exclusively within the competence of the Executive. Even after 1945, the discussions on foreign policy did not go beyond the ideological framework of the existing political parties. Indeed, the ideology and the social bases of the political parties was so limited as to leave little room for assessing or criticising the Turkish foreign policy with a new outlook. The appearance of ideological views on foreign policy, and the doctrinaire evaluation of world affairs in general and of Turkish stand and behavior in world politics in particular took place only after 1961, as a result of a wide range of freedoms, granted by the Constitution.

Therefore, by the time clashes between Turks and Greeks broke out in Cyprus in December 1963, unorthodox views falling counter to those promoted by the government as well as an ideological reassessment of Turkish foreign policy had lost much of their taboo character. Several developments coincided to make the Cyprus issue a catalyst of Turkish foreign policy. First, the Turkish public already very alert became interested in world politics. The United States involvement in the war in Vietnam increased while the principle of "peaceful coexistence" propagated by Khruschev as a pillar of foreign policy back in 1956, at the 20th Congress of the Soviet Communist Party, began to be extensively discussed in Turkey as if it were a brand new political idea. All this led to some public tendency towards a re-evaluation of the Turco-Soviet relations and possibly closer economic ties with East European countries. Such economic ties were deemed essential in order to stimulate the economy which had entered a period of stabilization and stagnation as a result of the haphazard economic policies of the Democratic Party. It was under the influence of such internal and external circumstances that the foreign policy views put forth by the radical left found the opportunity to pass an important "test". The Cyprus crisis prepared the ground, in fact necessitated a Turkish intervention on the island in 1964, in order to defend the Turkish community.

The Cyprus problem presented a paradox in itself. Although outside the specific area of interest of the alliance, it involved directly two members of NATO—Greece and Turkey. The Turkish Government, acting on the assumption that the United States was NATO's leading and most powerful member and one of the two super powers which would be affected by any major incident anywhere in the world, informed the U.S. Government of its intention to intervene on the island. The letter sent by President Johnson as answer to the Turkish Prime Minister Ismet Inönü in June 1964, marked the beginning of a change in the Turkish foreign policy. This letter, drafted in the style of a peace agreement dictated to an occupied enemy country, created first utter astonishment and, then, violent reactions not only among leftist circles, but among the public in general. The letter was an indication of the fact that the image of "Turkey" among the government circles in the United States, contrary to the assumptions generally held until then by Turks and propagated by various media, was not a positive one in the least. However, more important and interesting was the section reflecting the American interpretation of NATO. This section of the letter reads:

> I must call your attention, also, Mr. Prime Minister, to the obligations of NATO. There can be no question in your mind that a Turkish intervention in Cyprus would lead to a military engagement between Turkish and Greek forces. Secretary of State Dean Rusk declared at the recent meeting of the Ministerial Council of NATO in The Hague that war between Turkey and Greece must be considered as "literally unthinkable". Adhesion to NATO, in its very essence, means that NATO countries will not wage war on each other. Germany and France have buried centuries of animosity and hostility in becoming NATO allies, nothing less can be expected from Greece and Turkey. Furthermore, a military intervention in Cyprus by Turkey would lead to

> a direct involvement by the Soviet Union. I hope you will understand that your NATO allies have not had a chance to consider whether they have an obligation to protect Turkey against the Soviet Union if Turkey takes a step which results in Soviet intervention without the full consent and understanding of its NATO allies.

The provisions of the 1960 Treaty of Nicosia gave Turkey the right to intervene for the sole purpose of upholding her rights in the Island. But upon the receipt of this letter which arrived shortly before her intended intervention, Turkey abstained from this act. Government officials clearly confirm this fact today.

The section of President Johnson's letter quoted above is important in many respects. First, it indicated that the United States envisaged no enemy for Turkey other than the Soviet Union, and believed that Turkey's rights could be violated only by the Soviet Union. Thus, if another country, even a member of the NATO violated Turkey's rights and interests, the country should have not resisted such an act, let alone invoke the relevant provisions of the North Atlantic Treaty; the NATO interests prevailed over everything else. In other words, to put it more concretely, the American thinking on the Cyprus questions was the following: the important problem in the whole Cyprus issue was the protection of peace, or rather, prevention of war between the two allies of NATO. The violation of Turkey's interests in favor of or by another NATO ally, could not be construed to be a cause for war so far as these did not affect the "NATO community" unfavorably vis-a-vis the Soviet Union. It appeared in fact clear that the United States would apply utmost "influence" to prevent a war of this type. As a matter of fact, President Johnson's intimidating sentence "war between Turkey and Greece must be considered as 'literally unthinkable' ", quoted from the speech by Secretary Rusk, was a clear confirmation of this intention.

There is an even more important implication in President Johnson's letter; the United States did not intend to invoke the NATO mechanism in favor of Turkey, as long as no direct Soviet aggression occurred, even though the most vital Turkish interests were at stake. As the last sentence of the letter quoted above shows it clearly, the Americans tried to justify their stand by referring to Turkey's obligation to consult her NATO allies in this case. This, then, brings several questions to mind. Two of these are of special importance to our discussion. First, under what conditions is an aggression to be regarded as a "direct" one? Second, does the United States seek the approval of its NATO allies when engaging in acts likely to drag them into war? Prime Minister İnönü, in his answer to President Johnson, had the following to say on "direct" aggression:

> The part of your message expressing doubt as to the obligation of the NATO allies to protect Turkey in case she becomes directly involved with the USSR as a result of an action initiated in Cyprus, gives me the impression that there are as between us wide divergence of views as to the nature and basic principles of the North Atlantic Alliance. I must confess that this has been to us the source of great sorrow and grave concern. Any suggestion against a member of NATO will naturally call from the aggressor an effort of justification. If NATO's structure is so weak as to give credit to the aggressor's allegations, then it means this defect of NATO needs really to be remedied. Our understanding is that the North Atlantic Treaty imposes upon all member states the obligation to come forthwith to the assistance of any member victim of an aggression. The only point left to the discretion of the member states is the nature and the scale of this assistance ... In this connection I would like to further point out that the agreements on Cyprus have met with the approval of the North Atlantic Council as early as the start of the United Nations debate on the problem, i.e., even prior to the establishment of the republic of Cyprus, hence long before the occurrence of the events of December 1963.

As for Turkey's responsibility to consult the United States on the question of intervention, the Turkish Prime Minister said:

> In the first place, it is being emphasized in your message that we have failed to consult with the United States when a military intervention in Cyprus was deemed indispensable by virtue of the Treaty of Guarantee. The necessity of a military intervention in Cyprus has been felt four times since the closing days of 1963. From the outset we have taken special care to consult the United States on this matter. Soon after the outbreak of the crisis on December 25, 1963, we have immediately informed the United States of our contacts with the other guaranteeing powers only to be answered that the United States was not a party to this issue ... [When] Mr. George Ball [visited] Ankara [in February 1964], we informed again the United States of the gravity of the situation ... that we might have to intervene at any time.

However, it is clear that contrary to the allegations expressed in President Johnson's letter, the Turkish Government had informed the United States of the gravity of the situation—a type of behavior not usually exercised by the United States in NATO—only to be told that the latter preferred to stay out of the dispute. What is more important for our specific subject is this: how could one relate the policy of noninvolvement pursued by the United States, the strongest power in NATO, to the Explicit provision of Article 5 of the North Atlantic Treaty? If the Soviet Union attacked Turkey, without any provocation, can the United States stay out of the conflict although the conflict may not be of direct interest to her.

The reaction to this letter, the text of which had been kept secret for some time and later obtained by a daily newspaper in an unknown way, was so enormous that it pushed the question of Cyprus to the background. At the time the letter was revealed, the leftist circles had made foreign policy issues more popular than ever before. Subsequently, these circles which had limited themselves to advocating cooperation between Turkey and other developing, non-aligned countries changed their views and became vehemently anti-American and anti-NATO. Posters with slogans such as "No to NATO", "American Imperialism", and "Fully Independent and Truly Democratic Turkey", became visible in the street demonstrations organized by university students. Walls in major cities and in universities were covered with posters carrying these slogans. Beginning early in 1970, demonstrations were accompanied by bombing of American bases in Turkey and the kidnapping of American personnel. Naturally we do not intend to explain the animosity against America and NATO solely in terms of their particular stand in the Cyprus question. The problem may be posed differently. Assuming that Turkey had not faced such a problem as Cyprus and the United States had never been involved in it, or assuming that the turn of events there had favored Turkey, one may ask whether animosity against NATO and the United States would have developed at all? Undoubtedly it would have. Paradoxically, the animosity of the radical leftist circles is not, in reality an animosity directed solely against NATO and the United States, as an organization and as a state. It is a basic animosity towards "Western capitalism" and the "Western way of living". Since the most powerful and effective representatives of these concepts in Turkey are the United States and NATO, these have become the chief targets for attack. In other words, the forces underlying the reasoning of the radical left are ideological and have some public appeal for a variety of complex cultural and social reasons beyond the scope of this paper. Consequently, people with similar ideological aspirations would have seized opportunity to incite animosity against NATO and the United States and would have succeeded, at least partially in their efforts regardless of the Cyprus issue. Yet, we are of the opinion that the Cyprus question and the attitude of the United States on the issue accelerated the development of this animosity and helped its dissemination among the intellectuals and even among the neutral masses at large.

Thus, the American view of NATO that surfaced as a result of the Cyprus problem, affected indirectly the internal development in Turkey, and reactivated and accelerated negative factors of foreign policy. This mutual interaction between domestic and foreign politics, a most natural process certainly, intensified with the help of the communication media and by a rapidly organizing left, brought Turkish political life into a vicious circle from which she has not emerged yet. If one considers the situation objectively, one must admit that some of the criticism related to Turkey's relations with NATO and the United States is justified. But the critics raise also several erroneous objections alongside the justified ones purely on theoretical and ideological grounds, with little respect for the rules of international politics. The switch in policy proposed by the radical left on the issue of Cyprus and related problems provides ample proof to verify the previous statement. These circles displayed a most violent reaction against the United States because she prevented the Turkish intervention in Cyprus in 1964. But then, they made a complete turnabout, rejecting intervention and the partition of the island that would have followed it by labelling such an act "a trick of Western Imperialists". The Turkish Workers' Party (closed formally in 1971) and the other radical leftist organizations adhere to this view. This switch is a consequence of looking at these developments from an ideological point of view suggested by someone else. We believe that the strength acquired recently by the leftists in Cyprus, and the Soviet Union's anti-partition stand, are among the foremost reasons behind this new ideologically oriented line.

We have tried to summarize briefly the reasons underlying

Turkey's desire to enter NATO and the part played by the radical left (and some other segments of public opinion) against NATO. There is one point that needs clarification before proceeding further with more specific and concrete criticism of NATO. In spite of the reaction caused by the Cyprus problem in certain circles against NATO and the United States, and in spite of the anxiety and suspicion displayed by the public, the official circles of Turkey did not revise their original views and attitudes towards NATO. The original attempt to enter NATO was initiated by the People's Republican Party which was in power when the organization was first established in 1949. These efforts were kept alive after the Democratic Party came to power in 1950, and culminated in Turkey's entry into NATO in 1952. During the Democratic Party's tenure in office in 1950-60 there was almost no reaction against NATO, while relations between Turkey and the United States developed at a very rapid pace. Turkey found herself following the policies of the United States almost step by step both within and outside NATO, thus reducing herself to the position of a satellite. The military government which took power in 1960, as mentioned before, brought no important changes in Turkey's relations with NATO except for a change of tone.

Coalition governments headed by the People's Republican Party were in power between 1961 and 1964, that is, during one of the most acute phases of the Cyprus problem. The American attitude on Cyprus and the reaction it created among the youth compelled Prime Minister İnönü, a prudent statesman and a master of foreign policy, to issue the following warning statement: "A new world order could be set up under newly created conditions and Turkey would take her place in that world." But all this did not produce any immediate change since the relations between Turkey and the United States were so complex as to necessitate considerable time before any kind of change could be effected.

Meanwhile the Justice Party which won the elections in 1965, and 1969, with unchallenged majorities formed the government and stayed in power until the Memorandum of March 12, 1971, delivered by the Armed Forces. The Justice Party's domestic and foreign policies were in essence similar to that of the defunct Democratic Party. However, the national and the international situation during the Justice Party rule entered a process of development and change quite different from the one that had prevailed during the Democratic Party. Following the detente between the East and the West, agreement was reached on the partial limitation of nuclear testing, economic relations were improved, and talks on disarmament (SALT) were started. France quit NATO's military organization and Rumania began to follow a more independent foreign policy. These developments were followed by events in Czechoslovakia in 1968 and the internal conflicts in Poland in 1970.

The Turkish developments in the same period followed in a different direction; that is, into social and political restlessness.

The student movements which started at the end of 1968, brought to the foreground once again, alongside domestic issues, the foreign policy problems, especially Turkey's relations with NATO. A series of books, dailies and periodicals discussed at length the new strategy of NATO known as "flexible response", its impact on the security of states located on the flanks of NATO, such as Turkey and the "bilateral agreements" concluded between the United States and Turkey within the framework of NATO. These publications although often tainted by sentimental or ideological biases, nevertheless, shed light on many important points in the relations between Turkey, NATO and the United States, and had considerable impact on the official stand of Turkey on these issues. The Turkish Government, for example, engaged in "normalizing" her relations with the countries in the Eastern Bloc and the Third World, a process initiated in the early 1960's. It also initiated negotiations with the United States in order to reassess the situation pertaining to the "bilateral agreements", a subject of extreme irritation to the Turkish public opinion. Yet, the Turkish Government made no changes in its basic NATO policy and expressed repeatedly the view that there was no need to do so. This situation continued until the resignation of the Demirel Government on March 12, 1971. The new Government was formed by Prime Minister Nihat Erim. A section in the program dedicated to foreign affairs reads as follows:

> We find the strongest external guarantee to our security in our membership in NATO, a defensive organization since the time of its establishment and today. We believe that NATO conforms to our foreign policy objectives [and it is] also a kind of forum where the real conditions of a reliable peace are discussed.

II

Having reviewed the reasons leading to Turkey's admission into NATO and the ensuing reaction against Turkey's participation in NATO in several circles, we shall now turn to the study of two topics of specific interest for a better understanding of the subject under discussion: Why and how was NATO established? Why and how did the Western states admit Turkey into NATO?

The United States, after toying with the idea of returning to her traditional policy of isolationism, ended by renouncing it. Eventually she assumed new commitments in several parts of the world in line with the "containment policy". It is clear that the new American policy was adopted to protect freedom in the world, as much as to protect her own national interests which were challenged at the time. Much of this development was the consequence of the Soviet expansionist policy after the war. The weakness of Europe at the time coupled with a certain ephemeral U.S. view on world politics, as though these had changed overnight their age old nature, brought the Soviets close to achieving the centuries old policies of Imperial Russia. The Soviet Union imported communism into the Eastern European countries under its occupation and then turned them into satellites.

Indeed, the American hopes to continue the war-time cooperation with the Soviet Union came to a halt in 1947. At this time the Soviet demands began to take on a turn totally contradictory to the political and economic interests of the United States. Neither the Truman Doctrine and the Marshall Plan, nor the Mutual Aid Treaty between Britain, France and the Benelux countries, were powerful enough to stop the Soviet expansion. Finally the coup in Czechoslovakia and the Berlin Crises brought developments to a climax.

Meanwhile it became quite clear by the end of the 1940's that the American nuclear monopoly could not hinder Soviet expansion. Moreover, it was not too difficult to foresee that American nuclear monopoly would not last long, that sooner or later the Soviets would produce the atomic bomb and would, thus, create a nuclear balance.

NATO was founded amidst these conditions on April 4, 1949, with the participation of twelve North Atlantic countries, but without Turkey. At this date the Soviet threats on Turkey, though they had quieted down, had neither been completely lifted nor officially renounced. The uncompromising attitude of Britain and that of the United States regarding the Turkish Straits, undoubtedly contributed to this state of affairs. Still, what was most effective in preventing the Soviets from escalating their claims into an armed attack was the stand taken by the Turkish Government not to yield but fight if necessary to the end. The Turkish Army kept mobilized since the end of the Second World War was ready for war.

The Turkish application for membership in NATO in 1949 was rejected despite the fact that she was one of the first countries to receive American aid after the war. The rejection created anxiety throughout the country chiefly because in spite of American aid to Turkey, the Soviet policies continued to remain aggressive as evidenced by a series of incidents. Furthermore, the rejection created considerable anxiety as to the wisdom of carrying on with the policy of Westernization as amended after Ataturk's death. Westernization as a means of modernization was initiated by Ataturk. But the Republican Party in power until 1950, and especially the Democratic Party reinterpreted Westernization to mean intimate cooperation with the "Western" countries at all costs and under all conditions. Thus "Westernization" in this sense became a general philosophy of domestic politics and foreign policy. (This interpretation has survived to this day. As a matter of fact, the program submitted by the government of Prime Minister Nihat Erim to the Parliament on April 2, 1971 reads: "We maintain our close ties of friendship and cooperation with the United States on the basis of mutual respect and understanding. The fact that we differ on certain matters must be regarded as the natural expression of mutual understanding and sincerity between our countries, and as an open indication of their strength, and of the political philosophy of the Western world of which Turkey and the United States are members".) Finally, another reason for the disillusion caused by rejection of Turkey's application for NATO membership was fear of reduction in American aid to Turkey. It was assumed that the establishment of NATO would put an end to Soviet expansionist aims. This proved to be wrong since the Soviets did not officially renounce their claims for territories and bases on the Straits until after Stalin's death.

The reasons precipitating the admission of Turkey into NATO together with Greece in 1952, must be sought first in the Turkish decision to assign a contingent of 5.000 men for the war in Korea in 1950, soon after the United Nations resolution to this effect was passed. This decision and the prowess displayed by the Turkish soldiers on the battlefield gave rise to a belief among American leaders and the public that Turkey would be a rather useful ally in the future. The second reason, connected with the admission was the existence of twenty-two Turkish divisions. The meaning of such a force for NATO was suddenly dramatized by the establishment of a nuclear balance between the United States and the Soviet Union, and the priority regained by conventional armies. It became obvious that the rearmament efforts of Europe, and especially those pertaining to the building up of a conventional force, would not proceed as fast as had been supposed. Finally the admission of Turkey was achieved after Britain and the Nordic powers withdrew their objections. Initially Britain preferred to keep Turkey out of NATO on the grounds that she would rather have the Middle Eastern countries organized in a common alliance or pact. The commander of the military forces of the alliance in which Britain would be a natural member because of her interest in the region, would be a British general. This, in turn, would give Britain a chance to retain her hold of the Middle East, a region she was supposed to leave shortly. However, once Britain received word that Turkey would play a leading role in the establishment of such a pact if admitted into NATO, England withdrew her objections. After admission into NATO, Turkey fulfilled her promise to Britain by taking a leading part in the establishment of the Baghdad Pact. Some of the smaller members of the alliance had objected to Turkish membership because they feared a decrease in the amount of American aid, while others did not wish to risk an armed conflict with the Soviet Union on account of Turkey. Still others did not want Turkey as a member because they did not consider her as "part of the Western civilized world". But all these objections were withdrawn when the United States put her weight on the side of Turkey. Turkey became a member of the organization when the American proposal was voted for at the meeting of the NATO

Council in September 1951, in Ottawa. The Protocol of Entry was signed in February 1952, in Washington.

III

Having summarized under what conditions and how Turkey was admitted into NATO, we shall attempt to determine whether NATO membership was beneficial or harmful to the country, and whether any of the criticisms directed against NATO by certain circles in Turkey are justified at all.

As indicated before, the Soviet threat to Turkey was still present when Turkey became a member of NATO. For that matter, one may say that considering Turkey's geographical location she might have suffered the fate of Korea as long as the Soviets remained convinced that their policy of acquiring land or expanding their sphere of influence, initiated after the War, produced dividends. Therefore, it may be appropriate to conclude that the NATO membership has provided Turkey with a much more basic security than the Truman Doctrine and the Marshall Plan.

Stalin died on March 5, 1953, a year after Turkey's entrance into NATO. His successors, in a note submitted to Turkey on May 30, 1953, declared that they renounced their former claims on the Turkish territories and emphasized their sincere wish to establish ties of friendship within a very short time. Some anti-NATO circles in Turkey claimed that if Turkey had stayed outside NATO, she could have grasped this opportunity to pursue a more flexible policy towards her great neighbor which in turn would have led to an easing of tensions between the two countries. This reasoning, however, goes beyond our imagination. First of all, it was not possible to foresee that Stalin would have died one year after Turkey's admission into NATO, and that the new Soviet leaders would have adopted a different course of foreign policy. Anyway, antagonisms on the international level do not last forever but neither do they dissolve with the first peaceful initiative, but persist for some time to come. One may ask in fact whether the Soviet attempt at rapprochment would have occurred at all if Turkey were not a member of NATO. Therefore, Turkey's entrance in NATO must be assessed basically as a necessary and a positive foreign policy move.

As for Turkey's comportment, we believe that she made a

series of mistakes after her admission. For instance Khruschev's speech at the 20th Congress of the Communist Party of the Soviet Union on February 14, 1956, in Moscow in which peaceful coexistence was advocated—was not interpreted by Turks as a symptom and evidence of a real thaw in international relations. This was appreciated only recently. This speech attacked various Soviet domestic and foreign policy decisions of the Stalinist period and seemed to open a new phase in international relations. The Soviets were apprehensive at the time that their attack on Stalinist policies may be reinterpreted as a change of tactics forced by the international atmosphere and the gradual change in the internal Soviet structure. In order to counteract such a charge Kruschev declared:

> It has been alleged that the Soviet Union advances this principle of peaceful coexistence merely out of tactical considerations, considerations of expediency. Yet it is common knowledge that we always, from the very first years of Soviet Power, stood with equal firmness for peaceful coexistence. Hence it is not a tactical move, but a fundamental principle of Soviet foreign policy ... To this day, the enemies of peace allege that the Soviet Union is out to overthrow capitalism in other countries by "exporting" revolution. It goes without saying that among us Communists there are no supporters of capitalism. But this does not at all mean that we have interfered or plan to interfere in the internal affairs of countries where the capitalist order exists ... It is ridiculous to think that revolutions are made to order ...
> [Engaged in] building communism in one country, we are resolutely against war. We have always held and continue to hold that the establishment of a new social system in one or another country is the internal affair of the peoples of the countries concerned ...

Even if only tactical motives lay behind the new moves in Soviet foreign policy, it must be recalled that it is extremely difficult to separate tactics from substance. Tactical changes will, in time, inevitably lead to changes of substance. Anyway, the 20th Party Congress helped thaw somewhat the rigid bi-polarization of the two blocs and gradually gave way to a rapprochement which, paradoxically enough, benefitted from the "balance of terror" resulting from the Soviet launching of the first satellite in 1957, which implied that they had developed inter-continental missiles. However, no matter what the real reasoning was, it was obvious that the Soviet attitude towards the Western countries underwent considerable change. The moves for rapprochement were interrupted temporarily by the refusal of Khruschev to attend the Paris Summit Conference with President Eisenhower in May 1960, as a consequence of the incident caused by a U 2 spy aircraft which had taken off from an American base in Turkey and had been shot down over Soviet territory. The efforts however were resumed after the Sino-Soviet conflict errupted before some 81 Communist parties meeting in Moscow in November-December 1964. Subsequently events that led to a relative easing of tensions between the "East" and the "West" followed in succession. In December 1961, President Kennedy and the Secretary General of the Soviet Communist Party met in Vienna; on June 25, 1967, President Johnson and Prime Minister Kosygin met in Glassborough. A direct telephone line was established between the White House and the Kremlin in order to prevent at the last moment the outbreak of an accidental nuclear conflict between the two blocs. Among the very first concrete examples of these contacts were the partial nuclear test-ban treaty signed in August 1963 and the SALT negotiations presently taking place today.

These developments provided Turkey with an opportunity to pursue a more flexible policy towards the Soviet Union. However, Turkey failed to take advantage of the opportunity and followed a policy of blindfolded dependences on the West. Turkey turned herself into an outpost of the West on the Soviet border and remained as such until the middle of the 1960's. Behind the Turkish attitude lie not only ideological motives or security considerations but a variety of internal factors. The economic policy pursued by the government made Turkey increasingly dependent on foreign aid injecting the reasoning that the more obedient Turkey was in her relations with the United States, the more aid she would receive from the latter. However, this reasoning proved misleading and fallacious, as evidenced by other international examples. For instance, Yugoslavia or Spain have, from time to time, received more direct aid from the United States than Turkey despite firm adherence to their respective ideologies. Indeed, the blindfolded attachment to a rigid policy left Turkey far behind the developments and changes in the world. At a time when classical colonialism was rapidly eliminated, Turkey felt obliged to support the colonial powers because of her membership in NATO, as fully attested by the UN record of speeches and votes. Furthermore, a considerable number of NATO powers which interpreted the concept of strategic embargo according to their own interests did not hesitate to enter into commercial relations with the Eastern bloc. Turkey was a late-comer and probably lost markets for her goods in this region. A vivid example of her belated response to international developments is her policy with regard to mainland China. Many NATO members chose to recognize this country because of economic and commercial considerations. Turkey, however, hesitated to recognize this country until August 1971, most likely because of the influence of her powerful ally, the United States.

The image of Turkey as an American satellite within NATO in the eyes of the developing countries in general and the neighboring countries on her southern border in particular are among the disadvantages brought by NATO membership. For instance, after joining NATO, Turkey was used by the Western powers as an instrument to protect their interests in some of the developing countries. She was one of the few states that posed as the spokesman of the West at the Bandung Conference of 1955, and attracted the scorn of all the developing countries. In return for the British support for membership in NATO, Turkey played the major role in the establishment of the Baghdad Pact as part of the "containment" policy of the West. Furthermore, the stand taken by Turkey during the Suez Crisis of 1956 merely because she was a NATO member, despite some apparent support for Egypt, led to a further deterioration in the already poor relations between Turkey and the Arab countries. Finally the part played by Turkey in the Syrian and the Lebanese crises of 1957 and 1958, neither of which fell within the responsibilities of NATO, can again be said to be an indirect consequence of her membership in NATO.

One had to wait for the emergence of the Cyprus crisis in order to understand better the international image of Turkey created by the foreign policy of the Turkish governments. The United Nations General Assembly, proceeding from a series of resolutions detrimental to the interests of Turkey since March 1964, adopted on December 18, 1965, a resolution greatly limiting Turkish rights on the island. The vote was 47 for, 6 against, including the vote by Turkey—and 54 abstentions. We believe that this vote reflected best Turkey's standing on the international stage. The six negative votes, apart from Turkey, belonged to two CENTO allies, Iran and Pakistan, to Libya, with which Turkey maintained strong ties of traditional friendship, to the United States and Albania. Albania, completely isolated in the Balkans and Europe and hoping to be recognized by Turkey, cast a negative vote. The United States vote which was in total contradiction to her previous record on the Cyprus question, was an attempt to calm to some extent the reaction aroused by President Johnson's famous letter. The abstention votes belonged to all of the Eastern bloc countries, and the rest of the NATO members. These votes reflected the new tendency which appeared in the Turkish foreign policy prior to the voting. This new tendency consisted of efforts to better, or at least normalize the unfriendly relations between Turkey and the Soviet Union and other members of the Eastern bloc which prevailed since the middle of the 1940's. The first of these initiatives was the visit to Moscow after so many years, on October 30, 1964, of a Turkish Foreign Minister. This visit which paved the way for other visits at different levels was accompanied by declarations which created world-wide repercussions. Indeed, Turkey declared all of a sudden that she would not participate in the "Multi-Lateral Force (MLF). This proposal defended by the United States for some time in order to associate West Germany in the use of nuclear weapons had created vehement Soviet reaction. In a declaration on January 14, 1965, Washington officially announced that Turkey had refrained from participating in MLF and had simultaneously withdrawn her eleven man crew from the destroyer "Claude-Ricketts" manned by seven NATO members. At the time of these Turkish declarations, Moscow revised its pro-Makarios attitude and came out with an official announcement stating that the Soviet Union now accepted "the right of existence of two separate communities" in Cyprus, and considered suitable a "federative" administration for the island. This stand was more in line with the Turkish position on Cyprus. In May 1966, the Turkish parliament subjected NATO to criticisms for the first time in its history, while several youth organizations issued a declaration openly demanding the withdrawal of "our troops from NATO".

Thus, the Cyprus question brought to light the fact that Turkey had been isolated in the international scene and, indirectly, resuscitated the awareness of Turkish public opinion on matters of foreign policy. Perhaps for the first time in history the Turkish people became involved in a thorough discussion of foreign policy problems alongside domestic issues with a view to searching the best course to secure Turkey's national interests. The discussions and debates did not go unheeded by the government of the Justice Party which, in line with its political philosophy, had accepted without any reservations whatsoever the Western model of development. Consequently the government, while preserving the existing ties with NATO and the United States, made several attempts to normalize the tense relations between Turkey and the countries of the Eastern bloc. This was the real intention behind the official visits mentioned previously.

Naturally, as may be the case elsewhere, the extreme left in Turkey benefitted most from these developments. Those who advocated a Marxist-Leninist line for the development of Turkey believed that NATO was the major obstacle to the establishment of socialism in the country. The radical left believed that if Turkey stayed outside NATO, the possibility of American intervention against leftist activities would be largely reduced. It was based on this reasoning that the radical left initiated a violent campaign against NATO. The campaign which portrayed NATO as an instrument of American imperialism affected, after a while, even the sections of the public which had remained neutral so far, and contributed to the gradual loss of prestige of the Justice Party government. Some of the reasons advanced to justify the withdrawal of Turkey from NATO, although ideological and emotional in substance, nevertheless revealed many issues which had been concealed from the public. Two of these will be carefully reviewed here since they point to the other side of the coin in the relations of Turkey with NATO and the United States, that is, to the advantages and disadvantages stemming from these relations as far as Turkey is concerned.

The first of these issues concerns the bilateral agreements signed between Turkey and the United States within the framework of NATO, and the second concerns the position of Turkey vis-a-vis the recently altered strategy of NATO.

IV

The agreements concluded between Turkey and the United States after the Second World War within and without the framework of NATO on military, economic and financial matters are generally referred to by Turks as "bilateral agreements". Some of these agreements are open agreements, signed, ratified and promulgated according to the constitutional provisions of both parties. A good many, however, are executive agreements, concluded in accordance with Article 3 of the North Atlantic Treaty. As mentioned before, the latter agreements became the subject of public discussion in Turkey only after 1965. Turkish public opinion which was not interested even in the open agreements was completely unaware of the existence of the secret agreements. The commitments undertaken by Turkey vis-a-vis the United States through these international agreements was brought to the attention of Turkish public opinion for the first time with President Johnson's letter. A section of the letter reads as follows:

> I wish also, Mr. Prime Minister, to call your attention to the bilateral agreement between the United States and Turkey in the field of military assistance. Under Article IV of the Agreement with Turkey of July 1947, your Government is required to obtain United States consent for the use of military assistance for purposes other than those for which such assistance was furnished. Your Government has on several occasions acknowledged to the United States that you fully understand this condition. I must tell you in all candor that the United States cannot agree to the use of any United States supplied military equipment for a Turkish intervention in Cyprus under present circumstances.

The agreement, referred to in the letter, is the one concluded between the two countries setting up the conditions under which Turkey would receive aid under the Truman Doctrine. It will be necessary to examine briefly the provisions of this treaty in order to understand fully why President Johnson's letter caused such an uproar in Turkey. The preface to the agreement specified that aid would be extended to Turkey "on terms consonant with the sovereign independence and security of the two countries". Article 2 of the agreement again stated "The Turkish Government will make use of the assistance furnished for the purposes for which it has been accorded". Article 3 contained the following statement: "... in so far as may be consistent with the security of the two countries: (1) representatives of the Press and Radio of the United States will be permitted to observe freely and to report fully regarding the utilization of such assistance, and (2) the Government of Turkey will give full and continuous publicity within Turkey as to the purpose, source, character, scope, amounts and progress of such assistance". According to Article 4, "... The Government of Turkey will not ..., without the consent of the Government of the United States ... permit ... the use of any such article ... for any purpose other than that for which the article or information is furnished."

Once the circumstances under which the agreement was reached, and the text of the agreement are carefully examined, it will be much simpler to understand the causes of the Turkish reaction to the Johnson letter. First, the treaty was concluded at a time of an acute Soviet threat in 1947, when no ties of alliance existed between Turkey and the United States. The two countries became allied with Turkey's admission into NATO. Once Turkey was admitted into NATO, American aid was extended not according to the Agreement of 1947 but within the framework of the alliance. Consequently, the American view that the weapons Turkey intended to use in Cyprus in 1964, had been provided within the framework of the Agreement of 1947 seems to be deprived of a legal basis. Even if one agrees that all aid given to Turkey were to be used according to the Agreement of 1947, then one finds difficulty in reconciling the contradiction in the same agreement. Aid should be extended "on terms consonant with the sovereign independence and security of the two countries", says the agreement, but with the condition that the Turkish Government "obtain United States consent for the use of military assistance for purposes other than those for which such assistance was furnished".

It is public knowledge that the member states of NATO have divided military responsibilities among themselves in order to defend best the region covered by the alliance. According to this master scheme, Turkey, though the least developed of all NATO countries, was to maintain one of the largest land-forces. And again according to this division of responsibilities, the United States was to provide the Turkish army a large part of its weaponry. Can one then consider Turkey rightly a sovereign state if she cannot have access to these weapons at a time when her rights and interests are violated, or if she has to seek beforehand the permission of the United States? Therefore, one of the major causes of the reaction against NATO and the United States in Turkey lies in this peculiar American interpretation of the idea of "alliance" and "ally" as reflected in President Johnson's letter. If this line of reasoning were extended to its logical limits, one would arrive at the following conclusion: the enemies of the United States were automatically the enemies of Turkey whereas the United States was free to decide whether the enemies of Turkey were also its own enemies.

After becoming a member of the North Atlantic Treaty, Turkey concluded a series of bilateral agreements with the United States either directly with reference to Article 3 of the Treaty or with reference to the NATO Status of Forces Agreement signed between the member countries on June 19, 1951. Article 3 of the North Atlantic Treaty states: "In order more effectively to achieve the objectives of this treaty, the Parties, separately and jointly, by means of continuous and effective self-help and mutual aid, will maintain and develop their individual and collective capacity to resist and attack". The Status of Forces Agreement contains provisions regarding the status of the forces of a member country during their being stationed on the territory of another member country. Following her admission into NATO, Turkey became a party to this agreement on March 10, 1954.

The Status of Forces Agreement consisted of general provisions applicable to all NATO members, while the bilateral agreements, concluded either according to the Status of Forces Agreement or to Article 3 of the North Atlantic Treaty consisted of special provisions applicable only to the states directly parties to them. Turkey and the United States concluded nearly a hundred of these agreements, a majority of which remeined secret. Among these, the secret Military Facilities Agreement concluded on June 23, 1954, was in the nature of a general agreement, while the rest were agreements of implementation. In the course of the heated debate on foreign policy in Turkey after 1965, a great majority of these bilateral agreements were revealed either by the press or Parliament. Several points came out into the open. It was learned, for example, that the agreements had been concluded by different departments in the government, and that some were written while others were oral agreements reached either by face-to-face or telephone conversations. Actually the texts of some of these agreements could not be located when later the United States and Turkey began negotiations for a basic treaty to replace some of the bilateral agreements. It is likely that American officials, when rejected by one Turkish department for one reason or another, preferred to turn to another department to secure the concessions they sought, thus entering into a series of agreements with a multitude of government offices, each with no information on what the others were doing.

Possibly the most important point in the revelations on bilateral agreements concerned the American bases and sites in Turkey. The presence of some American bases, facilities and military personnel in Turkey was common knowledge. However, the status, the real nature of the bases, together with the amount, responsibilities, rights and privileges of the American personnel on the bases was not known since many of these were regulated by the Secret Military Facilities Agreement, of 1954, and by the agreements of implementation deriving from it. The Agreement of 1954 was concluded by the Ministry of Foreign affairs upon the authorization of the Council of Ministers while a majority of the agreements of implementation were concluded either by the Ministry of Foreign Affairs, the Ministry of National Defense, or directly by military officials themselves.

The American bases and sites established in Turkey under these agreements can be classified into four categories: (1) air bases, (2) strategic missile bases, (3) electronic communication facilities, and (4) establishments necessary to meet the needs of the American military personnel and their dependents working at bases and related sites, such as housing, hotels, schooling, hospitals, clubs, various recreation facilities, shopping centers (PX) and supply storage centers. The Turkish government made available 32 million square meters of land to the United States for the location of these bases and sites. The expropriation costs of this land and the responsibility for the protection of the bases and sites, the storage and care of weapons and the maintenance of environmental security was assigned to Turkey. The financial burden placed on the Turkish defense budget by these obligations was approximately 30 million Turkish lira or about 11 million dollars (2.80 TL per dollar until 1958, thereafter and 15 liras in 1970) annually. The agreements made possible the following: (1) The establishment of a joint Turkish-American air base at Çiğli (Izmir), and (2) the Incirlik Air Base at Adana, connected to the Strategic Air Forces Command of NATO, to be turned over to American control in case of a crisis; (3) access for American planes to the airports at Pirinçlik (Diyarbakir), Esenboğa (Ankara), and Eskişehir; (4) the establishment of electronical communication bases at Karamürsel, Samsun, Trabzon, Ankara and Diyarbakir; (5) permission for American ships to have shelter and repair service at the Turkish ports. In addition, the same agreements granted other rights ranging from juridical privileges to the establishment of a private postal service and tax-free shopping centers. These privileges and rights granted to the United States personnel in Turkey exceeded by far the rights stemming from the Status of Forces Agreement concluded among the rest of the NATO members. These were, in sum, a form of modern "capitulations". Many of these privileges and rights were misused to an embarrassing degree by some American officials and responsible officers. All this had its share in generating a wave of anti-Americanism in Turkey. For instance, the legal privileges granted to the American military personnel in Turkey by the same agreements prevented their trial in the Turkish courts for any offense committed. All American military offenders ranging from a colonel who ran over a child with his jeep, to drunken sergeants who tore up the Turkish flag and insulted Turkey publicly were exempt from trial in Turkish court by a simple statement issued by the highest ranking American officer in charge: "he was on duty". One of the bilateral agreements on legal matters ruled that offenses committed by military personnel while "on duty" were to be tried before American courts. The exemption of custom duties accorded American personnel deprived the Turkish treasury of an important source of income and encouraged the flow into the domestic market, illegally through the PX stores of a whole set of luxury goods whose entry had been officially forbidden. The historical and cultural treasurers of Anatolia accumulated over a period of nine thousand years were smuggled out of Turkey in unprecedented proportions. The postal service owned and operated by the United States in Turkey, without Turkish control over it, provided convenient channels to smuggle anything out of the country including thousands of ancient works of art.

This abuse of the bilaterial agreements, when given extensive publicity by the press and other media of mass communication bred rapidly anti-American feelings among the public. The initial sympathy and affection shown by the Turks, well known for their hospitality, contrasted sharply with their dislike and scorn displayd towards Americans at the end of the 1960's. Anyone who lived through both of these periods could discern easily the vast difference. Neither the Turkish nor the American official circles were too willing to notice or acknowledge for long the change in the Turks' attitude towards the United States and the Americans in Turkey. Finally, following a proposal put forth by the Turkish Government on April 7, 1966, and accepted by the United States on April 18, 1966, the two governments entered into preparatory talks in order to revise the Military Facilities Agreement of 1954 to clarify the thirteen secret bilateral agreements stemming from it, and to combine all the bilateral agreements into a single Basic Agreement. The press release issued on July 3, 1969, at the end of the preparation talks stated:

> Following careful studies carried out by the national authorities, the representatives of the two Governments officially started negotiations to this effect on January 20, 1967. After two years and four months of extensive and detailed negotiations which took place in an atmosphere of mutual understanding and cordial relationship that has always characterized the bonds of friendship between Turkey and the United States of America, the Government of the Republic of Turkey and the Government of the United States of America have today (July 13, 1969) concluded an agreement relating to the basic principles of the collective measures to be taken by the two Governments pursuant to Article 3 of the North Atlantic Treaty.

The details of this agreement, too, are secret like the majority of the rest of the bilateral agreements; only its basic principles were made public. One has the impression that some of the principles in the Basic Agreement were intended to avoid repeating the weakness and controversial aspects of the bilateral agreements. For example, the following provision of the basic agreement was made public: "The nature, purpose and duration of each common defense installation must be approved by the Government of the Republic of Turkey". It is generally assumed that this provision was inserted in the text of the Basic Agreement in order to bring an end to the *fait a compli* with respect to defense matters and to oral agreements. Another provision in the text said: "Within the terms of this agreement it is clear that the Government of the United States of America holds no secrets from the Government of the Republic of Turkey". The reason for such a provision may be attributed to the desire to avoid the recurrence of such incidents as that of the U-2 pane shot by the Soviets after it took off from Turkey without the prior knowledge of the Turkish authorities, or the American aircraft which was downed over the Black Sea in the same fashion. The majority of the provisions in the Basic Agreement give the impression that they were inserted in order to rehabilitate the Turkish Government in the public eye. The self defensive attitude of the government is evident in some of the provisions of the agreement: "The mutual cooperation between the two parties envisaged in the Agreement is based on reciprocal respect for each other's equal rights and sovereignty ... Turkey retains the right to assign Turkish military and civilian personnel to all facilities as it deems suitable ... Turkey has the right of inspection of all facilities to verify that the nature and purpose of the common defense effort under this agreement conforms to mutual goals of both nations as specified in implementing agreements". (This provision may be the result of the debate revolving around the fact that Turkish officials were not permitted to enter the military bases and its facilities which were thus placed under *de facto* American sovereignty.)

The signing of the Basic Agreement was accompanied with a reduction in the number of American military personnel in Turkey and a change in Turkish-American relations. A Turkish journalist related the opinion of an American official on the subject as such: "We first made the adjustments with respect to the bilateral agreements proposed by the Turkish Government. We now turn to the reduction of the American military personnel in Turkey to a minimum number adequate for the defense purposes of NATO and Turkey, this is a matter which reached a peak of sensitivity".

In fact, in order to "lessen the presence" of American personnel, especially in the bigger cities, their number was reduced from 27.000 to 6.400. A parallel undertaking was the transfer of Çiğli airport (Izmir) and the radar bases at Trabzon and Samsun to the Turkish armed forces, while the status of the radar bases at Karamursel, Sinop and Pirinçlik (Diyarbakir) and of the Incirlik airport (Adana) were adjusted to the principles of the new agreement.

However, in spite of all these adjustments, the question of bilateral agreements continued to remain subject to criticism in Turkey even by people who have a moderate or even pro-Western view on foreign policy. For example, the late Ismet Inönü, the leader of the People's Republican Party, the main opposition party, who had already indicated his dissatisfaction with these agreements earlier, came out openly against them later. The apprehension expressed by Inönü and other critics was based mainly on the special case of the Incirlik base.

The nuclear weapons placed in Turkey as a result of the NATO defense scheme are subject to the "double key" system, that is, a nuclear weapon cannot be fired without the consent of both parties which have access to the weapon. The "double key" principle is to be applied in the following manner: the weapon is in the hands of the American troops in Turkey; the means of delivery, however, are in the hands of the Turkish armed forces. Consequently, it is impossible to use the nuclear weapons without the consent of the Turkish Government. The only place where this system is not applicable is the Incirlik base. Short range American planes equipped with nuclear war heads are located at this base. According to the NATO defense plans, the airplanes located at the Incirlik base come neither under the command nor the control of the Turkish armed forces. These are directly related to the European Allied Command of NATO whose Commander is always an American. He wears both the cap of the NATO military command and the American armed forces. This means that the United States can, through this commander, move her air fleet equipped with nuclear war heads at Incirlik toward any destination it chooses, simultaneously dragging Turkey into a nuclear war without her consent.

Here, however, one has to remember a very important safety valve. The NATO commander in Europe has to consult the NATO Council before making a move that could trigger off a war. Since decisions in the Council are to be taken unanimously, in other words, since Turkey like every other member state has the veto right in principle in the Council, these planes should not undertake any action without Turkish consent. Yet, could this required consent impede the United States from a *fait a compli*? Incidents such as the transfer of American troops from their base at Incirlik to Lebanon during the crisis of 1958, the take off of the U-2 reconnaissance plane in 1960, and the removal of the strategic missiles from the same base without prior consultation with the Turkish government (possibly as part of a deal between the United States and the Soviet Union following the Cuban crisis of 1962) create deep apprehension in Turkey. On the other hand, it is possible to argue that in case of a nuclear attack on the Soviets by planes taking off from Incirlik, the Soviet Union would retaliate by bombing not only the bases in Turkey but also the NATO bases in Europe. The chances of a *fait a compli* which would sacrifice Turkey exclusively thus appear rather remote. However, the recently adopted NATO strategy known as the "flexible response" and the idea of the so called "limited war" enhance further the possibility of converting Turkey into a first degree target. In order to understand this question it is necessary to study the nature of this NATO strategy and the special place of Turkey in it.

The defense strategy of NATO has undergone several changes. Between 1950-57, NATO strategy rested on the understanding that the United States would activate immediately her total nuclear power in case of an attack on any member of the alliance. At the time, the conventional power balance between the European members of the Alliance and the Soviet Union was in favor of the latter almost beyond comparison. The balance of power could be established only with the aid of the American nuclear power. Yet, this balance changed suddenly in 1957, when the Soviets launched into space their first earth satellite, proving their mastery of long range missiles. In order to fill the missile gap created by this development, since the United States possessed only medium range missiles, it was proposed at the meeting of the NATO Council of Ministers in December 1957, that American missiles be installed and nuclear war heads be stored in Europe. Turkey was among the few NATO members which supported this proposal immediately. Prime Minister Menderes seemed at the time more than willing to allow the use of Turkish territory for American missiles and nuclear war heads. This attitude was due probably to his feeling that the Soviet missile superiority posed a new threat to Turkish security, and possibly to his hope that such a stand would be rewarded by a generous amount of American aid sufficient to pull out the Turkish economy from its miserable stand at the time. Thus, a new bilateral treaty was concluded between Turkey and the United States in November 1958, providing for the construction of a base for fifteen Jupiter missiles at the Çiğli (Izmir) Air Base. (It was the missiles at this base which became part of the U.S.–Soviet deal. The Soviets proposed that in return for the removal of Soviet missiles from Cuba, a neighbor of the United States, American missiles be removed from Turkey, a neighbor of the Soviet Union. The missiles were in fact removed from Turkey in 1963, apparently without consultation with the Turkish government.) This incident took place at a time when the American military circles were engaged in efforts to replace the NATO strategy of "massive retaliation" with that of "flexible response", which placed the European countries in a new position vis-a-vis the U. S. A. Therefore, on top of the anxiety caused by the removal of the missiles from Turkey came the uncertainties and the suspicions concerning the proposed new NATO strategy.

The questions arising from this development became the subject of discussion among the other NATO countries. This was, in fact, the main reason of De Gaulle's controversy with the United States, and the eventual withdrawal of France from the integrated forces of NATO. This was also the reason why West Germany desired to have closer ties with the actual nuclear weapons. In order to determine the position of Turkey towards this new development one must first analyze the very concept of "strategy".

The meaning of the term "strategy" obviously changes according to the technological characteristics of the period. Strategy, in its classical meaning can be defined as "recourse to force with skill". Clausewitz's dictum of, "war is the continuation of policy by other means", which was accepted generally as a basic premise until recently seems to have lost its validity today. Diplomacy and defense have become complementary factors. Today the basic function of strategy is to avoid war and to maintain defense by using force as an instrument of threat but without having recourse to it. The reason for this is the range and the terrifying power of weapons capable of covering the whole world.

The overriding concept in the nuclear strategy of our times is "deterrence", which means to cause the enemy to adopt a predetermined behavior. The most important condition for an effective deterrence is that it must be convincing. The threat will be effective if the would be aggressor is convinced that its preplanned action is considered most vital by the other party. But if, on the other hand, the would be aggressor is frightened by a powerful threat or deterred from the execution of the planned action, or the interests to be protected are not too vital, then the threat would not be as convincing as in the case of the first. The establishment of a complete nuclear balance through the development of inter-continental missiles caused considerable change in the degree of deterrence of a nuclear threat. Obviously, it will be unconvincing to assume that one would enter a limited nuclear war which would simultaneously mark one's own destruction. In a nuclear war of this type there would be no chances of survival for either side. This development brought forth by the establishment of the "balance of terror" made it indispensable for NATO to dismiss the strategy of "massive retaliation" in favor of the strategy of "flexible response".

The strategy of "massive retaliation", to be resorted to in case of lesser incidents, as an alternative of an "either all or none" type, has become completely unthinkable in the circumstances prevailing in the world today. If the forces in the hands of the Alliance were to be used according to the strategy of "massive retaliation", they would be paralyzed and unable to intervene in case of an attack, for example, on Turkey.

The adoption of the strategy of "flexible response" appears to be a necessary and even a helpful development, not only with regard to the security of NATO, as a whole, but also with regard to Turkey, provided certain conditions are fulfilled. Now, we can briefly take a look at the meaning of "flexible response" and then deal with Turkey's special position in it.

The strategy of "flexible response" was accepted unanimously in December 1967, by the NATO Defense Planning Committee in a meeting at ministerial level. The strategy, proposed by the United States originally in the early 1960's, had been opposed by some European members of NATO and by Turkey for a long time. In fact, Turkey was one of the last countries to accept this strategy. According to the declarations of the NATO Council and public documents, the strategy consists of three stages: the first, foresees a direct conventional response. This means that a conventional attack on one NATO member will receive a response of the same type. In the second stage, if aggression cannot be defeated by conventional weapons, tactical nuclear weapons, following consultations among member states, will be used but with utmost caution. This stage will prevent the expansion of war by escalation. The third stage involves a strategical total nuclear war which is practically unthinkable under the present circumstances. The presence of this stage, however, reveals the terror inherent in the danger of escalation, which forms the essence of the second stage, thus forcing deterrence to be both violent and convincing.

Various criticisms were advanced against the strategy of flexible response. Here we shall dwell on some of the more important ones. According to a view this strategy, while placing some of the territory covered by NATO, namely the North American region, outside the zone of war, turns the territories of the European members into zones of war. It seems as though the two super-powers wish to have the European countries pay the bill of a possible conflict among themselves. However, if the disaster is world-wide, then the sacrifice might be proportionate with it. According to another view, the interests of both super-powers call upon them in case of war to limit the scope of that war. Consequently, certain ideas may become the subject of a secret deal between them. The Soviet Union may, by occupying some areas within the NATO countries present the West with a *fait a compli*, which may very well be accepted by the United States on grounds of preserving the world peace.

The above criticisms may be answered in various ways. The would be aggressor cannot be sure whether its conventional attack would remain limited either in weaponry or in area. The thought that following a conventional response, tactical nuclear weapons may be used might be sufficient in itself to deter the aggressor. Secondly, it is impossible to imagine that American forces will not be involved in such an attack simply because these forces are found practically in, or the vicinity of every region vulnerable to attack. Therefore, the aggressor will inevitably face the United States. Finally, the would be aggressor will not make an attempt at a *fait a compli* however limited in size, since underneath deterrence lie essentially the danger of escalation.

One agrees that the technological developments in the world

forced NATO, as a whole, to adopt the strategy of limited war. Still, one is induced to believe that this strategy does not provide for the total security of countries such as Turkey situated at the flanks of NATO. For the critical questions above bring to mind further questions. For example, there is the question where to use the tactical nuclear weapons if a conventional attack cannot be repulsed by conventional means. The European zone of the Alliance where the attack is likely to occur will be used as nuclear war zone. Under these circumstances, the areas most vulnerable to attack—to a sort of trial attack, one may say—are the countries located at the flanks of NATO, which, for political, military and economic reasons, will cause minimum reaction if attacked. It is obvious that Turkey is among the very first countries which fits into this category. Thus, the strategy of the limited war, which is the inevitable outcome of the strategy of flexible response, protects the two super-states almost completely from being a target of nuclear weapons. It fails, however, to provide a similar security for the European members in general and for the members at the flanks in particular. On the other hand, since the use of nuclear weapons in Turkey are either dependent on the double key system or are solely in the hands of the United States, the degree of deterrence inherent in these weapons will be determined mainly by U.S. intention and determination to use them to protect the whole or just part of Turkey. The presence of American bases, sites and even personnel in Turkey does not change the situation much because it is not too difficult to suppose that some bases, facilities and even personnel can be sacrificed in order to save oneself from total annihilation. Thus, one reaches the conclusion that the question of NATO strategy as far as Turkey is concerned rests, in the final analysis, on the decision of the United States, the most powerful partner of the Alliance, to side or not with Turkey and to use or not use all her nuclear and non-nuclear weapons to defend her.

Some neutral observers in Turkey suggest that Turkey withdraw from NATO, because the above question has never been answered definitely by the United States. Others propose that Turkey stay in NATO but direct at the same time all her energies to lessening the disadvantages and maximizing to her benefit the advantages deriving from the Alliance. These ideas will be elaborated in the summary.

V

In drawing a conclusion concerning the relations between Turkey and NATO, one must pay attention to two considerations: first, whether Turkey has secured for herself politically, economically and socially a permanent place in the Western world through her membership in NATO, and secondly, whether or not Turkey fulfilled the military objective of achieving security within NATO.

It is not just coincidence that the majority of Turks unfavorably disposed towards NATO are members of the radical left. These circles believe that membership in NATO made Turkey lose her independence and made her dependent on the West, especially the United States. Besides, the leftists feel that the American bases, sites and personnel in Turkey, together with the U. S. aid undermine directly or indirectly their own power. They believe that Turkey's withdrawal from NATO would be followed by United States withdrawal from Turkey, and subsequently the Turkish people will have the chance to establish the government most suitable to the realities of their own country.

The above claims contain truth as much as prejudices and dogmas. It is true that following Turkey's acceptance in NATO, the Turkish statesmen pursued blindly a pro-Western and pro-American foreign policy with little regard for the national interests of their own country.

One may be justified to take a strong position against the intervention of any foreign state or organization in the domestic affairs of Turkey. However, one cannot blame another state or organization for the mistakes committed or likely to be committed by Turkey in her relations with the outside world. Turkey did not sign the NATO Treaty or the bilateral agreements with the United States by force or the threat of force. They were signed with the full and free consent of the Turkish Government. If these were detrimental to the interests of Turkey, then only Turkey and her leaders should be held responsible. And, by the same token the correction of these mistakes rests only in the hands of Turkey and her leaders.

Furthermore, one cannot suppose, as some do, that the unhappy state of the internal development and the foreign policy of Turkey can be attributed to NATO membership and other foreign commitments. It has been a well-known fact as put forth by Machiavelli that the smaller and less powerful states enter into an alliance only in case of vital necessity, since alliances generally favor the bigger and more powerful members. Obviously this observation should not be turned into an absolute principle, ruling out all alliances. Alliances should be formed and maintained only in case of vital necessity. The question at hand, therefore, is to determine whether Turkey deems it vitally necessary to continue her membership in NATO.

NATO is an alliance formed primarily against Soviet aggression and expansion. It would be sheer illusion to think that the Soviet policy of expanding her territory and sphere of influence adopted after the Second World War underwent a substantial change. One can easily prove this proposition by citing such examples as the Soviet occupation of several countries in Europe after the war, the Czech incident being the last in a series of moves of this sort. The Brezhnev Doctrine and the recent Soviet involvement in the Middle East are other examples. As long as Turkey is geographically located within the expansion zone of the Soviet Union and is incapable of meeting the Soviet expansion solely with her own powers, she has a vital interest, in fact a dire necessity to participate in a system of alliance to assure her security. Since there exists no other power outside of NATO to balance the Soviet power, Turkey's membership in NATO is a foregone conclusion. Consequently, the question facing Turkey today is not whether or not to stay in NATO, but to make every attempt to reduce the disadvantages of this membership and to increase its advantages. For example, it will be in Turkey's interest to try to establish normal relations with her big neighbor, the Soviet Union, and with other socialist countries of Europe, while staying in NATO. Experience has demonstrated that NATO membership does not constitute an obstacle to the establishment of such relations. Several members of NATO have tried this course before Turkey. Turkey, due to her geographical location, should and could have been one of the very first to do so. Turkey's bad relations which lasted until recently with her Arab neighbors were the result of the role she played in the formation of the Baghdad Pact, her stand at the Bandung Conference, her position adopted during the Suez Crisis, and her role as a relay station to the American troops during the Lebanese crisis. Turkey's own interest demanded abstention in all these endeavors. Although Turkey made slight alternations in her foreign policy after 1960, she could have easily taken additional steps and initiative in the international arena. She should not have abstained for so long from recognizing mainland China out of unconditional loyalty to the United States, thus depriving herself of certain economic and commercial advantages. A more active part by Turkey on such proposals as the convening of an "European Security Conference" and the signing of a "Non-aggression Pact" between the "Eastern" and "Western" blocs should be given high priority simply because Turkey is one of the countries likely to derive utmost benefit from their enactment.

As for the military aspects of NATO membership, in other words, as to the question of whether this alliance guarantees the security of Turkey, various factors must be kept in mind. First, there is the evident fact that no member country was ever subjected to an attack after the establishment of NATO. This obviously is not a mere coincidence but a consequence of the alliance itself. On the other hand, just because agression in its customary form of armed attack upon another country has not occurred in NATO, should not make one say that the bigger and the more powerful states have renounced to resort to other means with the purpose of influencing the smaller and less powerful countries, including NATO members, that is, of taking them into their spheres of influence. The geopolitical position of Turkey makes it necessary for this country to be especially sensitive towards any moves undertaken by the Soviet Union. Some writers and intellectuals assume that the rivalry and struggle for influence among the super powers, forces these giants to aid the smaller and weaker states, whether they are allies or not, when their own national interests are involved. The Turkish defense cannot be entrusted to a probability of this sort, although staying outside of an alliance is not an "immoral" act, as John Foster Dulles labeled it. But events change form and content drastically. Not long ago one could have not imagined that the Western powers would allow the Soviet to penetrate the Middle East to the extent she appears to have today. If Turkey were not a member of NATO, or had she left NATO, while Greece remained a member of the alliance, this would tip the power balance in favor of Greece and weaken the Turkish stand on Cyprus. In such a case, the chances are that the bigger Western powers would favor the unification of Cyprus with Greece, at least as far as their own security is concerned, and would make every effort to achieve this objective. On the other hand, Turkey has received until today approximately 3 billion dollars of military aid as grants and 2.5 billion dollars of economic aid from the United States especially because she was a member of NATO. The amount of military aid received in 1969 was 99 million dollars and in 1970, 92 million dollars. Were this aid not extended to Turkey, she could not have the well-disciplined army of about 500.000 people maintained today. Turkey has no interest to give up a source of power of this magnitude when nearly all the countries of the Middle East possess large and regular armies maintained largely by foreign aid. In the light of the circurmstances prevailing in the world today, it is folly to assume that military power serves no ends and that vital foreign policy objectives can be obtained merely through diplomatic, economic and moral means.

Turkey's position within the strategy of NATO needs some elaboration. NATO is an alliance system stretching over a large part of the world, which makes it difficult to formulate a strategy equally valid and acceptable for all the member countries. Therefore, it is expected that the member countries will come out with special demands stemming from the specifics and the geographical location of their respective countries. Turkey's special demands stem from her position as a weaker member of the alliance and her location on the flank of the NATO region. Since Turkey cannot deter a possible aggressor with her own nuclear capability and cannot improve her conventional power beyond a certain limit in a foreseeable future, she is bound to seek aid from the more powerful members of the alliance. There is one thing, however, that must be kept in mind: Turkey herself must see to it that, while she receives aid, she is not dragged into a war she does not wilfully intend to take part in. We have outlined above the measures Turkey has already taken to this end. Only the status of the Incirlik base remains unaffected. It is imperative for the security of Turkey to revise the status of this base and adopt the double key system in case of nuclear operations. This will place the base under the direct control of NATO European Command, and hence under the indirect control of the United States. The single key system presently effective at the Incirlik base, however, carries with it the threat of dragging Turkey into a war to a *fait a complis* against her will.

On the other hand, whatever the strategy agreed upon, it is simply impossible for a country threatened by this or that great powers to provide for her defense effectively only from outside sources. The further a country of this type is located from the center of gravity of the alliance, the more hazardous her defenses are. In the light of these circumstances, Turkey is bound to develop a well-equipped national conventional force with superior mobility and fire-power through her own resources with a view to creating local deterrence. A force of this type might prove to be a most important weapon against the aggressor, even if the other NATO members choose to refrain from helping Turkey. The state of the world calls for Turkey to secure the utmost protection through a regular army maintained through outside assistance within the framework of NATO, and with a force established and maintained through her very own resources.

TURKEY AND THE UNITED STATES

GEORGE S. HARRIS

School of Advanced International Studies, Washington D.C.

Turkey and the United States forged an alliance that operated with singular success and harmony in the years after the Second World War. It was a bold experiment to unite states of such disparate power and at such divergent stages of development. But Turkish-American collaboration prospered nonetheless. It was based on strongly perceived mutual interests and common concern, not only to resist Soviet aggression, but to see Turkey develop as a self-reliant Western-oriented state. Washington disposed the resources and the willingness to commit them to satisfy in reasonable, though never complete, degree Ankara's appetite for economic as well as military assistance. From the outset, too, the allies shared a devotion to the open society that reinforced their bonds of unity. Moreover, different as they were in tradition and experience, the two peoples quickly conceived a mutual respect on a personal level. These warm personal relations carried the collaboration through many of its inevitable growing pains. Those disagreements that did arise in the early years, then, were dwarfed by the broad coincidence of interests of the partners and by their commitment to each other.

More recently the bonds of alliance have begun to loosen.[1] After a dramatic conflict of interest in respect to Cyprus in 1964, a new mood became apparent in Turkey. Among the Turkish elite it became common to question US motives; a radical, though tiny, fraction of the Turkish populace has even had recourse to violence in an effort to disrupt Turkey's cooperation with the United States. Although the Ankara government remains committed to close ties with Washington, it too is making a shrewder calculation of its own interests and is reappraising the various facets of the alliance.

In light of Turkey's historical experience it should have come

---

[1] Joseph J. Sisco, then Assistant Secretary of State for Near Eastern and South Asian Affairs, assessed this change in his statement before the Foreign Operations Subcommittee of the Senate Appropriations Committee, November 26, 1969.

as little surprise that ties with the United States have relaxed somewhat in recent years. For in many ways the consumation of the postwar intimacy of Turkey and America had itself been a surprising venture for the heirs of Ataturk. Close involvement with European states in the 19th and 20th centuries had left a bad taste in Turkish mouths. European economic entanglements during the late Ottoman Empire sealed the Turkish fall into bankruptcy and culminated in the imposition of foreign financial controls through the Public Debt Administration. The experiment in military cooperation with Germany during the First World War had led the Turks into an abyss from which they barely escaped after being on the losing side in this conflict. Memories of these tribulations were still fresh when the Second World War broke out. With Ataturk's exhortations to remain masters of their own fate still ringing in their ears, Turkey's leaders then decided to stay outside the war.

Yet hardly was this conflict at an end when the Ankara government began to turn away from its neutral stance to seek open alignment with the Western powers and especially with the United States. Certainly the impetus for this move did not come from the West. For a time the British were reluctant publicly to reaffirm their defensive alliance of 1939, whose provisions for Turkish involvement had not been invoked during the war. Nor were the Americans willing at first to offer material assistance in any quantity for fear of spoiling hoped for postwar amity with the Soviet Union. Washington by the end of 1945 did make clear to Moscow its interest in Turkey's territorial integrity and in 1946 began making naval demonstrations to reinforce this point. But it was only in 1947, when the United Kingdom announced that it was abandoning its role of supporting Turkey, that the American leaders established a formal tie—the Truman Doctrine. Washington took this step partly in response to the continuing pressures from Ankara to establish a more coherent connection and partly because of awakening fears of Soviet expansion in the eastern Mediterranean and Caucasus region.[2]

---

[2] On the genesis of the Truman Doctrine, see U.S., Department of State, *Foreign Relations of the United States, 1945*, vol. VIII (Washington, 1969), pp. 1219 ff.; *Foreign Relations of the United States, 1946*, vol. VII (Washington, 1969), pp. 801 ff; Stephen Xydis, *Greece and the Great Powers, 1944-1947: Prelude to the "Truman Doctrine"* (Thessaloniki, 1963), *passim*.

One can only speculate about the complex of motives that ordered the actions of the Turkish government in the postwar years. Ankara's diplomatic archives remain closed even for the early days of the Republic; few Turkish leaders have yet published memoires dealing with foreign policy in the period since the war. But there can be little doubt that the need for a powerful Western counterbalance to set against the Soviets played a prominent part in Turkish thinking, even though, to be sure, there is evidence that the Ankara Foreign Office had judged the most immediate danger to Turkey to have been successfully passed by the time of the Truman Doctrine.[3]

There were domestic considerations as well that pushed Turkey toward the West. Ataturk had explicitly enunciated the goal that the Turk should be Western in civilization—for he and his associates judged Europe to represent the epitome of national power. During the 1930s, the Turkish elite had engaged in some dispute over the matter of a European model for Turkey; the depression of 1929 discredited laissez-faire capitalism and enhanced the prestige of the systems in vogue in Nazi Germany, fascist Italy, and communist Russia. But the victory of the "democracies" in the Second World War reestablished the prestige of England and the United States in Turkish eyes. Thus it was also the desire to share in the power offered by association with the Western democracies that animated Turkish statesmen after 1945.

Yet whatever the conjugation of circumstances that impelled the Turks to seek a Western alliance, few of those at the head of the Turkish state apparently believed at the outset that it would be necessary for their ally to enter extensively into Turkish life. In the beginning Ankara sought principally military hardware. It was only after the Marshall Plan demonstrated US willingness to grant large-scale economic aid to European countries that the Turkish government's interest was whetted for this sort of massive assistance. Then the Ankara authorities quickly mounted a campaign to overcome Washington's initial inclination to leave the Turks outside of this overarching aid mechanism.[4] Hence, it

---

[3] For the attitudes of the Turkish Foreign Office, see Feridun Cemal Erkin, *Les relations Turco-Soviétiques et la question des détroits* (Ankara, 1968), pp. 329 ff.

[4] As part of this campaign the Turks proposed a Five-Year Plan calling for $ 615 million in foreign investment. See Max Weston Thornberg, Graham Spry, and George Soule, *Turkey: An Economic Appraisal* (New York, 1949), pp. 288-315.

would appear that the deep and profound involvement of the United States generally throughout Turkish society was not planned in advance, but grew more or less spontaneously out of the circumstances of the early years of the association and even to some extent from events totally or largely unconnected with Turkey itself. And the very sprawl of the relationship laid the base for difficulties in the future.

After the European powers coalesced to form NATO in 1949, the Turkish leaders became dissatisfied with the Truman Doctrine and Marshall Plan arrangements. Ankara wanted to be part of the Atlantic alignment not only to bolster Turkey's defense, but perhaps even more to express identification with Europe and to tighten the grip on aid. Thus, following rebuff of its entreaties to join NATO, the Turkish government in 1949 sought to establish a Mediterranean alliance, including the United States, as a device to enter the North Atlantic pact through the back door. Obstacles to a seperate Mediterranean treaty organization proved insuperable, however, and the Turks were obliged to seek other ways to attain their desire.[5]

For Turkey, then, the path into NATO was strewn with thorns. In the end, it took skillful diplomacy, the opportunity of the Korean confligration in 1950, and generous amounts of luck to set the stage for Turkey's successful assault on the objections of the European powers. But the difficulties of gaining admission to the Atlantic Pact merely increased Ankara's ardor; while the example of the eagerness of Western states for an American connection broke down reservations among Turkey's leaders about entangling alliances. Indeed, the Democratic Party (DP) government of Adnan Menderes evidently judged that a comprehensive association with the United States stood to benefit Turkey far more than the limited collaboration of the Truman Doctrine years. As a result, Menderes was willing, if not eager, to agree to cooperate with the West in the Middle East—a region not till then generally considered in Turkey to be of high priority—as the ultimate price of entry into the Atlantic alliance.

In fact, it was the Middle East that formed a major testing ground for the Turkish-American alliance in the first decade of Turkey's membership in NATO. Turkey played a prominent role

---

[5] On the Mediterranean alliance, see Ankara University, *Turkey and the United Nations* (New York, 1961), p. 158.

in the abortive endeavor to create a Middle East Command in 1951.⁶ More important was Ankara's successful effort to forge the Baghdad Pact a few years later. Menderes had perhaps been sparked in this direction by John Foster Dulles, who in 1953 pointed to the "northern tier" as the best remaining hope for constructing a defensive grouping in the Middle East.⁷ Nevertheless, by the time that this alliance had come into being in 1955, Washington had become reluctant to join as a full-fledged member. The United States accepted merely observer status, although agreeing to serve on committees and to provide regular financial support. But all through the 1950s Ankara continued to press Washington to regularize its position in the Baghdad Pact.

The Suez imbroglio of 1956 posed a serious challenge to Turkey's Western alliance. But despite concern that international action in connection with the Suez Canal could create undesirable precedents for Turkey in the Straits, Ankara—albeit with continuing reservations—did support Washington's efforts to form a Canal Users Association following Egyptian nationalization of the Suez Canal Company.⁸ Some differences also appeared between the Menderes regime and the Eisenhower administration in regard to Turkey's crisis with Syria during the ensuing year. In the end, however, Ankara was reassured by proclamation of the Eisenhower Doctrine in January 1957 and by the subsequent categoric statement of US determination to protect the Turks against attack from any quarter arising out of the Syrian question.⁹ For its part, the Turkish government cooperated with Washington during the events surrounding the Iraqi revolution and the Lebanese crisis in 1958, permitting US troops to use the military airbase near Adana as a staging point for deployment to Lebanon in the summer of 1958. And the following year—after tension in the Middle East had abated considerably—the United States signed a treaty of "Cooperation" with Turkey.¹⁰ This last

---

⁶ For basic documentation on the Middle East Command, see U.S., Department of State, *American Foreign Policy, 1950-1955: Basic Documents*, vol. II (Washington, 1957), pp. 2183-87.

⁷ Ibid., pp. 2168-80.

⁸ Ömer Sami Coşar, "Türkiye ve Suez," *Cumhuriyet*, Aug. 19, 1956.

⁹ U.S., Department of State, *Bulletin*, Jan. 21, 1957, p. 83; Nov. 11, 1957, p. 741.

¹⁰ For the text of this treaty, see U.S., Department of State, *Treaties and Other International Acts Series*, no. 4191, signed Mar. 5, 1959. References in this treaty to "aggression, direct or indirect," were later cited by elements in Turkey hostile to the

arrangement did not go beyond the commitments inherent in NATO membership and the Eisenhower Doctrine, but was one of a triad of identical US bilateral pacts then concluded with Iran and Pakistan and designed primarily to reassure the Shah.

In the Menderes era Turkey's strategic importance grew partly as a result of its increasing military cooperation with the United States. Turkish forces were modernized according to plans accepted by NATO. At the same time, the United States established electronic monitoring sites, based reconnaissance aircraft, and later deployed intermediate-range ballistic missiles and tactical strike aircraft in Turkey.[11] As a result, the Turks began to assume for American military planners a new importance as part of the overall US deterrent in the continuing cold war. Turkish leaders too were delighted by the rising strategic importance of their country. They, like public opinion generally in Turkey, appeared to accept the notion that participation in the strategy of "massive retaliation" raised the cost of attack against their state, thus adding to Turkish security. And no doubt they recognized that Turkey's significance to its allies enhanced the claim to economic and diplomatic as well as military support from the West.

Whereas political and military cooperation blossomed in the 1950s, in the economic sphere US-Turkish collaboration soon ran into snags. Washington regarded aid to Turkey's development as an integral part of the NATO alignment; for the first six years after Turkey joined the Atlantic Pact, economic aid averaged some $ 80 million a year.[12] But American insistence that economic criteria should dictate development projects clashed with Menderes' disposition to allocate investments for political purposes. Hence, Washington was unwilling to provide the massive additional economic assistance that the Ankara authorities requested after 1954 to alleviate the strains of Turkey's serious balance of payments crisis. Controversy raged till 1958, when rapidly deteriorating economic conditions in Turkey brought the

---

United States as authorizing American military intervention to suppress legitimate Turkish opposition political parties. See A. H. Ulman and R. H. Dekmejian, "Changing Patterns in Turkish Foreign Policy, 1959-1967," *Orbis*, Fall 1967, no. 3, pp. 772-85.

[11] Prime Minister Süleyman Demirel gave a detailed explanation of Turkey's military cooperation with the United States at his press conference of Feb. 7, 1970.

[12] U.S., Agency for International Development, *US Economic Assistance Programs, April 3, 1948-June 30, 1968* (Washington, 1969), p. 22.

DP government to agree to a more conservative fiscal course.[13] But although acrimony between the United States and Turkey over economic policy led to the point where it once even appeared that the chief of the aid mission might be declared *persona non grata*, both governments took care not to let ill feeling spill over to taint other facets of the relationship.

Despite the lingering discord on development criteria, the United States undertook to finance dams, energy grids, and other infrastructure projects at this time in an effort to provide a sound base on which long-range economic development would be possible. American assistance was also devoted to fostering agricultural growth through increasing mechanization of farmers. In addition, proliferating educational and technical assistance programs saw Americans involved in support to Turkish universities on a broad scale and engaged as advisers widely in the Ministry of Education. Generally successful as these endeavors were, nonetheless, they were marred by the friction between the American aid mission and the Turkish government. They also suffered on occasion from faulty personnel and uncoordinated approaches; for example, the Political Sciences Faculty of Ankara University felt impelled to terminate the New York University project of assistance on these grounds.[14] And these flaws, particularly in educational ventures, laid the basis for later disenchantment felt by a significant segment of the Turkish elite with American aid.

Close cooperation between Turkey and the United States was not interrupted by the military coup which ousted the Menderes government in May 1960. The new military rulers were preoccupied with domestic concerns; they had little time or interest to devote to foreign affairs. Consequently, the momentum of previous arrangements continued, despite fears in some quarters lest the new regime encounter US opposition.

An area where past momentum was particularly visible was that of military cooperation. The Menderes government had welcomed deployment of Nike antiaircraft missiles and Honest John short-range battlefield missiles. Toward the end of the 1950s Turkey, along with England and Italy, agreed in principle to station Jupiter medium-range ballistic missiles on their territories.

---

[13] John White, *Pledged to Development* (London, 1967), p. 103.

[14] Walter Adams and John Garraty, *Is the World Our Campus?* (Michigan State University Press, 1960), *passim*.

During the Menderes era only preliminary arrangements for this endeavor had been concluded. Preparations to deploy the Jupiters were not slowed appreciably by the military takeover. Despite Soviet objections to this activity in 1961, Turkish crews were sent to the United States for training and construction of installations for the missiles was carried forward in the Izmir area.[15] In fact, the Turkish military rulers appeared far more eager to receive these missiles than Washington to provide them. Thus the Turks categorically rebuffed the Kennedy administration which in April 1961 requested permission to withdraw the Jupiters on the grounds that they would be rendered obsolete by the proximate deployment of Polaris submarines.[16]

When the Cuban missile crisis broke out in the fall of 1962, therefore, the Jupiters were still stationed in Turkey. They immediately became the object of intensive Soviet efforts to arrange a bargain with Washington. Reasonable as President Kennedy considered Krushchev's proposal to withdraw missiles from Cuba in exchange for removal of those in Turkey, the American President was unwilling to accept a deal in the heat of crisis. Informally he let the Soviets know that the Jupiters would be withdrawn once Moscow had pulled its missiles out of Cuba. While the Turkish government stood staunchly behind the United States through the critical days of the Cuban confrontation, it too was shaken by the proximity of war in which Turkey appeared destined to play a central role. Thus the civilian coalition regime which a little more than a year before had taken over from the military junta readily agreed early in 1963 to let the Jupiters go.[17]

This signaled a change in Turkey's strategic position. With the departure of these missiles, Turkey no longer had on its soil offensive weapons which seemed certain to be subjected to immediate attack in the event of conflict. It was true that American and Turkish strike aircraft did continue to be deployed in Turkey—indeed, their number rose somewhat after the Jupiters were withdrawn.[18] But these aircraft, even if armed with nuclear weapons, obviously did not pose such a compelling threat to

---

[15] *Ulus*, Feb. 25, 1961, carries excerpts from the Soviet note of Feb. 3, 1961, and the Turkish reply of Feb. 24, 1961.

[16] Max Frankel, "Mischief Seen in Offer of Bases Deal," *New York Times*, Oct. 28, 1962; Robert F. Kennedy, Thirteen Days (New York, 1969), p. 94.

[17] Kennedy, pp. 94-95.

[18] Demirel's press conference of Feb. 7, 1970.

Moscow, many of whose more important targets were already being protected by effective surface-to-air missiles. In this constellation of circumstances, Turkey no longer held the position of extreme importance in the cold war it had occupied heretofore.

In this situation, the dramatic flare-up of the Cyprus dispute in the closing days of 1963 posed a serious challenge to Turkey's alliance with the United States. By this time Cypriot President Makarios had concluded that the compromises painfully achieved at London and Zurich in 1959 to accommodate the Greek and Turkish communities within one independent Cypriot state posed insuperable obstacles to his design for a unitary state. Makarios' demands in November 1963 to abrogate their special political rights came as a profound shock to the Turkish community. When violence soon erupted, the Ankara government felt impelled to send planes in token passes over the island to demonstrate its involvement.[19] Thanks in no small measure to this show of force, a lull came about in the fighting on Cyprus. But on the ground a tense confrontation continued, punctuated by recurrent armed clashes.

Washington found itself rapidly drawn into this imbroglio which threatened to bring its common allies Greece and Turkey into direct conflict. Both mainland states felt irresistible pressures to support their respective communities on Cyprus. Hence, American efforts to calm passions and to forestall military action strained US relations with both Greece and Turkey. Finally, in June 1964, President Johnson, believing that Ankara's forces were about to land on Cyprus, sent a letter not only informing the Turks that they must not use US equipment in such an operation, but warning also that the NATO alliance might not act to defend Turkey in the event of Soviet retaliation against Turkish intervention on the island.[20]

President Johnson's letter marked a turning point in Turkey's association with the United States. To the Turkish leaders, this message, by calling into question the automatic operation of NATO commitments in regard to Turkey, struck at the sanctity of Turkey's whole system of alliances. Ankara authorities were especially shocked because they had since the Second World War

---

[19] *New York Times*, Dec. 27, 1963.
[20] The texts of the Johnson letter and of the Turkish reply were published in the *Middle East Journal*, Summer 1966, pp. 386-93.

predicated their entire foreign policy on faith in commitments from their allies. Various Turkish governments had gone to great lengths to cooperate with their alliance partners, even beyond formal treaty obligations. For example, after fellow CENTO ally Pakistan complained, Ankara reneged on its offers of aid to India at the time of the Chinese Communist incursion in the fall of 1962. Turkish governments had also been willing to incur great visible risk to stand with the United States, notably in the Cuban missile crisis when the Turks (unlike other European members of NATO) found themselves at center stage in a conflict between the superpowers. In consequence, those in power in Ankara were enormously shaken to discover that their most important ally, the United States, not only would not help them in a deeply felt cause, but apparently disagreed profoundly on the force of the NATO commitment to defend Turkey.

Inevitably, therefore, the impact of the message from President Johnson was visible in many areas of Turkish life. The contents of the American communication leaked out almost at once into the Turkish press. Public opinion focused initially on Washington's efforts to prevent a Turkish landing on Cyprus, castigating the United States for its inconsistency in acting freely first in Cuba, then in Vietnam, while forbidding Turkey to do likewise in its "Mediterranean Cuba."[21] Indeed, the notion now began to spread among the Turkish elite that the alliance was one-sided, i.e., that it served US interests far more than those of Turkey. The emotional response to the falling out between the Turks and the United States over Cyprus thus affected Turkish-American relations in a depth that previous irritants and disagreements of years of association had not been able to do. By the end of the summer of 1964, youth and opposition elements launched protest demonstrations against the United States; a few Turkish publicists even projected their suspicions of America to the point of accusing Washington of seeking to manipulate Turkish domestic politics to serve US international purposes.[22] And these exaggerated, often completely insubstantial accusations against the United States, henceforth became a constant feature of the more extreme Turkish opposition circles.

Another striking change came in Turkey's relations with the

---

[21] *Ulus*, Aug. 7, 1964.
[22] For example, see "Kıbrıs: 'Go Home!'," *Akis*, Aug. 28, 1964, pp. 8-12.

Soviet Union. Concern that the alliance with the United States no longer offered necessary security from the USSR led Ankara to be receptive to Moscow's blandishments. For, after initial hesitation, the Soviets had seized on Turkey's disillusionment with the United States as an opportunity to wean the Turks away from the West. But Ankara was not willing to let down all the bars in regard to the USSR. Rather, the Turkish government welcomed merely a normalization of state-to-state relations, exemplified by exchanges of state visits and parliamentary delegations. Ankara, however, showed no desire or willingness to put intimacy with the USSR on anything approaching the level of Turkish relations with NATO and the United States. Indeed, as Turkey's interest in normalizing Turkish-Soviet relations lay primarily in gaining flexibility to deal with the Cyprus issue, there were clear limitations on the amount of warmth toward Moscow that Ankara would be willing to permit.

Taken together, these circumstances dictated that the peak of American intimacy with Turkey had passed. After mid-1964, therefore, the stage was set for some loosening of the bonds.

One of the most important forces of change was the growing political debate in Turkey in the 1960s. The freer atmosphere bred by the 1960 revolution led to active questioning of all facets of Turkish life. From concentration on domestic issues, this debate soon involved Turkey's foreign orientation as well.

A major facet of this questioning centered on the value of NATO and the Western alliance. As the 20th anniversary of NATO approached in 1969, a date when the members could—if they wished—leave this pact, extremists (particularly of the left) intensified their efforts to induce the Ankara government to say "No to NATO."[23] Student groups and small extremist unions led in this endeavor, assisted by the tiny Turkish Labor Party (TLP), which had some 15 members in the lower house of parliament from 1965 until the end of 1969, when its representation was cut to 2. These views received perhaps inordinate attention in the press, where partisans of the TLP had disproportionately heavy representation. They were echoed in less extreme form by the left wing of the Republican Peoples Party, then the principal opposition party, some of whose members appeared uncertain as

---

[23] Türkiye İşçi Partisi Ankara İl Heyeti, *NATO'ya Hayır* (Pamphlet distributed 1968), *passim*.

to whether Turkey should remain in NATO.[24] The more moderate opposition looked to the stance of their European allies, especially France, as a model for Turkey's conduct. But, after it became clear that Paris did not intend to withdraw from NATO, all except the most die-hard opponents of the Atlantic Pact in Turkey shifted ground. Instead of calling Turkey to disengage from the alliance, they propounded extensive changes in the Turkish association with the United States to bring a new measure of "equality" into the relationship.

Demands among the left-of-center opposition for such alterations in relations with the United States reflected also a growing feeling that in the changing strategic situation of the 1970s the doctrine of "flexible response" left Turkey exposed to aggression without providing a firm guarantee in the event of attack. Thus, what most of those who advocate changes are seeking is the elimination from Turkish soil of weapons systems that appear likely to provoke Soviet attack in the event of conflict between NATO and the Warsaw Pact nations. In this context, these critics brand nuclear weapons and American strike aircraft as particularly undesirable. By far the majority of those who argue in this vein do not seek the interruption or reduction of military aid to the Turkish armed forces. But partisans of this view hold that Turkey would not be a sure target for retaliation if these weapons were entirely removed from Turkish territory.[25]

The debate on the benefits and detriments of alliance with the United States also reflects Turkey's rising nationalist fervor. The thrust of this powerful force has been easily channeled into hostility against the United States, especially under the allegation that Washington benefits from the alliance more than does Ankara. However incomprehensible this claim may be to Americans who recall the massive amounts of US aid to Turkey, increasing numbers of Turks have nonetheless come to believe that the

---

[24] The position of the left wing of the Republican Peoples Party was set forth in a preliminary report published in *Milliyet*, July 5, 1968. For views of individuals in the party, see, for example, Doğan Avcıoğlu, "Kıbrıs ve Ötesi," *Yön*, Dec. 31, 1965, p. 3; Ahmet Şükrü Esmer, "NATO ve Türkiye," *Milliyet*, Dec. 17, 1966; Muammer Aksoy, "Atatürkün Işığında 'Tam Bağımsızlık İlkesi'," in Siyasal Bilgiler Fakültesi, *Abadan'a Armağan* (Ankara, 1969), pp. 689-799. See also George S. Harris, *Troubled Alliance: Turkish-American Problems in Historical Perspective, 1945-1971* (Washington, 1972), pp. 141-43.

[25] *Milliyet*, July 5, 1968.

United States now contributes little to Turkey, but gains use of strategic territory of immense value against the Soviet Union. Those at the head of Turkey's military establishment and major political parties do not share the view that relations are badly out of balance—although they too may have some doubts as to whether Turkey's needs are sufficiently met by the present terms of collaboration.[26]

Yet even those who have been most satisfied with the workings of the Turkish-American association have been pushed hard by university and other radical circles. Already before the Cyprus crisis popularized a certain suspicion of the United States in the mid-1960s, some in the universities had long been preaching distrust of America as an imperialist power.[27] As a result, a generation of educated Turks is on its way to maturity who have imbibed profound suspicions of American intentions and actions. Almost all of Turkey's student organizations have traded on hostility toward the United States in addition to their other issues of protest.

Indeed, the efficacity of student organizations in inflaming passions against America has no doubt been important in spurring their greatly increased activism toward the end of 1960s. Student protest against the appointment of American Ambassador Komer at the end of 1968 provided a focus of cohesion and direction to the student movement which had been lacking in the past. When he was soon removed from office by the newly elected American President Nixon, student leaders in Turkey easily exaggerated the importance of their agitation in securing this result. Continuing campaigns of violence against visits of the US Sixth Fleet to Turkish ports also contributed to bolstering the self-confidence of Turkish student demonstrators. By the end of 1970, the radical student movement had gained such momentum from this chain of events that the Revolutionary Students Federation—a highly extremist organization, dedicated among other things to the expulsion of all Americans from Turkey—succeeded in kidnapping first one lone American soldier, then four of his compatriots at once. It was these events in February and March 1971 that formed the background for the ouster of

---

[26] Abdi İpekçi examined the attitudes of the Turkish military toward America in his series of articles on US-Turkish relations in *Milliyet*, May 18-27, 1970.

[27] For views of university professors, see Aksoy, *passim*.

the Justice Party government of Süleyman Demirel under pressure from the Turkish armed forces and its replacement by the Erim regime in March 1971.[28]

The military-backed Erim government, and its successors up to the elections in the fall of 1973, put an effective damper on student activists and other radicals. Using martial law, these Turkish governments arrested numerous agitators, cracked down on terrorists, and even tried numerous intellectuals whose ideas were held responsible for inflaming youth. Although these actions were designed to restore law and order within Turkey, they also served to remove from the public arena most of the more virulent critics of the United States. And the ensuing respite from public attack took some of the intensity out of the criticism of America.

Even after the return to more normal party politics in the campaigning for the 1973 elections, the issue of the Western alliance has remained muted. Particularly with American disengagement from Vietnam, Turks appear widely to credit the "Nixon Doctrine" with being one of limited involvement in the domestic affairs of other nations. Hence the fear of active American intervention in Turkish domestic politics, fear which fueled much of the suspicion of American motives, seems to have abated.

Military cooperation between Turkey and the United States reflected the growing Turkish nationalist sensitivity. It was also affected by the shifting equation of American budgetary contraints and rising Turkish economic strength. Moreover, the increasing divergence of interests between the allies, with Turkey focusing more and more on regional concerns and interested in mollifying the USSR, all served to change the relationship.

A major effect of these alterations was the restriction of the freedom of American activity in Turkey. For example, after a reconnaissance aircraft crashed in international waters in the Black Sea, such flights ceased and were never subsequently resumed.[29] Turkey, which had once been the host to a U-2 squadron, thus ceased to be a base for active surveillance of the USSR.

---

[28] On the kidnappings, see *New York Times*, Feb. 16, 1971; "Turkey: The Welcome That Wore Thin," *Time*, Mar. 1, 1971; *Cumhuriyet*, March 5, 1971; "Kidnappers Free 4 G.I.'s in Turkey," *New York Times*, Mar. 9, 1971.

[29] *Hürriyet*, Apr. 1, 1966; Demirel's press conference of Feb. 7, 1970 in Harris, pp. 229-38.

Similarly, after Turkish Labor Party leaders mounted a concerted campaign to attack the United States for exercising "sovereignty" over "35 million square meters" of Turkish territory, the Justice Party government in the spring of 1966 requested Washington to open negotiations to regularize and formalize American access to military facilities in Turkey. [30] These lengthy negotiations resulted in the Defense Cooperation Agreement of July 1969, a document which explicitly affirmed ultimate Turkish sovereignty over all installations and emphasized their NATO character. Operating procedures for the use of these facilities were relegated to "implementing agreements" which are still under negotiation some five years later. Yet the general provisions of the 1969 accord clearly did place additional limits on American freedom of action.

At the same time, Washington in reassessing its operations concluded that some activities in Turkey were no longer needed. Starting in 1968, the United States began cutting back operations, pulling personnel out of facilities, such as the "site 23" communications complex outside of Ankara. [31] Likewise, Americans were withdrawn from two of the three major installations on the Black Sea coast; US strike aircraft were removed from the Çiğli NATO base near İzmir. This left sizable concentrations of US military personnel at installations only near İzmit, Sinop, Diyarbakır, and Adana, in addition to headquarters complements at Ankara and İzmir. From a peak of some 24,000, therefore, the number of American military personnel and their dependents dropped to some 16,000 by mid-1970. [32]

With the decline in numbers came also a decline in the dollar valuation assigned to US military assistance. Assistant Secretary of Defense John McNaughton had proposed a five-year program of modernization for the Turkish armed forces calling for $ 134 million a year in American military aid starting in 1967. [33] This already represented some decrease in the stated amount of

---

[30] *Cumhuriyet*, May 1, Nov 8, 1965, reported these accusations against the United States. For the initiation of negotiations, see *Hürriyet*, Apr. 1, 1966; Demirel's press conference of Feb. 7, 1970.

[31] *New York Times*, June 8, Aug. 9, 1968; A. Şükrü Esmer, " 'Manzaralı' Tesisinin Devri," *Ulus*, June 17, 1968.

[32] U.S., Senate, *United States Security Agreements and Commitments Abroad*: Part 7: *Greece and Turkey* (Washington, 1970), p. 1831.

[33] *Milliyet*, Aug. 16, 1966.

US assistance as compared with previous years. But in the economic stringency generated by the Vietnam conflict Washington fell short of even this level after the first year. Although in practical terms the decline in dollar amounts of military aid was somewhat offset by reductions in the price of items supplied and by the donation of surplus American equipment, it was hard to belie the impression that US assistance was waning.

Nonetheless, these changes in the scope of military cooperation were not directed at gradually phasing out the relationship between Turkey and the United States. The Turks continued to look to America as the major source of military equipment. And the Turkish military commanders persisted in ambitious efforts to modernize their forces after the end of the McNaughton program. For example, in August 1972 Turkey committed its own resources to buy 40 Phantom jet fighter-bombers (F-4s), after Greece concluded similar arrangements. [34] A substantial American aid program continued as well. Indeed, by 1974 the United States was still providing grant military assistance valued at nearly $ 100 million.

A more radical transformation took place in the field of economic assistance. Here two essentially unrelated processes were at work. On the one hand, Turkey's economic position underwent a veritable revolution in the decade following 1964. From a state with a perennial deficit in its foreign account that could be met only by continuing infusions of economic aid from abroad, Turkey swiftly passed to the point of having large annual surpluses of foreign exchange. Unaccustomed to such fortunate circumstances, the Turks rapidly built up their reserves, until by 1974 the Central Bank held over $ 2 billion in hard currency. [35] This windfall came from remittances from the million or more workers who streamed to Western Europe (mostly to West Germany) to find employment during these years. Not only, therefore, did Turkey benefit from this massive inflow of foreign exchange, the domestic economy was relieved of the necessity to

---

[34] *Milliyet*, Aug. 9, 1972, reported Republican Peoples Party leader Ecevit's opposition to the "arms race" between Greece and Turkey. The agreement signed on Aug. 10, 1972, called for delivery of the planes by 1976 at a cost of $4 million each. *Cumhuriyet*, Aug. 11, 1972.

[35] International Monetary Fund, *International Financial Statistics* (Washington, March 1974), p. 359.

absorb these workers at a time when unemployment and underemployment were already high.

Though there was some cost in inflation, a problem made far more severe by the skyrocketing price of petroleum in 1974, the accretion of such sizable reserves freed Turkey from dependence on concessionary assistance from abroad. It also dwarfed the amount of aid which the United States then disposed for Turkey.

The other process which affected economic assistance was the growing reluctance of Washington to continue large economic outflows at a time when the United States itself was experiencing an unfavorable trend in its balance of trade.

As a result of the convergence of these two factors, American economic assistance to Turkey gradually petered out after 1968, but with little untoward effect on the Turkish economy. Indeed, by 1974 Turkey was experiencing a net outflow of resources as previously contracted debts were repaid.

The gain to Turkey from nearly a quarter century of economic assistance ran beyond the impact of the some $ 3 billion divided nearly equally between grants and loans.[36] The access to American technology and know-how was also of significance to the Turks. The necessity to justify and plan the use of aid and to account in detail to aid givers, especially the international consortium sponsored by the United States, stimulated an economic awareness and promoted a level of expertise that is standing Turkey in good stead. These experts, institutionalized in the State Planning Organization, have become a permanent feature of the Turkish economic landscape.

While the ties of alliance were thus slowly relaxing in these ways, the allies have had to face two particularly challenging problems: opium and Cyprus. Both remain overhanging the alliance and both have the potential to disrupt it.

Of these problems, opium is the newest to trouble Turkey's relations with the United States. In the years immediately following the Second World War, narcotics did not loom as a contentious matter between the United States and Turkey. The Turks had long been major exporters of opium for the licit medicinal trade. Since adhering to the League of Nations convention to

---

[36] AID, Office of Statistics and Reports, Bureau for Program and Policy Coordination, *U. S. Overseas Loans and Grants and Assistance from International Organizations* (Special Report Prepared for the House Foreign Affairs Committee), May 1974, p. 28.

control the production and sale of narcotics in 1932, the Turks had operated the production and marketing of opium gum as a state monopoly. Further, Ankara acceded to the international opium control convention which took effect in 1964.[37] This instrument imposed rigorous obligations on the government to prevent the diversion of narcotics into illegal channels, and committed Turkey to curtail—or cut off entirely—poppy cultivation in the event that it proved unable to police the legal trade effectively.

By the mid-1960s, American interest in the traffic of narcotics was rising rapidly. Drug abuse had begun to emerge as a major problem in the United States. From experience in combatting the heroin trade, American authorities soon became convinced that the major proportion (some 80 percent was the common estimate) of the heroin illegally introduced into the United States was derived from opium diverted from legal channels in Turkey.[38] This conclusion led Washington to approach the Turks for joint action in dealing with the poppy problem.

Despite the fact that there was little consumption of narcotics in Turkey, Ankara took seriously the obligation to curb the illicit international trade. The Turks joined American narcotics agents in cooperation to prevent opium from falling into illegal hands. But, as this action seemed insufficient to stop the illegal traffic, the Justice Party governments which ruled Turkey from 1965 to 1971 also undertook to restrict poppy acreage. There, was even a press report that Prime Minister Demirel had agreed to end all poppy cultivation by 1971.[39] But when a military ultimatum brought down his government in March 1971, poppy raising was still permitted in four provinces. Given the political importance of the poppy producers in these provinces, it was clearly difficult for any elected regime to reduce cultivation further.

The nonparty government of Nihat Erim installed after the military ultimatum in March 1971 did not suffer from these constraints. Erim himself was thoroughly persuaded of the hu-

---

[37] Harvey R. Wellman (Special Assistant to the Secretary of State for Narcotics Matters), "Speech before the American Turkish Society," Dec. 14, 1970, p. 3.

[38] U.S. Department of State, Press Release no. 108, April 2, 1970, p. 13: "Address by the Honorable Elliot L. Richardson, Under Secretary of State, to the Philadelphia Bar Association."

[39] Felix Belair, Jr., "U.S. Loan to Turkey Dismays Narcotics Officials," *New York Times*, June 14, 1970.

manitarian obligation to end the planting of poppies. After intensive negotiations with the American ambassador, he used his legal authority to regulate the areas of poppy cultivation to issue a decree banning production entirely following the 1972 harvest. In return, Washington undertook to provide Ankara $ 35 million in loans to be used to compensate the farmers and to promote the transition to other crops.[40]

This was not a popular bargain in Turkey. In the atmosphere of free debate that preceeded the military intervention in 1971, the United States had been heavily criticized for pressing Turkey to abandon poppy cultivation. The congressional testimony of Attorney General John Mitchell, raising the possibility of economic sanctions in the event Turkey did not stop the illegal trade, roused a furor in the summer of 1970.[41] Even in the general moratorium on criticism induced by the arrest of the government's more vociferous critics after mid-1971, Erim's move to end poppy planting occasioned renewed attacks. Deputies introduced legislation calling for a resumption of cultivation.[42] But given the constraints of that era, circumstances were not conducive for parliament seriously to challenge Erim's action. Even under the procession of governments that followed until the elections in the fall of 1973, the same restraints applied.

Return to more normal party politics with the 1973 elections brought with it, among other things, renewed debate on the poppy decision. In their election campaigns almost all the parties had called for review of the ban on poppies. Thus it was not altogether surprising that, when the Republican Peoples Party finally managed to piece together a coalition with the National Salvation Party some three months after the election, one of the government's first acts was to ask Washington to join in reexamination of the ban on poppy growing. Public sentiment in Turkey strongly favored resumption of cultivation. And despite American urging to maintain the ban, at the end of June 1974, Prime Minister Bulent Ecevit announced that planting would be permitted in the fall of 1974 in seven provinces.[43] To soften the blow

---

[40] Dana Adams Schmidt, "Poppy-Ban Cost to U.S. Disclosed," *New York Times*, Nov. 21, 1971.

[41] Harris, pp. 191-92.

[42] *Milliyet*, Dec. 23, 1971.

[43] *Cumhuriyet*, July 2, 1974. The text of the decree was carried in a special issue of *Resmi Gazete*, July 1, 1974.

to Washington and to carry out the obligation to prevent diversion, Ecevit also appealed for suggestions for improved methods to control production.

Congressional reaction in the United States was quick and unfavorable. The mood of Congress was to penalize Turkey until it could demonstrate effective controls. American lawmakers showed little disposition to credit the Turks with the will or the capability to carry out promises this time to institute a control system with teeth that would work.[44]

But Ankara soon made clear that despite preoccupation with pressing domestic and foreign problems, it was serious about applying strict controls. On September 16, 1974, the Turkish delegate to the United Nations Division of Narcotic Drugs in Geneva announced his government's decision to adopt the so-called "poppy straw" process of harvesting poppies, i.e., to buy the whole unincized plant from the farmers.[45] This procedure bypassed the production of opium gum by the peasants, thereby obviating the greatest opportunity for diversion. This change "was warmly welcomed by the United Nations," as providing assurance of strict compliance with international obligations.

Under these circumstances, the Turkish government appears to have succeeded in forestalling, at least in the short run, major damage to relations with the United States from the decision to resume poppy cultivation.

The Cyprus problem presents an even more precarious face. American efforts under Dean Acheson to mediate a compromise settlement at Geneva in August 1964 failed when terms of his plan leaked prematurely.[46] Thereafter until 1967, an uneasy cold war persisted between the Greek and Turkish communities on the island. But the advantage lay with the Greeks; and Athens was able to introduce thousands of troops onto the island to reinforce the military preponderance over the Turks. In November 1967, shooting between a Greek patrol and Turkish villagers led to a number of casualties. Challenged by this incident, Ankara again began preparations for a landing. Again the United States found itself in the middle, for both Greeks and Turks

---

[44] David Bird, "Wolff Pressing Turkey on Opium," *New York Times*, July 9, 1974.

[45] Press release, the UN Division of Narcotic Drugs, Geneva, Oct. 8, 1974.

[46] Harris, pp. 117-18.

looked to Washington for assistance. Yet colored by disappointments of the past, neither side was confident of securing the American backing it desired.

The mission of Cyprus Vance in November 1967 did not repeat the precedent of the Johnson intervention three years earlier.[47] This time, Washington sent no strong threatening letter. Instead, Vance shuttled between the three capitals involved working out an acceptable compromise to avert the war nobody wanted. With a military regime in Athens which did not have the goad of public reaction to take into consideration, the Greeks agreed to remove their offending troops and the Vance mission succeeded in its central aim: to prevent war. In Turkey, therefore, Vance's conduct and the outcome of his efforts served to dissipate some of the suspicion and concern about American policy toward Cyprus.

While the possibility of a new outbreak on the island remained a threat to Turkish-American relations, the period until July 1974 passed uneventfully for the alliance. Intercommunal negotiations began on Cyprus in 1968. Though they made little progress, the talks did serve to lower tension. None of the parties actively looked to the United States for assistance in pressing its cause.

But the renewal of the Cyprus crisis in July 1974 posed new strains on the alliance. The overthrow of President Makarios and his replacement by Nicos Samson, whom the Turks held responsible for the killing of many of their compatriots in December 1963, was a red flag for Ankara. Recognizing the dangers inherent in this situation, Washington sent Under Secretary Joseph Sisco to attempt to reach a diplomatic solution.[48] Unable to find any acceptable compromise in the short time available, his mediation was not able to avert Turkish military landings on the island.

The effort to head off war having failed, Washington encouraged the parties to agree to armistice talks in Geneva under the auspices of British Foreign Secretary Callaghan. Although Secretary Kissinger remained in frequent contact with Turkish Prime Minister Ecevit all during this period, it was clear that he was employing persuasion, not coercion, in seeking to find ways to make possible effective negotiations between the Greeks and the Turks.

---

[47] Harris, p. 123.
[48] *Milliyet*, July 19-20, 1974; Richard Eder, "Greece Pressed, Plans to Replace Cyprus Officers," *New York Times*, July 19, 1974.

It was widely believed in Turkey that the administration of President Ford understood and sympathized with the Turkish position. This conviction was strengthened when Ford and Secretary Kissinger publicly opposed congressional efforts to force a cut-off of aid to Turkey in protest against Turkish military intervention on the island.

Yet the continuing possibility of a suspension of American military aid to Turkey threatens the alliance in a fundamental way. An aid cut in these circumstances would leave deep psychological scars. Indeed, it would be this aspect—far more than the physical or economic impact of losing American-supplied equipment and credit—that would haunt the relationship for a long time to come. Even the threat of an aid cut-off has already provoked Turkish reaction. During deliberations on assistance in the American Congress, Turkish Foreign Minister Turan Güneş made clear that Ankara would reexamine the matter of American's access to facilities in the event aid were stopped.[49] But such a reappraisal would be most painful in Turkey which has based its foreign policy squarely on cooperation with the United States. Equally, Washington would find it troublesome and disturbing should any fundamental alteration in the alliance become necessary.

On the other hand, if the Cyprus imbroglio can be overcome without an interruption in aid, the auguries for Turkish-American relations seem good. No doubt return to the deep intimacy of the early 1960s is out of the question. The maturing of Turkish attitudes and the change in Turkey's need to receive and in America's ability to give would seem to rule it out. Moreover, Turkey's growing involvement with Europe also seems destined eventually to cut into American ties. Nonetheless, save in exceptional circumstances, there appear to be clear limits on how far disengagement will go. None of the major Turkish political parties wishes to dismantle relations with the United States in any fundamental way. Nor do the Turkish armed forces have any interest in disrupting ties. Hence, provided that the damage of the Cyprus dispute can be limited within reasonable bounds, the chances seem good for a close if not quite as intimate a relationship between Turkey and the United States to continue for many years to come.

---

[49] *Milliyet*, Oct. 26, 31, 1974.

TURKISH SOVIET RELATIONS

KEMAL H. KARPAT
University of Wisconsin, Madison, Wisconsin

History has been very generous to Turkey, locating her on the most strategic and traditionally most coveted piece of territory on the globe, thus her role in world politics has been far greater than the size of her population or economic power would warrant. But history has also been extremely cruel to Turkey by placing her next to the Soviet Union and by depriving her of enough resources and power to counteract alone the colossus in the north. The irony of history has not ended here. The Soviet Union, like its predecessor, Czarist Russia, has accepted in angry impotence the necessity of sailing its ships through the Bosphorus and the Dardanelles under the muzzles of the Turkish guns, and of allowing the Black Sea coast, comprising one of the most populous and developed sections of Soviet territory to remain vulnerable to attacks by an enemy which could enlist Turkey's support. The Soviet note of September 24, 1946, given to the Turkish Government and asking for bases on the Straits, clearly documents this situation. "It would be unjust," states the note, "to forget that the Soviet shores on the Black Sea are 2.100 km. long and give access to the most important regions of the country. The need to assure their security through the direct participation of the Soviet Union in the defense of the [Turkish] Straits has its source in the vital interests of the U.S.S.R." Indeed, the Paris Treaty of 1856 resulting from the Russian defeat in the Crimean War of 1853, and the Berlin Treaty of 1878 which altered the San-Stefano Treaty and deprived Russia of some of her gains secured in the Ottoman-Russian War of 1877, were in large measure the consequence of the joint European-Ottoman control of the Straits and the Black Sea.

The recent opinion put forth by some uninitiated observers that the strategic importance of the Turkish Straits has diminished because of nuclear weaponry is not supported by facts. The Straits have gained additional importance due to the rapid rise of Soviet maritime power. As Harry N. Howard has pointed out,

Soviet commercial tonnage sailing though the Straits rose from 1.2 million tons in 1955 to 26,365,346 tons in 1969, which accounts for about 43 percent of the total Soviet tonnage. In 1969 a total of 17,159 ships or 61,545,535 tons passed through the Straits, which was about five times more than the 12,322,012 tons registered in 1935. The Soviet fleet in the Black Sea comprises 31 percent of her shipping and 50 percent of her total tonnage. By 1980 the Soviet cargo to and from the developing nations is expected to reach an estimated total value of 11 billion dollars. A substantial part of it will pass through the Straits. The number of Soviet warships crossing the Straits rose from 90 in 1964 to 284 in 1969 and is likely to increase further. Indeed, the importance of the Turkish Straits has been especially enhanced during recent years by the entry of the Soviet naval units into the Mediterranean.

It is obvious that in case of an armed conflict between East and West the Soviet ships could be easily bottled up in the Black Sea. Even though nuclear weapons might have superseded all other conventional means of war still, NATO control over the Straits and Gibraltar, as well as the extreme vulnerability of the Suez Canal would continue to have a powerful restraining impact on the Soviets and play a significant part in checking her influence among the African and Middle Eastern nations. Moscow has quietly but insistently put forth the view that the Soviet Union has become, by extension, a Mediterranean power because she is a Black Sea power, and that her presence in the first sea would have political and military consequences. Such contentions are designed to convince world opinion that the Turkish Straits have been bypassed and establish in due time grounds for claiming that by custom the Straits have become part of the Soviet sphere of influence. It must be stressed that the status of the Straits is still governed by the Montreux Convention of 1936. However, the Soviet denouncement of the Treaty of Friendship of 1925 with Turkey, which had paved the way for the Montreux Convention, and their unsuccessful effort to create a new status for the Straits in 1946, may be used as arguments for claiming that the Convention has lost its validity, and for imposing at the proper moment a new regime on the Straits favorable to the USSR.

The strategic position of Turkey, affecting vital Soviet interests such as defense, navigation, and world influence, has been so pervasive as to compel the Soviet Union to use every device to subvert and dominate, to win over, or at least to neutralize Turkey at all costs. The efforts of the Soviet Union to fulfill her objectives in Turkey surpass by far the usual means employed by states in their normal relations. Indeed, the overwhelming importance attached by the USSR, a super power, to such a relatively small and powerless country as Turkey invites the suspicion that additional factors, besides the strategic ones, are inducing the Soviets to seek control or at least the "friendship" of Turkey. A closer scrutiny may reveal the existence of such factors.

A rather unique amalgam of strategic, historical, cultural, and psychological-ideological factors give to Turkey a special place among Soviet foreign policy objectives. First of all, the Soviets seem to have assessed accurately the special position held by Turkey in the Muslim world. For centuries Turkey occupied a central place as the seat of the Caliphate and the defender of Muslim independence, culture, and territorial integrity against the onslaught of the West. In the twentieth century Turkey has probably been the Muslim country most successful in achieving a true modernization and assuring herself relative peace and prosperity by establishing friendly relations with the West. There are few Muslims who would not acknowledge, although maybe a bit grudgingly, Turkey's achievement in past and modern times. And conditions permitting they may follow her leadership in a scheme of common appeal to all of them. It was not, after all, by chance that the Soviets used mainly Turkish leftist intellectuals in organizing the Congress of Eastern Peoples at Baku in 1920, with the idea of starting an anti-imperialist revolution in Asia. Close relations with the USSR and, even better, the full adherence of Turkey to Soviet foreign policy, would have a fundamental impact in winning over the Muslim peoples in the Middle East and Africa. Turkey is painfully aware that historically these intangible cultural forces, had conditioned the relations of the Ottoman state with Czarist Russia, and are affecting her own present relations with the Soviets. It is a well-known fact that the Russian Empire expanded through a series of wars into Crimea, South Ukraine, the Caucasus, and occasionally the Balkans, depriving the Ottoman state of its best lands, until exhausted by repeated defeats, the Ottomans lay powerless at the mercy of international intrigue and the whims of the great powers. The idea of defending the Orthodox Christians, and then Pan Slavism were ideological weapons which admirably served the expansionist aims of Czarist Russia. The sense of mission, the self-righteous posture in any internal or external problem which characterizes the actions of the Soviets are a carry-over from that messianic spirit developed by Czarist Russia in her struggle to destroy the Ottoman state and raise the cross on Saint Sophia in Tzarigrad ("the city of Czars") or Istanbul. Indeed, the Russians' political personality and sense of nationality were built on religious foundations which later, in the age of nationalism gained new strength through Pan-Slavism.

The allusion to the historical background of Turco-Soviet relations is not intended to revive the memories of an ugly past or to buttress the Western sterotyped concept that Turkey's fear of the Soviet Union is so deep as to make her ready to undertake any sacrifice in order to assure her survival. The point is made in order to bring forth the fact that in their relations with the Turks the Soviets rely on a special historical knowledge in manipulating cultural and ideological weapons, which they have not hesitated to do recently with rather devastating effect. By the same token, Turkey has developed a refined understanding of the policy and the means used by the Soviet Union toward her, and a rather deep insight into the strengths and weaknesses of the USSR, an understanding which she cannot exploit for lack of means. It is this understanding which has enabled the Turks in their own unobtrusive fashion to use the Soviet ambitions to neutralize their influence, often by appearing to give in to Russian pressures while promoting their own interests. It is the dangerous, but unavoidable game between a big power and a small state whereby the latter learns how to use in defense the weapons of the first, including the manipulation of cultural and ideological factors.

There have developed in Turkey during the past decade, two schools of thought which run contrary to the above classical view of continuous historical rivalry between Turkey and the Soviet Union. One of these schools claims that Turkish modernization and political progress in terms of national self-assertion has been more rapid during periods of rapprochement and friendship with the Soviets. Furthermore, this school maintains that the Soviets have not hesitated to share their technological skill and industrial power with the less developed nations such as Turkey, while the friendship of the West with the third world powers has been motivated by economic interest and a desire to establish cultural supremacy. Another school claims that friendship and a continuing dialogue with the Soviets will give Turkey a better bargaining position in world politics and allow her to acquire a better understanding of the methods and philosophy through which the Russians industrialized and made their country a world power. Indeed, the rapid technological, cultural, and scientific advancement achieved by the Soviets has created among some groups in Turkey an admiring interest in the Russians, which is often manifest in political sympathy for the USSR. These schools of thought have had considerable bearing upon the foreign policy of Turkey as shall be seen later.

Turco-Soviet relations are indirectly but profoundly affected by another cultural-ethnic factor which is seldom mentioned, namely, the existence of Turkic groups in the Soviet Union. As is too well known, Central Asia, the original home of the Turks, and parts of the Caucasus are inhabited by some forty million people whose language, culture, and religion are common to those in Turkey. Traditionally, a nationalist Turk motivated by cultural and religious considerations regards as Turk an Azeri, Khirghiz, Uzbek, Khazak, Turkmen, Tatar, or Chechen. The Soviets, while accepting the existence of cultural and linguistic similarities between these groups and the Turks of Turkey, regard them as different nationalities. Hence some writers refer to these groups as Turkic and others as Eastern Turks. We shall use the second expression.

This problem became an explosive issue early in the twentieth century when the ruling Committee of Union and Progress (CUP) made pan-Turanism, that is the unity of all Turks in one country named Turan, a cardinal point of its foreign policy in the period 1908-1918. The transformation of Russia from a Czarist nationalist state to a socialist regime, strangely enough, coincided with the transition of Turkey from a multinational religious state to a national secular one. It is important to note that the Eastern Turks, with the exception of those living in the Caucasus, were never under Ottoman sultans, who, guided by dynastic preoccupation, did not emphasize national identities. The Young Turks' Pan-Turanian dream formally came to an end with the Ottoman defeat in 1918, but its repercussions continued in the establishment of an independent Azerbaijan in 1919-1921, and the death of Enver Paşa, one of the three leaders of CUP, at the head of the rebellious Basmachi tribes in Central Asia.

The Republican regime, established formally in 1923, repeatedly repudiated Pan-Turanism or Pan-Turkism. Yet, the issue has reappeared in one form or another in Turco-Soviet relations. Early in 1930, the Russian ambassador in Ankara complained that the Turk Ocakları ("Turkish Hearths") the nationalist organization, disseminated Pan-Turkist ideas. These were eventually replaced by the People's Houses, whose program conspicuously omitted the principle of cultural unity or *hars*, which figured prominently in the program of the Ocaks. Between 1941 and 1944, Turkey witnessed a resurgence of Pan-Turanism, now called Pan-Turkism, under German influence, which was brought under control through suppression of existing organizations and arrest of leaders. Today the apologists for Pan-Turkism no longer demand the unity of all Turks in one country, but have limited their objectives to asking independence for Eastern Turks, similar to that of the third world nations of Asia and Africa.

A number of scholars claim that economic and cultural development under the Soviet regime resuscitated national consciousness and solidarity among the Eastern Turks and increased their sense of cultural affinity with the Turks of Turkey, paradoxically enough mostly among the intelligentsia raised in marxist schools. These scholars claim that the Soviets are increasingly apprehensive that an independent, economically prosperous, modern Turkey will stimulate nationalist feeling among its own Soviet-Turks. There are some indications to back these views. Very often Turkish groups in the Soviet Union migrate and settle by preference in Turkey, given the chance to do so, and assimilate rapidly. Most have their cultural organizations in the country and are active in anti-Soviet propaganda. It is difficult to assess the accuracy of these views and the extent to which Soviet officialdom is truly worried about the national movements among its people. Yet, the rich literature on the subject, the Soviet irritation at even the slightest allusion to the Turks of the Soviet Union in other than their officially designated fashion, and the fact that most leftists in Turkey regard any effort to relate the "Turks of Central Asia" to those from Turkey as a cardinal sin, reinforce one's suspicions that the Soviets are indeed concerned about this potentially explosive issue. Consequently, it would be accurate to state that various problems connected with the Eastern Turks have some impact upon Soviet relations with Turkey. However, Turkish foreign policy makers have consistently refused to exploit any issue involving the Eastern Turks or even to acknowledge its existence. They emphatically stress the fact that Turkey is interested exclusively in conducting its relations with the Soviet government in the most correct fashion and is not interested in anything else, least of all in nationality problems. Whatever the truth, these allegations add new complexity to the background of Turco-Soviet relations and give them additional dimensions.

The objectives of Soviet policy toward Turkey and the means used to reach them are conditioned in large measure by the factors cited above. Indeed, the territorial security of the USSR, her long-range interests in the Middle East and in the Mediterranean basin, and the need to assimilate the Eastern Turks without any interference from outside, however small, give Turkey top priority in the general framework of Soviet foreign policy. Normal or friendly relations do not provide permanent guarantees. The Soviet interests are so basic as to call for definitive solutions. Consequently the annexation of the country, the establishment of a pro-Soviet regime and government, or the involvement of Turkey in a regional pact dominated by the Soviets, and finally, her neutralization, appear by order of priority to be solutions most satisfactory to the Soviets.

It is interesting to note that the Soviets have attempted to reach all those objectives, except for the first, while openly declaring respect for Turkey's political regime and international commitments. The strategy of the Soviets during their own period of weakness, from 1921-1936, was to establish friendly relations with Turkey. But even during this period, known at the "Lenin-Ataturk era of friendship," the basic Soviet strategy was to keep Turkey isolated as clearly evidenced by the Soviet reaction to the Turkish formal alliance with France and England in 1939, which, incidentally, was aimed at providing a defense against Germany, as shall be indicated later. For a brief period in 1944-46, Turkey was isolated because of the Allied displeasure over Turkish procrastination in engaging in war against Germany.

The Soviets used this opportunity to claim territories in the north and bases on the Straits. Consequently, Turkey committed herself to a full alliance with the West as the only solution for the defense of her territory and independence. In sum, one can say that the policy of Turkey toward the Soviet Union has been motivated almost exclusively by defensive purposes.

So far the means used by the USSR in the effort to realize her objectives in Turkey have not involved military action, despite frequent threats and troop movements at the border. The Soviets have made, nevertheless, continuous efforts to establish direct land frontiers with Bulgaria, her most trusted ally in the Balkans. The latter, which borders Turkey and wants to annex Rumanian Dobruja, hopes to bring the USSR within striking distance of the Straits and the Aegean Sea which are about 30-60 miles from the Bulgarian border.

The failure of the USSR to wrest concessions from Turkey in 1946-1950, has forced her to modify her tactics. Her new policy began in 1953, with a sustained campaign urging friendship and better relations, and entered a decisive stage only in 1964. The Soviets have used successfully the Cyprus issue to better their image in Turkey, as well as economic and ideological means to widen their influence in the country. Industrial credits extended on relatively easy terms, technical assistance, support from some leftist elements in the universities, a few trade unions, and the press have helped the Soviets in their effort to come to terms with Turkey. Interestingly enough, the Soviets have recently reversed their policy of considering the Eastern and Western Turks as separated from each other. They have encouraged mutual visits by properly selected people in order to publicize through them the progess registered by the Eastern Turks under Soviet rule. The policy, which had some impact among intellectuals, was intended to prove that nationality, separate cultural identity, socialism, and Soviet citizenship are not exclusive, as claimed by some nationalists in Turkey, but are mutually compatible. An extensive study of this aspect of Soviet Turkish relations, which surpasses the scope of this study, could uncover interesting developments.

Official Turco-Soviet relations originated in 1919, under a set of new conditions. Both countries had or were on their way to overthrowing their theocratic and absolutist monarchies and establishing in their place modern regimes. Faced by a hostile West, both countries were subject to military intervention from outside and were denied for a long time diplomatic recognition and membership in the League of Nations. The Soviets had denounced as early as 1917-1919 the secret treaties concerning the annexation of Istanbul to Russia, concluded by the Czar and his Western allies, and explicitly stated that the city must remain in Turkish hands. Consequently, Mustafa Kemal (Atatürk) and Lenin established close relations. The result was the Treaty of Friendship of March 16, 1921, calling for mutual solidarity against expansionism. It was followed by the Treaty of Nonaggression and Neutrality of December 17, 1925, after Turkey was compelled by England to renounce her claims to Mousul, and the Soviets were left out of Locarno Treaty. The validity of the second treaty was reaffirmed on December 12, 1928, when Turkey seemed to move closer to France and England, and signed a pact of neutrality with Italy. Through these treaties, especially the first, both states gained considerable advantage. Turkey secured her eastern borders and consolidated the position of the National Assembly gathered in Ankara in defiance of the Sultan, while the Soviets, assured of safe borders in the South, expanded their rule into the Caucasus and Central Asia by subduing the independent states of the area.

The Treaty of 1921, had a clause stipulating that the regulation of the Straits would be settled in a conference attended by the Black Sea states only. The same treaty contained in Article 8, significantly enough, another provision whereby each government agreed to abstain from activities designed to oust the government of the other. This, in practice, implied that Turkey would not promote Pan-Turkism or Turkish nationalism in the USSR and the Soviets would not promote communism in Turkey. However, as early as 1921, Bekir Sami, the Turkish foreign minister who had returned from Moscow in time to attend the London Conference, expressed deep misgivings about the absolutist tendencies of some Soviet leaders, and eventually Ataturk had to restrain the activities of the communists at home. The Soviet Union participated in the Lausanne Conference of 1922-1923, which brought peace between Turkey, the West, and Greece, but only as directed by England in the sessions dealing with the Straits. The Soviets signed but did not ratify the Straits Conventions at Lausanne, which left the waterways demilitarized and open to the warships of all nations. Consequently, the Soviets became strong supporters of Turkish efforts to militarize the Straits, which culminated eventually in the Montreux Convention of July 20, 1936. The Turkish foreign policymakers during this period went out of their way, more as allies than friends, to provide the Soviets with the utmost feeling of security so as not to give them any pretext for complaint or grounds for seeking a change in the existing status of the Straits. As Tevfik Rüştü Aras, foreign minister from 1923-1937, expressed it, Turkey hardly made a move without consulting the Soviets and thus a "practical collaboration, whereby each side consulted the other before undertaking an action of interest to the other" had emerged. But Soviet writers have described the era of friendship between 1921-1939, as due to the good will and generosity of the Soviet Union rather than the mutual interests of the two parties. In fact, after 1946, Soviet historians, in order to dramatize the "Turkish ingratitude and bad faith" in siding with the West, claimed that the Soviet Union had listened sympathetically to Ataturk's call for help in 1919, despite her own difficulties, and has assisted him in every way to liberate and modernize his country. The Big Power mentality in these writers is so pervasive as to make them believe that any sign of friendship coming from the Soviet Union, as though by divine grace, must be answered by Turkey with total and unconditional surrender.

Turco-Soviet relations began to deteriorate in 1939. The Soviet Union once reassured about the survival of her regime and the extent of her military strength, began to use Turkey as a pawn in her international dealings. Early in 1939, the Soviets, expecting Turkey docilely to follow their advice, urged her not to yield to German pressure, and to give her support to the Allies. Turkey signed an agreement with France and England on October 19, 1939. Meanwhile the Soviet Union had agreed to a pact of non-aggression with Germany on August 23, 1939, which left Turkey totally disoriented. Following the established custom of mutual information, Turkish Foreign Minister Şükrü Saracoğlu went to Moscow to inform the Russians about the Turkish pact with the Western Allies. The Soviet Union, however, informed the Turkish minister of the need for joint defense of the Straits, neutrality in the event of Soviet acquisition of Bessarabia and Bulgarian accession of Dobruja, noninvolvement of the Soviet Union in a Turco-German armed conflict, and especially restriction of passage through the Straits of warships belonging to the non-Black Sea powers. Moreover, Molotov, the Soviet Foreign Minister, scolded the Turks for signing the Mutual Assistance Treaty with France and England, the "belligerent imperialist states," and accused Turkey of trying to "spoil German-Soviet relations" and of "dragging the Soviet Union into an anti-German scheme." Later Molotov agreed with Germany and Italy to free Turkey of her obligations toward her Western allies and to bring her "through the necessary military and diplomatic measures" to the Germano-Soviet-Italian side. The Soviets also secured a promise from Von Ribbentrop in 1940 about acquiring a sphere of influence in the direction of the Indian Ocean and on the Turkish Straits. The Soviet policy toward Turkey, thus, had radically changed.

It was under these circumstances that Turkey, with the full knowledge of her Western allies, who saw gains in a neutral Turkey, signed a nonaggression pact with Germany on June 18, 1941, just a few days before Hitler attacked the Soviet Union. During the war years, despite German efforts to rekindle Pan-Turanic sentiments and despite the presence of large units composed of Soviet Turks fighting on the German side, Turkey remained neutral. Meanwhile, in 1943, the Soviets put pressure on the Allies to bring Turkey into war knowing well that ill armed as she was, Turkey would be occupied by Germany and probably would have to wait for the Soviets to "liberate" her. Yet by 1944, when German defeat appeared certain, the Soviets opposed Turkish entry into the war, possibly in order to isolate and exclude her from any voice in the post war reorganization of the world. Indeed, on March 19, 1945, the Soviets informed Turkey that they would not renew the Treaty of Friendship of 1925, due to expire soon. A few months later Molotov officially informed the Turkish ambassador in Moscow that a new pact between Turkey and the Soviet Union depended on a rectification of the Turco-Soviet borders, that is, cession of territory in the north and bases on the Straits for joint defense, and a revision of the Montreux Convention. Already at Potsdam in 1945, the Soviet Union had sought to obtain an Allied consensus that the problem of the Straits was a matter to be settled between Turkey and herself. Great Britain objected, while the U.S. agreed. Left isolated and at the mercy of the Soviets, the Turks sought to change the U.S. stand. Eventually The United States agreed as she had indicated she would, that passage through the Straits was a matter of international concern and thus supported the Turkish position.

The Soviet Union finally presented a formal note on August 7, 1946, asking, in effect, for bases on the Straits, well after the British and U.S. opposition to Soviet demands had crystallized and Turkey, thus, had been pulled out of her temporary, but dangerous isolation. The Soviet note prompted President Truman and his top officials to back Turkey in rejecting the Soviet demands, which, if accepted would have weakened Greece and changed the balance of power in the Mediterranean. A second Soviet note of September 24, 1946, expressed indignation that Turkey dared to slander the Soviet Union by thinking that the joint defense of the Straits proposed by the Soviets was intended to violate her sovereignty. All these Soviet notes appear in retrospect, not only ill timed, but quite illogical if the general trend in world thinking is properly weighed.

Turco-Soviet relations after 1946 deteriorated proportionately to Turkey's commitment to the West through the Truman doctrine in 1947, her NATO membership in 1952, and the Baghdad Pact of 1955. Possibly the most meaningful commitment of Turkey to the West and to its political system during this period was the acceptance of a parliamentary regime based on free elections and of a scheme of economic development centered largely on free enterprise. Each move made by Turkey to consolidate her relations with the West was followed by stern and often threatening Soviet notes, which only moved her closer to her Western allies.

The Democratic Party government, which came to power in 1950, found that full identification with the West offered Turkey military and political security, some capital resources for economic development, and, as a combined effect of all these, victory at the polls for itself. Prime Minister Menderes embarked upon a policy of economic modernization, according to the Western model, mostly forced by the growing mass demand for employment and higher living standards. Economic development gradually became the dynamics of Turkey's domestic politics. All this in turn consolidated the parliamentary system. Thus, inadvertently perhaps, the Soviet Union helped the Westernization of Turkey.

The initial policy of the Menderes government was based on a violent, almost irrational anticommunist and anti-Soviet stand which he promoted actively. The Turkish government denounced incipient efforts at achieving a detente in the relations between East and West as another Soviet device intended to deceive the world. It was under these circumstances that the Menderes government was faced with an unexpected Soviet note on May 30, 1953. Barely three months after Stalin's death in March 1953, the Soviet government informed Turkey that, in order to preserve good relations and strengthen peace and security, Armenia and Georgia, the two Republics through which the USSR had put forth her territorial demands in 1945-1946, "have found it possible to renounce their territorial claims on Turkey." Furthermore, the note expressed the Soviet view that the security of the Straits could be assured on conditions acceptable to the USSR and Turkey, and that the USSR did not have any territorial claims on Turkey. This was, indeed, a sudden and total position reversal on a fundamental issue, which gave credence both to Krushchev's view that the Soviet policy toward Turkey was Stalin's aberration, and to the view that the overwhelming importance of Turkey would make the Soviets undertake the most improbable moves, as well as sacrifices.

The Soviet peace offensive, which began in 1953, continued intermittently without visible results until 1960. Although the Soviets did not hesitate to occasionally use the threat of war and concentrate troops on the Turkish border, as happened during the Syrian and Iraqi crises of 1957 and 1958, respectively, their attitude was markedly more mellow than in 1946. In the process, the USSR made it clear that an improvement in Turco-Soviet relations was not conditional on Turkey's withdrawal from NATO and CENTO. The Russians also proposed economic aid, increased commercial relations, assistance to private entrepreneurs, and even suggested a high-level conference to discuss impending differences. They accused "a third party," that is, the United States, of opposing a Turco-Soviet understanding. Turkey first regarded the Soviet peace notes as new tactics designed to tear her away from the West and treated them as such. This attitude created indignation among the Russians, who felt that Turkey did not show gratitude for the Soviet renouncement of their claims on Turkish territory. "Even an uninitiated reader," P. Moiseev and I. Rosaliev, who were experts on Turkish affairs, wrote in 1958, "would realize by reading this document [note of 1953, renouncing the claims] the generosity and magnanimity of the Soviet foreign policy. But in spite of this generous act of the Soviet government, certain circles in Turkey opposed to the establishment of friendly relations with the Soviet Union have continued to invoke the mythical threat [embodied] in the Soviet Union."

In a way it was difficult for Turkey to move closer to the USSR since, in 1958, NATO had established nuclear missiles in the country with an intermediate range designed to offset the tactical superiority in ballistics achieved by the Soviets through the launching of Sputnik in 1957. The refusal of Turkey to participate in a Soviet scheme in 1959 to establish a zone free of nuclear weapons in the Balkans and the Adriatic did not deter the Soviets from resuming their peace offensive in 1959. This time the action produced results. In December 1959, Lutfi Kirdar, Turkish Minister of Health, visited the Soviet Union and on his return, expressed hope for improved relations between the two countries. On January 9, 1960, Fatin Rüştü Zorlu, the Foreign Affairs Minister, declared that the world military balance made unlikely a Soviet attack on a NATO power, that is, Turkey, and that the Russians were respectful of Turkey's international commitments. Consequently, some improvement in Turco-Soviet relations was possible. Finally, on April 11, 1960, the Turkish government announced officially that Premiers Menderes and Krushchev would exchange visits. The plan was well set. Not even the downing by the Soviets of an American U-2 spy plane, which had taken off from the Incirlik base near Adana, could spoil the Turco-Russian dialogue.

The Soviet Union attached great importance to the Menderes visit. Cemal Feridun Erkin, Turkish Ambassador in Paris in 1960, reports in his book on the History of the Straits, which also contains his memoires, that Krushchev, who was visiting France in 1960, expressed repeatedly to him his desire to ease Turco-Soviet tensions, and asked Erkin, who was returning to Turkey, to help improve relations between the two countries. The need for economic aid as well as the East-West detente were some of the principal reasons which prompted Menderes to accept the Soviet invitation, but he could not carry out his plan. He was ousted by a military coup on May 27, 1960, and Turco-Soviet relations remained at a standstill for another four years.

The military had originally favored a reexamination of Turkey's foreign policy, but did not want to begin by reviewing the relations with the Soviets for fear this would antagonize the West, which the new government suspected of nurturing great sympathies for the ousted Menderes. Soon the military became involved in domestic issues, while the new Minister of Foreign Affairs, Selim Sarper, a former Ambassador in Moscow, and known as a conservative anti-leftist, did not see much gain in improving relations with the Soviets. However, the Russians, who sensed an actual neutralist mood among some officers, claimed in a note that if "Turkey had remained neutral, undoubtedly some close relations between our countries would have been established ... instead of spending large sums for military preparations Turkey would have used the money for economic development and the welfare of her people." Ready to acknowledge the existing differences in foreign policy, the Soviets proposed to begin by concentrating only on common points, but President Cemal Gürsel, in his answer, stressed the continuity in Turkey's pro-Western foreign policy and left unanswered the Russians' overtures for a meeting. Sometime later in 1962, the Soviet Ambassador visited Premier Ismet Inönü, who had also been Premier most of the time from 1923-1937, that is the first period of Turco-Soviet friendship, and asked him whether he would accept an invitation to visit Moscow. Moreover, the Soviet Ambassador reportedly promised 500 million dollars credit for economic development if Turkey fulfilled some changes pertaining to her relations with NATO. The Turkish answer was an embargo on her ships carrying cargo to Cuba, in accordance with a U.S. request, and a reaffirmation of her solidarity with the West.

Meanwhile, however, the thinking in the Foreign Ministry began to shift toward a rapprochement with the Soviets, while the public, subject to powerful socialist writings, began to show impatience with the slow pace of economic development, and to have doubts about Turkey's foreign policy. Furthermore, bad relations with the Arabs, and the Third World in general, had increased Turkey's sense of isolation, while her products found fewer and fewer buyers in foreign markets.

The new phase in Turco-Soviet relations began amidst these conditions with a series of official visits initiated by the President of the Senate, Suat Hayri Ürgüplü. He and a parliamentary delegation visited Moscow from May 29 to June 14, 1963, and returned with, in addition to excellent impressions, Soviet promises for friendship, economic aid, and easy financial terms for industrial projects. In return, the Russians asked only good will, possibly planning to present their counter demands, with compound interest, at a later date.

It would be an error to deal with Turco-Soviet affairs without briefly analyzing Turkey's relations with the Balkan countries in the same context. The Balkan Peninsula was for centuries a part of the Ottoman state and complemented economically and strategically its Asian domains. The defense of the South Balkans and Asia Minor are inseparable. This explains how Turkey, possessing a relatively small, but prosperous territory in the Balkans, that is, in Eastern Thrace, bordering Bulgaria and Greece, was able to play a leading role in the politics of the region from 1923-1939. Turkey was able to establish friendly relations during this period with practically all the Balkan countries, first, by renouncing all claims to former Ottoman domains even to those areas thickly inhabited by ethnic Turks, and second, by creating, in concert with Greece, a system of regional alliance. The Balkan Entente formally established in 1934, after a succession of meetings in previous years, brought together the anti-revisionist states, that is, Greece, Rumania, Turkey, and Yugoslavia, and successfully contained the expansionist aims of Bulgaria. Eventually Bulgaria, feeling rightly threatened and insecure, established close relations with Italy and Germany, and briefly from 1941-1944, after the Entente lost its effectiveness, fulfilled her dream for a Greater Bulgaria by acquiring Macedonia and Southern Dobruja to the detriment of Yugoslavia, Greece, and Rumania. At the end of the war, Bulgaria was forced to return to the former sovereigns all the captured lands, except Dobruja, but without renouncing her old expansionist dreams. Thus, the basic territorial problems which underlay the Balkan politics of 1923-1940, remained more or less the same after World War II. Turkey, which had no territorial claims on any of her neighbors, could again play a pivotal role in Balkan politics, provided conditions permitted.

The Soviet influence over Rumania and Bulgaria after 1945, was so absolute as to limit extensively Turkey's political potential in the area. In fact, the position of Turkey was aggravated by the fact that the foreign policies of Rumania and Bulgaria were literal extensions of the Soviet policy in the area and of the Warsaw Pact of which they were members. Bulgaria, in particular, which had a deep sympathy for the Russians, became fully identified with the Soviet policies toward Turkey. With a substantial and rapidly expanding Turkish minority, which constituted fifteen percent of her total population, Bulgaria tried to secure her long-range security against Turkey through whatever Soviet support she could muster. Apparently following Stalin's suggestion, she expelled 150 000 Bulgarians of Turkish origin with the purpose of wrecking the incipient economic development of Turkey.

Turkey and Greece tried to consolidate their relatively weak positions in the Balkans by taking advantage of the Yugoslav-Soviet conflict. Threatened by the Soviets, Yugoslavia agreed to enter into a pact with Greece and Turkey which was signed on April 28, 1953, and confirmed as the Balkan Defense Pact, a military defensive alliance, at Bled, on August 9, 1954. However, shortly afterward, Yugoslavia lost interest in the pact, because of improved relations with the Soviets and President Tito's emergence as one of the leaders of the nonaligned, neutralist bloc. The potential moral support likely to be derived from the Third World seems to have out-balanced in Yugoslav eyes, the advantages offered by the alliance with Turkey and Greece. Anyway, the rapid death of the Balkan Defense Pact proved decisively the overwhelming influence exerted by the Soviet Union in the area.

It appeared certain in the early 1960's that an improvement in Turco-Soviet relations would inevitably better Turkey's relations with Bulgaria and Rumania, and indirectly restrain Greece, which assured of Turkish support in her persistent territorial and national conflicts with Bulgaria, Yugoslavia, and Albania, had turned her attention to the annexation of Cyprus. Furthermore, by 1963-64, Turkey was fully aware of Rumania's desire to follow an independent foreign policy, especially after a Soviet-Bulgarian scheme to create a regional economic unit along the Danube, mostly to the detriment of Rumania, was publicly put in print by its proponents. In fact, a Balkan Pact, proposed in September 1957, and again in 1959, by Chivu Stoica, Premier of Rumania, and rejected flatly by Turkey and Greece as a Soviet plot, might have been a subtle Rumanian effort to find a way for a more independent foreign policy.

The real thaw in Turco-Soviet relations started with the visit of Feridun Cemal Erkin, the Turkish Foreign Affairs Minister, to Moscow from October 30 to November 6, 1964, just a few days after a new Turkish Ambassador, Hasan Işik, presented his credentials to the Soviets, on October 26, 1964. Meanwhile, Krushchev, who had worked hard to promote Turco-Soviet relations, had been ousted from the premiership on October 15, 1964, but his departure did not hamper Erkin's visit.

It may be interesting to note that Erkin, a prototype of the Turkish foreign official who was dedicated to total Westernization and nurtured profound distrust toward the Soviets, was one of the first to acknowledge the inevitability of improving relations with the USSR and persuaded Premier Inönü, to take the necessary steps in this direction. Erkin claims in his memoirs that the rapprochement began because the Soviet threat to Turkey decreased due to the NATO alliance, the rise of China, her economic difficulties on the domestic front, and demands for autonomy by the USSR's allies in Eastern Europe. Actually, behind the move lay a series of other factors affecting each country. The Soviet Union seems to have viewed the increasing friendship and the economic and military cooperation between West Germany and Turkey with considerable misgiving. The Russians, already suspicious of any German moves at the time, and fully aware of the strange Turkish fondness for Germany, whose Pan-Turanist instigations in the past were all too well known, had bitterly denounced the "Germanization of Turkey." Early in January 1964, it was announced for instance, that a military mission would visit Turkey to study the possibility of German military aid to Turkey within the framework of NATO. Indeed, on May 2, 1964, Von Hassel, the West German minister of Defense, signed a treaty with Turkey providing 50 million marks as the first installment of a long-range program. Germany also adopted a position favorable to Turkey on the Cyprus dispute. And already Germany was employing Turkish workers, whose number continued to increase, reaching eventually a total of 386,000 early in 1971 and over a million by 1974.

Meanwhile, the Soviet call for a regional disarmament and the lofty idea of transforming the Black Sea into a sea of peace went unheeded. On the other hand, the removal by the United States of Jupiter missiles from Turkey early in 1963, apparently in response to the removal of Soviet missiles from Cuba, had increased Turkey's feeling that her security had been impaired, and that the big powers were deciding vital issues concerning her without even consulting her.

Turkey's rapprochement with the Soviets was precipitated by the Cyprus issue, which, by the middle of 1964, had acquired top priority in Turkish foreign policy. The unfortunate aspect of the Cyprus dispute lay in the fact that it created a conflict between Turkey's national interest and her commitment to NATO, as well as with the U.S. interests in Greece and the Eastern Mediterranean. Turkey was unable, largely because of the opposition of the United States, to exercise her rights of intervention in Cyprus, as entitled by the existing treaties, and thus safeguard the lives and property of the Cypriot Turks. The latter had become, in fact, synonymous with Turkey's long-range strategic interests in Cyprus. Unable to use her treaty rights, Turkey was militarily immobilized, while Greece and the Cypriot Greek government, which had unilaterally abrogated the Cypriot Turks' constitutional rights, were free to act as they wished.

The Soviet Union originally adopted a policy more or less opposed to the Turkish position on Cyprus. Consequently, Turkey counteracted the Soviet attitude by postponing the departure to Moscow of Foreign Minister Erkin, at first scheduled to take place on March 18, 1964. Indeed, originally the Soviet Union accepted the existence of a unitary government in Cyprus as a whole, without openly recognizing the existence of separate Turkish and Greek communities on the island. But the Turkish decision to postpone the long awaited visit produced results. On August 8, 1964, after Turkish planes strafed the Greek positions on the island, the Soviets, instead of sabre rattling, as in the past, sent just a mild telegram urging Ankara to stop the attacks which would increase the danger of war. And on August 15, 1964, the Soviet Ambassador in Nicosia visited Fazil Küçük, Vice-President, and the leader of the

Turkish community in Cyprus. This was the first Soviet visit since the strife on the island began late in December 1963, and a clear indication that the Soviet position on Cyprus had changed. Obviously, the practical-minded Soviet foreign policy makers could not exchange the great promises involved in friendly relations with Turkey for the limited rewards offered by Cyprus. Meanwhile, the insulting letter addressed by President Johnson to Premier İnönü, which was becoming known among the intellectuals spurred their anti-Western feelings. Thus, the Turkish Foreign Minister began his visit to Moscow amidst these circumstances, rather unfavorable to the West.

The joint communique issued at the end of Erkin's visit called for the strengthening of good neighbor relations between Turkey and the USSR based on mutual respect for territorial integrity, independence, and differences in social systems, and emphasized the need for increased commercial relations. Turkey was to export agricultural commodities and import construction material, drilling machinery, and capital goods. On the Cyprus dispute, the Soviets endorsed a peaceful solution which would allow for the "peaceful coexistence of the two national communities, on the basis of recognition of legal rights of the two national communities and for the independence and territorial integrity of Cyprus." Turkey also signed a cultural agreement which she considered a concession in exchange for endorsement of her position on Cyprus. The cultural agreement, originally of much broader scope, including exchange of students, was scaled down in the final version and was enforced in the form of a protocol renewable every year. The importance attached to the cultural agreement was evident in the fact that on November 12, 1964, just a few days after the minister's return from Moscow, an interministerial committee was formed to draw up the necessary plans. Meanwhile, *Pravda* published an interview with Foreign Minister Erkin, who made special efforts to emphasize the value of the cultural pact. Reasons for the importance attached by both sides to this cultural agreement, which was hotly debated in the National Assembly of Turkey, may be sought in the deeper sociocultural factors underlying Turco-Soviet relations. It is safe to state at this stage that the cultural agreement, and the subsequent friendly relations between the two countries, not only helped substantially to better the Soviet image in Turkey, but also quickened the transition of Turkey's intelligentsia, already caught in a deep identity crisis, to a new stage of ideological and cultural development of important consequence.

The effects of the Turco-Soviet rapprochement soon became evident. Already on October 30, 1964, the day of Erkin's departure for Moscow, the Greek government, showing a belated homage to Turkish deftness in the conduct of foreign affairs and implictly confessing its own shortsightedness, agreed finally to hold bilateral talks with Turkey to solve the Cyprus dispute. This was an awkward and unsuccessful move intended to thwart Turco-Soviet agreement on Cyprus.

The beginning of the Turco-Soviet detente was instrumental in initiating, expanding, or influencing a series of agreements in other fields of activity. The agreements on railways of October 11, 1961, and on telephone, radio, and telegraph signed in Ankara in 1962 and ratified in 1963, were supplemented with new ones, such as the agreements on trade and payments in 1961 and 1964, in accordance with the original instrument signed on October 8, 1935.

A few months later, after the return of Erkin from Moscow, Soviet President Nicolai Podgorny, visited Ankara early in January 1965, to return the visit of the Turkish parliamentarians in 1963. He told the Turkish National Assembly that the relations between the two countries were progressing to the advantage of both and expressed hopes for continuous mutual visits, especially among parliamentarians. Indeed, tourism, like ping-pong, proved to be an excellent vehicle for developing diplomatic relations, in this case Turco-Soviet relations. The Soviets seemed to have discovered the great weakness of the Turkish parliamentarians, like their counterparts in other lands for visits abroad, preferably extended ones. (During March 1971, when Turkey was going through an acute crisis, which threatened her entire regime, a rather large group of parliamentarians happily left on a one-month trip to South America.)

Meanwhile, on January 13, 1965, the United States Department of State announced that Turkey refused to participate in the Multilateral Force (MLF) as she had announced she would do several months earlier. Soviet President Podgorny praised the Turkish action publicly on Moscow Radio and expressed the wish that the "border of Turkey and the USSR become a link of friendship and the Black Sea a means of commercial activities."

The burgeoning relations between Turkey and the USSR, still more in words than deeds, showed signs of strain after the budget presented by Ismet Inönü's coalition government received a vote of nonconfidence in Parliament. The Justice Party, headed by its newly elected chairman, Suleyman Demirel, had engineered Inönü's downfall. Originally the Justice Party had opposed extensive relations with the Soviets. But the new coalition government, which remained in power for about nine months, seemed determined to pursue a policy of detente with the USSR. The new Premier was Suat Hayri Ürgüplü, the head of the Senate and of the first Turkish parliamentary mission which visited Moscow in 1963. He appointed as Foreign Minister Hasan Işik, the Turkish Ambassador in Moscow. After a brief period of uneasiness, caused by reports of Czechoslovak arms shipments to Cyprus, the exchange of visits between Turkey and the USSR resumed. The visit of Soviet Foreign Minister, Andrei Gromyko, on May 17, 1965, was followed by the visit of Premier Ürgüplü on August 7, 1965, while Vasil Isaev and Vladimir Fedorovich, Mayors of Leningrad and Moscow respectively, exchanged visits with their counterparts in Istanbul and Ankara. Meanwhile, Premier Alexei Kosygin told Metin Toker, a distinguished journalist and Inönü's son-in-law, that the Soviet Union would be interested in a Treaty of Friendship and Nonaggression, similar to the one of 1925, which they had denounced in 1945. The communiques issued at the end of these visits repeatedly stressed the themes agreed upon in 1964, except for an additional consensus on general disarmament and the end of colonial rule.

The general elections of October 14, 1965, gave a clear majority to the Justice Party and Suleyman Demirel became Premier. Demirel was already on record with a statement that he would favor relations with any country respectful of Turkey's interests, although his views on an agreement concerning the use of Soviet technicians and investment, while couched in technical terms, indicated certain apprehensions at the speed with which Turco-Soviet relations had developed. He brought to the head of the Foreign Ministry Ihsan Sabri Çaglayangil, a former governor, who adroitly left the conduct of foreign affairs to the professionals on the staff. As usual, stark realism and pragmatism in Turkish foreign affairs prevailed.

Sometime after the new government was formed, it was reported that Nikita Ryjov, the Soviet Ambassador in Ankara, had discussed with Çaglayangil the possibility of Soviet mediation between Turkey and Greece in the Cyprus conflict. About the same time, paradoxical as it may sound, Senator Hugh Scott of Pennsylvania, in a letter, asked the Department of State about alleged restrictions on matters of education imposed by Turkey on the Orthodox Greek Church in Istanbul. He had been conspicuously silent when Turks were wantonly butchered by Greeks on Cyprus. Obviously, Turks thought sympathies in the United States were still shaped by religious affiliations rather than objective principles, as indicated early in the Cyprus dispute.

The Demirel government eventually, like its predecessors, declared emphatically that the relations with the Soviets would not impair Turkish commitments to NATO and CENTO, and that her adherence to the Western system of alliance had priority over any other consideration. In any event, the Soviet Union had clearly acknowledged the fact that Turkish membership in Western alliances was not an impediment to improved relations with her.

During 1964-1965, Turkish relations with Bulgaria and Rumania, which began with a round of visits parallel to those with the Soviets, improved fast. Already in March 1964, Todorov Zhikov, party leader of Bulgaria, declared that his country had no plans then or in the future to expatriate the Turks of Bulgaria. But a few years later he did not hesitate to close all Turkish schools, abolish Turkish language publications, and embark upon a policy of assimilation with an unknown outcome. About one year later, Ivan Budinof, Minister of Trade, and the first Bulgarian Minister to do so in twenty-one years, visited Turkey with the purpose of expanding commercial ties and improving relations. Already, by the end of 1964, Turkish delegations had visited Bucharest and Sofia to discuss the improvement of trade and tourism. And, by 1965, tourism began to figure prominently in the Bulgarian and Rumanian plans for acquiring hard currency. They offered summer holidays at their beach resorts on the Black Sea at bargain rates for West Europeans (about $ 150 including air transportation) which often included an additional attraction; an overnight trip to Istanbul.

On December 20-27, 1966, Premier A. Kosygin of the USSR,

in the first visit by a Soviet head of government, came to Turkey. After a round of talks, the parties issued the customary joint communique stressing the determination of the Turkish and Soviet governments "with a view to the traditions of the Lenin-Atatürk period ... to continue efforts to advance friendly and good neighbor relations and to further mutual confidence." The Soviets now supported the Turkish position on Cyprus, causing the mercurial Greeks to stage angry demonstrations in Nicosia; their scheme of playing the USSR against Turkey had backfired. Significantly enough, a few months earlier on July 7, 1966, Turkey had withdrawn her last troops from Korea, which had been stationed there since 1950 and had played an important part at the time in preparing psychologically the ground for Turkey's entry into NATO in 1952.

Relations between Turkey and the USSR and the Balkan countries continued to develop. Already, while Kosygin was visiting Turkey, a working group of experts on tourism from Bulgaria, Yugoslavia and Turkey began discussions in Sofia to publicize a Trans-Balkan highway running through Belgrade, Sofia, Istanbul, and Ankara and ending in Antakya in the province of Hatay (Alexandretta) near the Syrian border. Since most of the highway ran through Turkey, it should have been called more appropriately Trans-Asia Minor. Greece, it must be noted, was being bypassed. In 1966, Turkey also was host to Gheorghe Maurer, Premier of Rumania and to Ivan Bashev, Bulgarian Foreign Minister. While the first sought an implicit endorsement of his country's new line of foreign policy independent of Moscow, the second discussed a series of important issues. Most of the outstanding problems brought up at these meetings, such as regulation of boundaries, consulates, fisheries, improvement of transportation and communication, including the building of a railway to bypass Greece, migration, and the like were concluded after Premier Todorov Zhikov visited Turkey in March 1968. Economic and commercial relations with the Soviets and their Balkan allies, negligible at the beginning of the decade, expanded fast. Already in 1965, trade with the Soviets reached 20 million dollars or double the amount of the previous year. In 1964, the volume of Turkish trade with the Eastern Bloc based on bilateral agreements was placed at a total of 65 million dollars in imports. The Soviets also proposed to build ten cement factories in Turkey with an annual capacity of 300,000 tons each, and an electric energy center and to supply electrical equipment, in addition to seven other industrial projects agreed upon previously. Agreements to build a new glass factory and expand the existing one at Çayirova, a steel mill with an annual capacity of one million tons, and an oil refinery of 3 million tons capacity, were among the most important projects. Similarly, Turkey signed civil aviation agreements with all countries in Eastern Europe and their planes began to land and refuel on their way to and from the Middle East and Africa.

The first phase of Turco-Soviet relations was concluded by Premier Suleyman Demirel's visit to the Soviet Union, including visits to Central Asia and the Caucasus, on September 19-29, 1967. Actually, the Justice Party government, despite early expectations to the contrary, expanded the relations faster and more profoundly than its predecessors. The joint communique stated that "in the relations between the Soviet Union and Turkey there are no questions which could cause clashes of fundamental interests. On the contrary, a broad and propitious field of activity is opening up for the development of relations ... in the interest of both countries." The two sides strongly backed the return of Arab lands lost to Israel in 1967, stressed the desire to see the Middle and Near East become a zone of peace and security, and called for bilateral contacts and exchange of opinion between Turkey and the USSR. Already in May 1967, Turkey, in an obvious reference to the United States troop landings in Lebanon in 1958, had declared that she would not allow the use of her territory for attacks on Arab countries. However, the expected broadening of Turco-Soviet relations did not materialize. The bombing of Greek positions in Cyprus by the Turkish air force brought in stiff Soviet protests, whereas the armed repression of the liberalization movement in Czechoslovakia, and the Brezhnev doctrine claiming a right of intervention for the Soviets to uphold the socialist regime in any country had more than a sobering effect in Turkey. Indeed, the Czechoslovakian affair was instrumental in turning many neutralists into strong apologists for NATO, and caused fatal dissensions in the Turkish left, notably in the Marxist Labor Party, whose final collapse in 1971, can be traced to the bitter fights among its members, some supporting and most opposing the Soviet intervention in Czechoslovakia.

The second phase in Turco-Soviet relations began again through the customary visits at high levels. The visit of the Turkish foreign minister in 1968 paved the way for the visit of President Cevdet Sunay in 1969. Now, in contrast to the past when the Soviets did most of the courting, Turkey was quite willing to resume the dialogue, partly due to mounting pressure from a section of the intelligentsia and the press asking for closer relations with the USSR, and mostly in order to secure long-term agreements and finance a series of industrial projects. The communique issued at the end of Sunay's visit reaffirmed the commitment of the USSR and Turkey to mutual respect for independence, sovereignty, territorial integrity, and noninterference in each other's internal affairs and expressed satisfaction over the improvement of neighborly relations and the increase of commercial and economic ties. They agreed, in addition, to enact an agreement on consulates, a land transportation agreement which would allow Soviet civilian vehicles to travel south to Arab countries and Turkish vehicles to the north, chiefly to Finland. Both sides praised the preparations made for a Conference on European Security and urged all interested countries to participate. On this last point, Turkey seemed to back the Soviet position more strongly than her Western allies, although this backing amounted to little in practice.

The effect of Sunay's visit was soon evident in a Soviet loan of 113.7 million dollars to finance further the steel mill being built at Iskenderum as part of a basic agreement signed on October 10, 1969. Similarly an agreement finzalized on March 25, 1967, to build a dam on the Arapçay was being brought to near completion. Meanwhile, the Turco-Soviet trade, which had risen to 74.8 million dollars in 1969, was estimated to have reached 84 million dollars in 1970, or more than four times the figure in 1965.

The hijacking of a Soviet airliner to Turkey and the shooting of the stewardess by two Lithuanians was followed by the hijacking of a light Soviet plane by two youths. The refusal of Turkey to return the hijackers did not cause deterioration in the Turco-Soviet relations. Eventually the two Lithuanians were tried for manslaughter by a Turkish court and the two youths, bored with life in a camp, returned to the USSR on their own. At about the same time, a United States Air Force plane, carrying one Turkish and two American officers violated, by error, the Soviet air space and was forced to land in Armenia. This last incident did not have visible effects on Turco-Soviet relations either. What caused growing apprehension in Turkey were two major, ominous developments which surpassed the scope of diplomatic relations between the two countries. The first was the Soviet naval presence in the Mediterranean, and the second was the growing ideological impact of socialist doctrines within Turkey.

The growth of Soviet naval power in the Mediterranean and her claim that this sea was an extension of the Black Sea rather than the other way around directly concerned the status of the Straits. It is difficult to envisage at this date the next Soviet strategy concerning the Turkish Straits. It is possible for the USSR to argue that the Straits become subordinate to the agreement which the Big Powers may reach with regard to the Mediterranean. Or they may argue, as mentioned before, that by continuous usage and through the right of custom and prescription embodied in international law, the Straits have become an integral part of the Black Sea and the Mediterranean, and hence outside Turkish jurisdiction. It must be stressed that so far, while the Soviets have not denounced the Montreux Convention, they have not proposed a new conference to revise or replace the existing arrangement either. It is obvious that the Soviets are waiting for the appropriate moment to secure an arrangement favorable to them, either by improving relations with Turkey to the maximum and making her dependent on the USSR or by isolating her completely from the Western defense system. Meanwhile, the Soviet Union has protested the visit of NATO ships to Turkish ports and kept a very close watch over the passage of such ships into the Black Sea, which she regards as having a special status.

The second set of developments stemming from Turco-Soviet relations and affecting both countries in different ways and degrees are of a cultural and ideological nature. The intensification of relations with the Soviets as far as Turkey was concerned, coincided with a crucial change in the meaning of modernization, nationalism, and economic development among the new Turkish intelligentsia. The economic development, the vastly expanded educational facilities, and the relatively free democratic life since 1946 have combined to create a sizeable intelligentsia whose social origin, philosophical and political outlook, and goals are markedly different from its predecessors. The bulk of this intelligentsia, originating in the towns and villages of Anatolia, received its schooling in the big centers, such as Ankara, Istanbul, and Izmir, which, until very recently, were islands of modernization and comfort in a sea of tradition and underdevelopment. Social, cultural, and economic contrasts between village and city, as well as change of status, and the unfavorable spectacle displayed by a Parliament bogged down in interparty feuds caused among the intelligentsia profound disillusionment with the existing system. Democratic-minded and motivated by social, populist, and egalitarian goals, the intelligentsia came to regard rapid economic development not only as the solution to all problems, but also as the essence of modernization. Consequently, the intelligentsia concentrated its attention almost exclusively on the means necessary to achieve rapid economic development. The shift of a good part of the Turkish intelligentsia to the left, as can be deduced from the above analysis, resulted originally from a desire to achieve national progress. The intellectuals' search for the causes of economic backwardness and the ways to remedy it, coincided with the improvement in Turco-Soviet relations, which brought forth by necessity a softening in the official restrictions imposed on socialist proselytizing. The liberal constitution of 1961 also played a major part in the ideological liberalization of Turkey. It was at this point, around 1966-67, that the serious discussions on economic development were adroitly converted by a handful of university professors and newsmen into political and ideological debates which had definite foreign policy implications. It was stressed, for instance, that the so-called economic development of Turkey followed a Western pattern, which enriched a few people to the detriment of all, wasted national resources, and delayed modernization. The socialist model, as provided by the USSR and the Balkan countries, was described by some leftist newsmen and writers returning from visits there, as tailored to suit Turkey's developmental needs. Eventually, as expected, the discussion on development and modernization culminated by placing all the blame for Turkey's ills, both currently and in the past, on the real culprit, the West. Interestingly enough, by 1970, the press, with the exception of the right wing, made hardly any critical allusion to the Russians or the Soviets, or the drama of the Straits in 1946. A book on the early Soviet-Turkish relations written by Semyon I. Aralov, Soviet Ambassador to Ankara in 1922-23, but published only in 1960 in the USSR and translated into Turkish in 1967, made a special point of attacking Ataturk's friends, such as Rauf Orbay and Refet Paşa who were oppressed to the Soviets as supporting a "bourgeois comprador" group of businessmen and landlords. In fact, by 1970 a rather insidious campaign was launched against Ataturk. He was accused by some leftist groups as having initiated modernization by following the Western model. The purpose of the attacks was to downgrade him and destroy the national unity created by allegiance to his reforms and to his memory as the creator of modern Turkey.

The bitterest public attacks came to be directed against NATO and the United States, which were accused of infringing upon the territorial integrity and national sovereignty of Turkey. The debates on development had become debates on foreign policy. By this time many of the ideas on development and foreign policy put forth by leftists had come to be shared by moderates and even the public at large. The Cyprus issue added a new, and culturally a rather biased dimension to these ideas. As mentioned before, the preoccupation of the Turkish intelligentsia with problems of development and modernization stemmed from an urge for national achievement. The Cyprus dispute, which touched upon a deep psychological cord in the personality of the modern Turk, acted as a catalyst to consolidate all issues into a new form of nationalism and turn its wrath against the West. In other words, some Turks came to regard the refusal of NATO and the United States to support Turkey on the Cyprus dispute, some, as a clear discrimination in favor of the Christian Greeks. Turks could not understand, as one indignant man put it, how the West could bear to see Archbishop Makarios with the "cross in one hand and the Bible in the other, marching over the corpses of Turks murdered by Greeks." And this, after all Turkey had done almost since the turn of the century to accomodate and identify herself with the West. Turks had regarded Westernization as a meeting of minds, a mutual acceptance of universal values and forms of thought. Now they were utterly disillusioned. Many of them thought that the West gave preference to Greeks simply because they were Christians. Although presumably, Turkey was the party in the right, the West was not prepared to extend full support—and implicitly accept her and her people—simply because they were Muslims. Even if accepted, they would be treated as the second class citizens of an underdeveloped country.

The Cyprus issue, the attitude of the West, and the dilemma of development deeepened the lingering crisis of identity and compelled the new generations to seek a solution in socialism and in identification with the cause of the Third World. Thus, the rapprochement to the left called for a new look at the Soviet Union which appeared as the champion of the underdeveloped countries, and most important of all, did not hesitate to call itself proudly Asian, as Dostoyevsky, in a fit of anger at the West's refusal to accept the Russians, had urged them to do almost a century before. For many Turkish intellectuals to be a leftist and a socialist was a way of identification with the Third World, and implicitly with the USSR which in a short time had risen from backwardness and posed a lethal challenge to the West. In essence this was an act of profound emotional redemption. Many intellectuals felt proud now to call themselves Asians and join the crusade of the Third World against imperialism, colonialism, and backwardness. Books on these subjects were translated by the dozen and sold overnight. By the end of 1967, the universities became targets for attack, first, because of "professional shortcomings," that is, inability to train the youth in accordance with the prevailing needs. About a year later, subjected to pressures and controls, the universities, especially the most modern ones, became leftist strongholds. Signs such as "NATO 'ya Hayır" (no to NATO) and attacks on American sailors visiting Turkish ports became a common occurence. On the other hand, Soviet singers, artists, and ballet dancers enjoyed immense popularity, mostly among the intelligentsia, while the rank-and-file still formed long queues at the cinemas playing the glamour films of Hollywood. Soviet works of art became highly appreciated. One intellectual told this writer that he paid a fortune to buy the Russian opera Ivan Susanin, ignoring that the original name Glinka gave to his opera was "A Life for the Czar" and that it was a glorification of the Russian deeds on the battlefield against the Poles. The paradox of the situation lay in the interest shown by the Turkish radicals toward the Eastern Turks of the Soviet Union.

Turkish journalists returning from Moscow wrote with admiration about the beautiful and famous artist from Uzbekistan reciting with abandon the poems of Fuzuli, the sixteenth century Azeri mystic poet who was all but forgotten by the modern "Westernized" Turks of Turkey. Crowds in Istanbul and Ankara listened in rapture to Hanlarova of Azerbaycan sing the beauty of her native land while many Turks of Turkey were ready to admire every land and culture except their own. Records from Azerbaycan not only sold fast, but were also played on the state radio. This was a way of acknowledging the progress registered by these Turks, but also a means of expressing deep affinity toward them, which, in most cases, was fully reciprocated. The Eastern Turks of the Soviet Union showed more than a literary interest, for instance, in Aziz Nesin, the well-known socialist and social satirist during his visits there, while Suleyman Demirel, the Premier, was met with such huge crowds and such uninhibited cries, as "kardeş" (brother), during his visit to Baku and Tashkent that at least in one place the Soviets shortened the visit. The Turkish leftists were not complacent either. Upon his return from a visit in Bulgaria, Aziz Nesin protested in writing the forced assimilation of Turks in that country. One can deal at great length with the side effects of the visits by Soviet dignitaries and artists to Turkey and vice-versa. The point is that by 1970 much of the stereotyped imagery about the Soviet Union as a perpetual enemy of Turkey was cast aside and the country began to be looked upon with new interest and curiosity. For instance, in 1964, the year of the Turkish foreign minister's visit to Moscow, there were published in Turkey twelve books dealing with Russians and the Soviets. Six of these dealt with the red peril, four with the occupation of the Urals and Turkistan by the Russians and the ill treatment accorded to the Turks living there. In 1965, the number of such books rose to fourteen, but only two of them took an anti-Soviet stance, while the rest described the country and tried to familiarize the public with it. The trend continued during the next years.

It is difficult to assess the Soviet influence over leftist activities in Turkey. First, one must stress the fact that following a long-established custom of blaming others for their shortcomings, many Turks tend conveniently to accuse Moscow as soon as some disturbance erupts in the country. Rumors have circulated that many student radicals were financed by foreign sources, and that a number of "secret" papers dealing with American interests in Turkey and the activities of the CIA were leaked to the press by the same sources. Moreover, it was rumored that some members in Parliament were adroitly used to incite anti-Western feelings and that some high echelons of the police and security were infiltrated by pro-Soviet and leftist agents. (In the crackdown which followed the coming to power of Nihat Erim's government in 1971 two high-ranking police officers were arrested for collusion in sharing with the radicals the money obtained from bank robberies.) It is known also that since the early 1950's the Soviets and their allies have made special efforts to win over Turkish intellectuals and have infiltrated many of the Turkish student organizations abroad, especially in France and Germany. However, as far as students are concerned, the growing influence of Maoism among them should have become a matter of concern to the USSR. Chinese influence in Turkey is bound to increase as the Chinese see the rise of nationally oriented leftist movements in Turkey and the surviving popular suspicion of the Soviet Union as favoring their own stand. There are several indications to support the contention that China is very much interested in Turkey as a possible friend or ally to outflank the USSR in the Southwest. Immediately after the revolution of 1960 in Turkey, the Chinese press heralded it as the beginning of a truly revolutionary and populist era in Turkish history and offered support to the revolutionary forces. Later, in 1965, Chou en Lai told the correspondent of the left wing *Akşam* that there was no impediment to establishing diplomatic relations between China and Turkey and that these could begin through scientific and economic contacts. "Both China and Turkey," declared Chou en Lai, "are Asian countries and there are very old and deep historical and cultural ties between them." One year later on November 30, 1966, a trade delegation from the People's Republic of China came to Turkey for unofficial contacts. The relations continued at a very low level until August 1971, when Turkey finally extended official recognition to mainland China. For all practical purposes the Sino-Turkish relations are bound to have a profound effect on Turkey's relations with the Soviet Union. The Chinese rely heavily in their struggle against the Soviet Union in Central Asia upon the Eastern Turks living there, although these fear the Chinese much more than the Russians who have allowed them some cultural freedom.

In summation, Turco-Soviet relations have been conditioned since 1960, first and above every other factor, by the relaxation of tensions between East and West and the renouncement by the Soviet Union to claims for military bases and territory in Turkey. Her isolation from the Third World countries including the Arab Bloc, and her Balkan neighbors, which was dramatized by the Cyprus dispute and the voting results in the U.N. General Assembly in 1964-65, have compelled Turkey to seek an accomodation with the Soviet Union. The Cyprus dispute, the cultural-ideological developments within Turkey, and her economic-commercial needs were the principle factors which enabled the Soviet Union not only to better her relations but to achieve a degree of influence over Turkey. In all these three areas it must be noted that the Soviet penetration was achieved through their objective estimation and understanding of internal conditions in Turkey.

In balance, however, the Soviet Union seems to have failed so far to attain fully her chief objectives: the neutralization of Turkey and possibly her inclusion into the Soviet sphere of influence. Turkey remains in NATO, CENTO, and the Common Market and a variety of other West European organizations. So far Turkey has not concluded a pact of neutrality or friendship or nonaggression with the Soviet Union. On the contrary, the leftist radical upsurge which undermined profoundly the authority of the Demirel government in 1971, and made the possibility of a basic change in Turkey's internal regime and foreign policy appear imminent, was checked through military intervention on March 12, 1971, and the establishment of a new government under Nihat Erim. The rapid expansion of foreign trade with the socialist bloc, which had reached about fourteen percent of the total, received a severe setback in 1971, after the new government decided to reconsider the bilateral trade agreements with these countries and thus "put an end to the policy of buying and selling at high price from these countries." On the other hand, the rapprochement to the Soviet Union has consolidated the Turkish position in Cyprus and has permitted her to break out from isolation and improve her relations with her Balkan neighbors and the Third World in general. Soviet economic aid has contributed to Turkey's development and industrialization while increased commercial ties have secured markets for some of her agricultural products. The relative lull in Turkish-Soviet relations after 1971, was caused by apprehension that much of the communist activities in Turkey were directed from USSR, through the Turkish Communist Party established abroad and its propaganda media, such as publications and the broadcasts of the *Bizim Radyo* (Our Radio) from East Germany. This view proved to be only partially correct, since the bulk of the leftist groups in Turkey, especially the militant ones, sympathized with China and Maoist teachings or had little to do with the Soviet Union. Consequently, despite the harsh treatment of leftists in Turkey in 1972, when thousands were arrested and imprisoned, Turkish-Soviet relations remained constant, especially after Nikolai Podgorny arrived for a one week visit in April 11, 1972, and agreed in a communique that the two countries will not allow their territory to be used for aggression or subversion against other nations. By the beginning of 1973, Turkey resumed her policy of expanding her economic and especially trade relations with East European countries as indicated by the Czech Foreign Minister's six day visit to Turkey in March 14, 1973, and Turkish Foreign Minister Halük Bayülken's visit to Bulgaria.

The electoral victory of the Republican Party in October, 1973, and the subsequent formation of a coalition government under the Premiership of Bülent Ecevit augured well for the future of Soviet-Turkish relations, or at least it seemed so, largely because of the moderate leftist stand of this party. The new government did in fact try to expand further the dialogue with the socialist bloc and paid special attention to improving relations with China. It also thought to recognize East Germany. Yet, the Ecevit government contrary to some expectations moved to establish better and even closer relations with the United States, especially after a few minor questions were clarified. In fact, one may say that American-Turkish relations improved along with Turkey's relations with the socialist bloc largely in accord with the spirit of the East-West detente. Turkish-Soviet relations were suddenly brought under severe strain by the crisis in Cyprus in July and August 1974 (see section on war in Cyprus).

Soviet relations with Cyprus intensified considerably especially after Archbishop Makarios turned to court the Soviets in the hope of balancing the pressure of the junta in Athens as well as the threat of Turkish intervention in Cyprus. The junta's ousting of Makarios on July 15, 1974, and the Turkish landing in Cyprus five days later put a sudden end to the Soviet hopes for expanding her influence in Cyprus. Consequently, the Soviets backed strongly the Turkish intervention in Cyprus in the hope that this would save Makarios' regime, safeguard the independence of Cyprus and allow the Soviets to maintain a foothold there. However, after the President of Turkey refused pointedly to follow the Soviet suggestions concerning Cyprus and reminded them that Turkey was defending her own interests and not playing the game of any big power in Cyprus, and after further Turkish expansion into Cyprus, the Soviet attitude changed somewhat. Though officially Turkish-Soviet relations remained outwardly cordial, the Communist Party of Turkey, through its clandestine organizations, and *Bizim Radyo* attacked Turkey vehemently as a warmonger and tool of NATO. The Soviet Union rejected categorically the Turkish plan for a geographical federation and insisted on an international conference to solve the crisis while asking also for a restoration of the situation prevailing before the July events, that is, on the evacuation of Turkish troops and reinstatement of Archbishop Makarios as President. Though the Soviets made efforts to maintain good relations with Turkey—a supplementary trade agreement for 30 million dollars was signed and a Turkish parliamentary delegation visited Moscow in 1974 and loans for industrial plants and a new steel plant were negotiated—they insisted also on the withdrawal of Turkish troops from Cyprus. Today, Turco-Soviet relations are at a crossroads. The factors which permitted the Soviet Union to achieve influence in Turkey, such as the Cyprus dispute, the need for economic development, and the cultural-ideological crisis are still present. The options of Turkey in solving all these problems by herself are limited. But the West and the Soviet Union have considerable freedom to affect each problem and determine the course of Turkish foreign policy in the future. Ultimately the foreign policy of Turkey will have a fundamental effect in determining the ideology and the country's political regime.

TURKISH AND ARAB-ISRAELI RELATIONS

KEMAL H. KARPAT

University of Wisconsin, Madison, Wisconsin

The communiques issued at the end of visits by Turkish and Arab statesmen to each other's country during the past few years refer invariably to the "brotherly feelings and the profound cultural and historical ties which unite" them. Indeed, a series of recent internal and international developments have brought to the surface among Turks and Arabs alike the memories of a common cultural heritage which not very long ago was denounced by both parties as having retarded their modernist emancipation. Anyhow, it would be literally impossible to study Turkish-Arab relations without some reference to the historical background which has conditioned and will condition these relations in the future. The chief factor conditioning the Turkish-Arab relations after both World Wars has been Turkey's political alignment with the West, and/or espousal of its political, cultural and social ideas. Indeed, throughout history the alignment by one or by several countries in the area with a Western power or the adoption of its ideas has produced a divisive effect on the Arab-Turkish relations. Thus, Mehmet Ali of Egypt and his pro-French policy was the chief single reason, early in the nineteenth century, which led to *de facto* separation of Egypt from the Ottoman State, and allowed for British and French penetration and eventual domination of the area. The rapprochement of the Ottoman government to the West after the Crimean War of 1853, and the Paris Treaty of 1856, was followed by an Ottoman policy of Europeanization, which produced among the *ulema* who represented an Islamic viewpoint the first reaction against the government. Their reaction was paralleled by a very complex socio-cultural and political development—a pre modern ideological upsurge—among the intelligentsia known as the Young Ottoman movement. In part, as a consequence of these events as well as the loss of territory in the Balkans in 1878, that is, of areas with large Christian population, Sultan Abdulhamit II (1876-1909) adopted a Pan-Islamic policy which had anti-imperialistic and anti-Western undertones. Subsequently, in the last quarter of the nineteenth century, Arabs, and especially Arab culture in general gained a prestige unparalleled throughout Ottoman history, and indirectly became an important stimulus in the rise of Turkish nationalism itself. Prior to the nineteenth century, roughly from 1517, that is, from the conquest of Syria and Egypt by Sultan Selim I (1512-1520) to 1805 and 1860, that is, to the date the challenge posed by Mehmet Ali to the Porte became menacing, and Mount Lebanon gained some autonomy under French pressure, the Arab question was not politically important as far as the Ottoman government was concerned. Even when it became important the issue appeared as a matter involving the protection of Christians rather than Arabs. Earlier, that is from the sixteenth to the end of the eighteenth centuries the main tension areas were in the Caucasus and Central and South Europe. Consequently, the Ottoman power was concentrated in these areas and prevented the Russians and the Austrians from advancing into the Middle East, and except for Napoleon's invasion of Egypt in 1798, it secured relative peace and tranquility for the Arab lands, at least as far as foreign interference was concerned. The Arabs, like most other Muslim groups living not in the immediate vicinity of tension areas did not contribute any soldiers to the Ottoman army well into the second half of the nineteenth century when general conscription was introduced. Moreover, the Arab lands enjoyed a large degree of self-rule and non-interference on the part of Ottoman authorities, except for strategically important areas, such as Baghdad, Basra and Yemen. Moreover, the religions, cultural and judiciary establishments in the Ottoman state were filled to a large extent by people of Arab origin.

The changes occurring in all major fields of activity in the nineteenth century, and the effort of France and especially of England to fill the vacuum caused by Ottoman loss of power, produced a series of rather unpredictable political and cultural effects. England occupied Egypt in 1882, and France, already in Algeria since 1830, occupied Tunisia in 1881. Thus, Pan-Islamism which merged under Abdulhamid II appeared among other things as a movement of self-defense against the political, cultural and military pressure of both Russia and the West. It had a religiously and culturally unifying effect upon the Muslim peoples while at the same time rising nationalism was dividing them politically. Indeed, Islam as a cultural system united them, while philosophical and political currents undermined the theological bases of the very culture that seemingly brought them together.

The anti-imperialist doctrine of Pan-Islamism originated mostly in Egypt in the Islamic revolutionary teachings of Afghani, and even of Mustafa Kiamil, while its organizational and institutional aspects were formulated in Istanbul. The Turks' skill in administration and organization, and especially their realistic understanding of power and its uses blended successfully as it did for centuries, with the imaginative, missionary-religious spirit of the orthodoxy to produce a powerful political movement with long lasting effects.

The Turkish-Arab relations were conditioned also by the eventual disintegration of Pan-Islamism through the emergence of secularism and nationalism which inspired by Europe, have dominated the Turkish and Arab thinking since the first World War. The major Arab-Turkish rift occurred in 1908-11, after the ruling Committee for Union and Progress adopted a nationalist-secularist policy with the express purpose of bureaucratizing the multnational Ottoman comity and transforming it into a centralized national Turkish state, and used secularism to justify it. This policy challenged *de facto* autonomy of local rulers, as well as the Arabs' cultural and linguistic heritage for it posed for them an insurmountable difficulty in separating culture, state, language, community and politics from each other. The combination of all these factors bred dissatisfaction and brought about the Arab revolt of 1916, in which thousands of helpless and wounded Turkish soldiers on the Palestine front were massacred by Bedouin tribes, more because of lust for booty than national feeling. All this eventually culminated in the establishment of independent Arab states in the area. The collapse of the Ottoman front in Palestine was followed soon by the move of British troops into the area, and the occupation of southern Turkey by French armies. The high ranking elite which ruled Turkey after 1922, was composed largely of military officers who never forgot or forgave the Arabs for the revolt of 1916, which brought Turkey to the threshold of extinction, and incidentally opened a series of developments which culminated in the imposition of the French and British mandate over eastern Arab lands. Nationalism continued to sow strife and bitterness in the area during the next decades. The closing of the Sheriat courts, the replacement of the Arabic script by the Latin, the purge of Arabic words from the Turkish vocabulary, the abolition of the Caliphate in 1924 undertaken by the Republican leaders of Turkey on behalf of a nationalist secularist policy of modernization caused profound mistrust among Arabs. All these measures were deemed by many Arabs as being deliberate efforts by Turkey to abandon or at least to weaken her own ties to Islam and join Europe not only in outward appearance but also in spirit. Turks in turn did not hesitate to blame Islam and Arabic cultural influences as major obstacles to their own modernist emancipation.

On the other hand, the successful war of liberation undertaken by Turkey in 1919-22, and the establishment of a relatively modern state caused profound admiration in the Muslim world, especially among the younger generations. Mustafa Kemal (Atatürk) became the symbol of enlightened leadership as later acknowledged openly by Gamal Nasser of Egypt, and lately even by Mujibul Rahman of Bangladesh.

Arab-Turkish relations since the first World War moreover have been marred by a variety of territorial problems. First, the boundaries between Turkey, Syria and Iraq were drawn by England and France in the most arbitrary fashion largely to the Turks' detriment. Consequently some 300.000 Arabs were left in Turkey and about one million Turkish speaking people remained in Syria, and especially in Iraq. The fact that much of this population living on either side of the border was tribal in organization and outlook, and possessed relatively limited national consciousness prevented the rise of ethnic conflicts in 1923-1970. Since the first World War Syria and Iraq have assimilated some of the Turkish speaking groups while Turkey did the same, though on a reduced scale, to the Arab stock living within her own boundaries. Moreover, the haphazard drawing of boundaries cut off towns and villages on either side of the border from their economic and geographic centers which were left almost by design in the other country. Furthermore, the headwaters of the two major rivers of the area, Tigris and Euphrates, which are among the main sources of water for Syrian and Iraqi agriculture are located in Turkey. These rivers are a continuous source of friction. Turkey has built the Keban Dam on the Euphrates, one of the largest of its kind, in order to meet her growing need for electric power. Already this project is causing tension in Syria and Iraq which fear that Turkey is establishing some sort of control over their water resources. Finally, the Syrian-Turkish border, 835 miles long, which offers endless possibilities for smuggling livestock and hashish to Syria and beyond, and manufactured goods to Turkey, offers also opportunities for illegal crossings as dramatized recently by the relatively unhampered travel of Turkish radicals to and from Syria and Jordan to receive guerilla training there. The difficulty of sealing off this border to infiltration from Syria has been a major cause of alarm in Turkey, especially after the establishment of radical regimes there in post WW II period.

All these territorial difficulties with Syria and Iraq were aggravated by the problem of Mousul and Hatay (Alexandretta) two areas in south Turkey, whose status was not fully settled in the Lausanne Treaty of 1923. Mousul, despite the existence of large Turkish groups in the Kirkuk and Suleymaniye districts, and despite the vital importance of its oil for Turkey, was left to Iraq through extensive British pressure in 1925. Hatay on the other hand, whose population had a slight Turkish majority joined Turkey in 1939, in good part through the assent of France, the mandatory power. Syria has not recognized the incorporation of Hatay to Turkey, and the issue remains a thorny problem in the relations between these two states.

It is rather difficult in some way to speak of genunine Arab-Turkish relations between the two World Wars, since the Arab countries hardly had any independence at all during that period. Even the Saadabad Pact of July 8, 1937, concluded among Turkey, Iran, Iraq and Afghanistan as a non-aggression treaty of limited consequence, concerned mostly the non-Arab states located on the Northern Tier along the Soviet border. Consequently it may be correct to state that Arab-Turkish international relations developed chiefly after World War II and that the previous period was a background to it.

The emergence of Israel and Israeli-Turkish relations had an immediate bearing upon Turkish-Arab relations. Consequently it may be useful to deal briefly with the Jewish question within the framework of Ottoman history. It is a well known fact that Jews in the Ottoman state enjoyed special recognition as the third *millet* along with the Armenians and Orthodox Christians. This officially recognized status maintained even after the reorganization of the *millets* in the 1860's, permitted Jews to preserve and continue their culture in its original environment—some communities had a continuous existence of at least ten centuries—until recent times. As "People of the Book" and because of their attachment to tradition and religion, always a high mark in Ottoman eyes, Jews, as believers enjoyed special protection. The sanctuary offered by the Ottoman sultans to Jews after their expulsion from Spain in 1492, and from Europe at various dates, as well as the freedom of trade granted them are too well known to warrant further discussion. Moreover, the Khazars from whom some East European Jews descend were of Turkish stock, while the Turkish-speaking Karaites of Crimea who accepted the Torah as basic Book but rejected rabbinical authority were trusted subjects who exercised some influence in the Ottoman court. The *dönme* of Turkey on the other hand are the Jews, followers of Sabbatai Zevi, (1626-76) who converted to Islam, and are Turkish speaking. Moreover, Vambery and Leon Cahun, both Jews, were among the first intellectuals in the West to point out in the nineteenth century to the Turkish achievements in Central Asia, while many European writers were racing with each other to downgrade the Turks as "barbarians" and interlopers squatting on Christian lands. The Jews of Salonica played an important part in the Masonic lodges of Salonica, which had apparently some role in the ideological formation of the Young Turks and their Revolution of 1908. As late as the 1930's after the Nazi persecution drove many Jews out of Germany, Turkey accepted many Jewish refugees, and with stern measures stopped short an anti-Semitic campaign which had been started in a small town by a self-styled Turkish racist. Thus, it is important to note that historically speaking friendly relations between Turks and Jews prevailed, that as communities and as states they never confronted each other; and they were spared violent conflict even in the era of Zionism.

However, the Ottoman government had no sympathy for Zionism and all that it entailed, including the establishment of a Jewish national state. It allowed for individual but not mass settlement of Jews in Palestine after 1880. Zionism was a form of nationalism and the Ottoman government opposed it as determinedly as it opposed all other forms and brands of nationalism. Hence the very negative attitude of the Zionists towards the Ottoman state.

The Turkish policy towards the Middle East in general and the Palestine issue in particular was relatively neutral in 1923-45. This remained in fact also her basic policy towards the Arab-Israeli conflict after 1948, despite some change in this policy which occurred after 1966. Originally Turkey opposed the partition of Palestine. But after the establishment of Israel, Turkey was the first Muslim nation to recognize her in 1949, and exchanged ambassadors in 1952. From 1949 to 1963, Turkey looked upon Israel chiefly as a country which achieved rapid modernization and progress in a relatively underdeveloped area. Thus, the Israeli educational and industrial establishments, the dynamism of her people became the subject of envy and admiration in the Turkish press. Moreover, the existence of Israel was considered a necessary means for containing Syria which backed by all Arab countries insisted on the return of Hatay. All this, it must be stressed were the by-products of Turkey's full identification with the foreign policy of the West and the United States towards the Soviet Union and the Middle East. Consequently, Turkey's relations with the Arabs remained subordinate to her commitment to the West in general and the United States in particular. Therefore, as might be expected, Turkish policy towards both the Arab nations and Israel began to change only after Turkey's position in the Western alliance and her relations with the United States began to deteriorate in 1964-69.

The Soviet territorial demands in 1946, and the support offered by the United States and England to Turkey against these demands became the fundamental factors which conditioned Turkish foreign policy in the years 1946-64. Consequently Turkey regarded her Middle East policy as an extension of her pro-Western policy whose main aim, overriding all other considerations, was to create a defense system against the Soviet Union and communism. Moreover, this pro-Western foreign policy gave new impetus to Turkish urge for cultural and ideological identification with the West, which in turn increased her foreign policy commitments. One should not overlook the fact that the Allied victory in World War II, the United States involvement in world affairs and her old untainted image as a country of progress opposed to colonialism and imperialism contributed to Turkey's desire to identity herself with the USA and its policy in the Middle East. Turkey in fact welcomed the involvement of the United States in the Middle East defense since the British appeared militarily unable to defend the area against the Soviets, and since she, like most countries in the Middle East, feared that the English still nurtured colonial ambitions. It must be stressed that despite alignment with the West, Turkey was definitely opposed to colonialism. Thus, the immediate or related objectives of the Turkish foreign policy in the Middle East in the late 1940's were subordinated to her general pro-Western policy. These may be summarized as aiming at achieving first, national security, second, economic aid, and third, at expanding her influence in the area. However, Turkey had defined her foreign policy objectives in the Middle East without understanding the trend of development and the political objectives of her Arab neighbors. In fact, it may be proper to state that Turkey viewed her relations with the Arab countries more or less as a continuation of the policy which prevailed in 1923-1945, when she dealt with the problems of the area more through France and England than with the Arabs. Though strongly in favor of Arab independence, nevertheless, Turkey assumed erroneously that the Arabs will follow after World War II a pro-Western policy in opposing the Soviet expansion, and somehow accept the British and French as their foreign policy tutors.

During 1946-50, while Turkey was preoccupied with the Soviet demands, and independence struggle among Arabs was localized in a few urban centers, Turkish-Arab relations followed a more or less normal course, despite the ill feeling caused by Turkish recognition of Israel. However, the idea of establishing a defense organization in the Middle East, controlled by England and aiming outwardly at preventing Soviet penetration (but also at controlling the spread of nationalist and socialist ideologies in the area) in which Turkey would have a leading role, had a profoundly negative impact upon Arab-Turkish relations. Early in 1951, Azam Paşa, the Secretary General of the Arab League visited Turkey in order to discuss the scope and nature of the proposed defense organization and apparently counseled against it. The Turkish answer to Arab misgivings was spelled clearly in a statement by then Foreign Minister, Fuat Köprülü. "We believe that the defense of the Middle East" stated Köprülü "is absolutely necessary for the economic and strategic defense of Europe. Consequently, after joining the Atlantic Pact, Turkey will perform in an effective fashion her role in the Middle East and will be ready to enter into negotiations with the interested parties in order to undertake the necessary common measures." The opposition Republican Party, however, cautioned the government not to assume military obligations on behalf of the British. Meanwhile, Egypt was engulfed in a series of anti-British demonstrations which carried also warnings to Turkey. The newspaper *al-dawa* of the Muslim Brotherhood labeled Turkey a "second Israel" and called for her destruction. Egypt eventually refused to join on an equal basis with the USA, UK, France and Turkey a proposed Middle East Command whose headquarters were to be in Cyprus, and continued to denounce Turkey. In Turkey proper, a number of people, especially contemporaries of Atatürk who were faithful to his neutralist policy, objected to membership in NATO if in exchange Turkey assumed obligations incompatible with her interests in the Middle East. Eventually Turkey was admitted into NATO in 1952, after the British withdrew their objections, obviously after being fully assured of Turkish support for a Middle East pact likely to defend UK interests in the area.

The first major concrete result of all these background developments was the establishment of the Baghdad Pact in 1955. There is hardly any other alliance in the recent history of foreign affairs as unnecessary, ineffectual and harmful to all parties as the Baghdad Pact. Indeed, it caused immense harm to the Western interests in the area, it precipitated the Arab countries' alignment with the Soviet Union, it stimulated the rise of radical ideologies, and cast Turkey in the image of a docile tool of Western powers.

The Pact had its origin in the Western preoccupation with the security of the area including the creation of the Middle East Defense Organization as mentioned above. The initial plan foresaw the organization centered around Egypt. However, Egypt, fully dedicated to ending the British rule in the country and striving to achieve it, even by violent means, refused to participate. A new plan was necessary. Meanwhile, John F. Dulles preoccupied with the idea of securing the Northern Tier against

USSR tried to reconcile the need for a defense organization in the Middle East linked to NATO in the West and SEATO in the East with the deep concern over national independence shown by the newly emerging states in the area. Consequently, during his visit to the area in May 1953, Dulles discussed the idea of a regional pact based on the nations in the area. Turkey, as a NATO member obviously was the keystone to this project. Meanwhile in Karachi, Vice-President Nixon discussed the Pakistani demand for aid to protect herself against India, and eventually a US—Pakistan agreement was signed in 1954. The same year Turkey and Pakistan concluded an agreement based on a previous Treaty of Friendship signed in 1951, to exchange information in the technological field, to assist each other in the manufacture of arms and ammunition as well as in case of attack. It left the membership opened to other nations willing to join it. Meanwhile Iraq led by General Nuri es-Said, the strongman at the time, signed an agreement for military aid with the USA in 1954. Then, on February 24, 1955, Iraq signed a Pact with Turkey, similar to the Turkish-Pakistani agreement, which included a clause leaving the Pact open to non-Middle East countries concerned with the security of the area, that is, United Kingdom and the USA. This was in essence the Baghdad Pact.

Each country had its own special aim in joining the Pact, which differed considerably from the others' goals. Turkey wanted to discharge her obligations to England and NATO and secure her south eastern flank. Pakistan wanted to consolidate her defense against India and to receive armament and economic aid. Nuri as-Said felt that cooperation with NATO through Turkey would give Iraq a leading position in the Arab world, and assure her support against Kurdish unrest, and strengthen her bargaining position towards Israel. Nuri es-Said seemed to have believed that the Arab-Israeli conflict and the Suez problem could be solved in the near future and that all Arab nations following the leadership of Iraq would side with the West. Incidentally, the Pact enacted between Turkey and Iraq included a clause to the effect that the signatories recognized and would implement the U.N. plan for the partition of Palestine. This was an anti-Israeli gesture designated to placate Arab public opinion.

The signing of the Baghdad Pact, it must be mentioned, was preceded by Turkish Premier Adnan Menderes' visits to Baghdad with stops in Damascus and Beirut where he issued invitations to Syria and Lebanon to join the Pact. The reaction was ominous. Menderes was met with street demonstrations in Beirut and criticism in the Syrian Parliament since the younger generation of Arabs, and some of the revolutionary regimes emerging from long foreign domination, looked with deep suspicion upon any pact backed by the West. Nasser of Egypt sensing a diplomatic trap had already turned down one year earlier a Turkish invitation to discuss the issue, and objected violently to a clause in the Anglo-Egyptian treaty of October 19, 1954, which allowed the British to occupy the Suez Canal in case of attack on Arab countries but also on Turkey.

England joined the Baghdad Pact on April 4, 1955, and signed a new agreement with Iraq replacing the old agreement of 1930, to make military aid available to her in case of attack. Pakistan joined the Pact formally on September 23, 1955, despite an almost identical pact signed with Turkey in 1954, and Iran joined it on November 3, 1955. Thus, a defense organization which had started actually through U.S. initiative materialized fully by giving to England a strong commanding position in it and in the Middle East as a whole. Possibly, the U.S. was not happy with the outcome and did not hesitate to uproot the United Kingdom from the Middle East when the chance presented itself in 1956.

The Baghdad Pact created profound and long lasting conflicts in the Arab world. The Arabs felt threatened by division and infiltration by pro-Western powers and tried to devise protective measures. A move by Egypt to exclude Iraq from the Arab Defense Pact was eventually abandoned as was the Syrian-Egyptian-Saudi Arabian counter project for a regional defense pact since Jordan and Lebanon opposed it.

Meanwhile at the Bangdung Conference in 1955, Nasser received an accolade as a leader of the Third World, while Turkey became isolated because of her strong defense of NATO and blistering attacks on non-alignment, neutralism, socialism and communism.

The Baghdad Pact increased further the often irrational apprehension and belligerent attitude of Syria towards Turkey, and was the major factor which compelled her to sign a military agreement for a unified command with Egypt on October 20, 1955. Meanwhile, the Baghdad Pact members began to put pressure on Jordan to join the Baghdad Pact. President Celal Bayar of Turkey visited Jordan and made a grandiose gesture of promising her Turkish support in case of Israeli attack. It was clear that support or opposition to Israel were emerging as the major means which Turkey could use to affect her relations with the Arab countries. However, the pressure put on Jordan backfired. King Hussein dismissed Glubb Pasha, the British commander of the Arab Legion and aligned himself with the nationalist Arab movement. Israel didn't like the Baghdad Pact either. Besides leaving her out, the Pact carried implications against Israel as made clear by some Iraqi letters. Turkey recalled eventually her ambassador in Tel Aviv while assuring the Israelis privately that her action was intended merely to strengthen the Baghdad Pact, and would not impair Turkish-Israeli relations. It was diplomacy at its worst, hardly compatible with the usual Turkish adroitness and correctness in the conduct of foreign affairs. Perhaps Turkish foreign policy makers at the time felt that these standards did not apply to the Middle East.

The Pact increased Egyptian fear of attack and was one of the reasons which compelled her to seek arms and support in the USSR in 1955. In turn, Egypt's move towards closer relations with the USSR left the USA with no other alternative but to support the Baghdad Pact. Consequently in the spring of 1966, the United States joined the economic and anti-subversion committees of the Pact.

Upon the French, British and Israeli attack on Egypt in 1956, the Baghdad Pact members met without inviting England, criticized and asked her to consider her action, although privately the Turkish Foreign Minister showed little sympathy for Nasser whom he accused of having courted trouble. In any case England eventually declared that she pulled out of Egypt partly heeding the criticism of her Middle Eastern allies; this was a convenient way to salvage some goodwill out of an adventure which ended in an otherwise total diplomatic rout. The Suez War of 1956 eliminated the British almost entirely from the Middle East and left the area open to further turmoil, even though Turkey inwardly was somewhat relieved by the British departure at long last from the Middle East. Paradoxically enough, it was the Ottoman State, the predecessor of Turkey, which helped England to take a foothold in the Middle East in the 1830's in order to offset the pressure of Mehmet Ali of Egypt, and then to provide a defense against Russia. A major responsibility now fell upon the US to prevent not only the spread of Soviet influence and communism into the area as a whole, but also of Nasserism into Lebanon and Jordan. The result was the Eisenhower doctrine stated on January 5, 1957, and accepted by the US Congress on March 9, 1957. The doctrine was dutifully approved by the Baghdad Pact members on January 20, 1957, while the UK remained cold to the doctrine which she regarded as a form of American intrusion into her traditional preserve in the Middle East. Henceforth the Baghdad Pact appeared, however ineffective, as a vehicle for the USA to implement its policy in the Middle East. Indeed, soon James P. Richards, special assistant for Middle East affairs, arrived in the area to conduct high level talks in all countries except Syria, Egypt and Jordan, in the hope of establishing a common front against revolution (subversion), socialism and communism, all of which seemed to be embodied in various ways in Nasserism. Meanwhile a plot to kill King Hussein turned Jordan against leftists and the supporters of Nasser, who fled Syria, and engaged there in a campaign against Jordan. Finally, the ascendancy of Colonel Bizri, known as a communist, to the head of the Syrian army compelled King Faisal of Iraq and Hussein of Jordan to undertake hurried trips to Ankara and engage in discussions concerning measures to combat possible leftist coups thought likely to originate from Syria. Soon Loy W. Henderson, the U.S. representative, joined the talks.

Syria, in Turkish eyes, had become now an armed center of subversion aiming at the overthrow of the existing regimes in the area, while the Ba'ath, the party in power in Damascus was regarded as a communist front, although the actual, domestic situation of Syria was rather different from the image formed by Turkish leaders. Some Turkish troops were massed at the border and a few land and air incursions into Syria and skirmishes followed. The Soviet Union appeared now as the sole defender of Syria. She sent threatening notes to Turkey and engaged in troop movements and delayed the incipient Turkish-Soviet detente. Eventually the USSR saw to it that the issue was brought before the United Nations as a Turkish threat to Syrian security. Meanwhile, Saudi Arabia mediated successfully between Syria and Jordan. The latter declared promptly that she would consider an attack on Syria as an attack on all Arab nations, although it was Jordon which had played initially an important part in inciting the Turkish-Syrian tension. Turkey as usual bore the brunt of unpredictable Arab politics, and was forced to beat a hasty retreat by informing the Lebanese President of peaceful intentions towards Syria and by sending a delegation to Saudi Arabia hoping to see her, as agreed previously, act as mediator between Turkey and Syria. However, prodded by the USSR and Egypt, which were bent on castigating Turkey as an agressor, Syria kept the issue on the U.N. agenda of the General Assembly. Syria also staged mass demonstrations in her major cities to claim Hatay, and to declare that peace in the Middle East would come only after all Arab lands have been returned to their proper owners. The allusion was obviously to Turkey and Israel whose relations had improved.

The Turkish pressure helped the Communist party increase its influence in Syria to the detriment of the ruling Ba'ath party. The latter threatened by a true leftist takeover finally found the salvation in union with Egypt, thus the United Arab Republic (UAR) was born in 1958. Turkey recognized immediately the union in the hope that it would limit Soviet influence and prevent a communist takeover in Syria. (A little earlier Nasser had assembled the Afro-Asian solidarity conference in Cairo, which met from December 26, 1957 to January 1, 1958, where Muslims from the USSR participated for the first time and were given a place in the permanent organization. Turkey and especially Pakistan though somewhat eager to increase their influence among Muslim nations, didn't participate. Nasser had emerged for all practical purposes, as the leader of Muslims.)

Kassem's revolution in Iraq on July 14, 1958, which overthrew and murdered King Faisal and Nuri es-Said left the Baghdad Pact in complete disarray. Once more Turkey massed troops on the Iraqi border, while U.S. marines, using in part the NATO military facilities in Turkey, landed in Lebanon on July 15, 1958, supposedly to prevent a takeover by Nasserites or leftists. The British troops did the same in Jordan a few days later. The heads of Muslim states, mostly from conservative countries, meeting at this time in Istanbul sent a message to President Eisenhower thanking him for his action while the young generations of Arabs were torn with rage at this subservient attitude of their elders.

The generation gap was widening. However, all this saber rattling failed to dislodge Kassem from power in Iraq or keep the country in the Pact though it might have restrained the partisans of Nasser from attempting to take over the government in Lebanon. Eventually, on March 24, 1959, Iraq declared that she would leave the Pact; the seat of the Pact had already been moved to Ankara. The Pact itself was re-named Central Treaty Organization (CENTO) on August 21, 1959, and dealt henceforth with the problems of the Northern Tier countries. Meanwhile, the Turkish policy in the Middle East, as well as the use of military bases in Turkey by U.S. troops for landing in Lebanon in 1958, caused the first major disagreement on foreign policy among political parties at home. The opposition showed openly its sympathy for the Iraqi revolution because it overthrew the despotic rule of Nuri es-Said, thus hoping that es-Said's fate would serve as a warning to Premier Menderes and induce him to refrain from pursuing further his totalitarian policies.

The withdrawal of Iraq from the Baghdad Pact and the massacre of some Turkish-speaking Iraqis in 1959, contrary to all expectations didn't keep the two countries apart for long. The Kurdish problem, the sharing of the Tigris and Euphrates waters, the transmission of natural gas were pressing problems which brought eventually an inprovement in Iraqi-Turkish relations. However, a timid attempt on the part of Turkey to normalize relations with all Arab countries after the revolution of May 27, 1960, was thwarted quickly after Syria launched a propaganda campaign to annex Hatay. Syrian action was backed by the National Union at its Cairo convention and by the joint statement of Arab ambassadors in Ankara. Eventually General Cemal Gürsel, the new President of Turkey, declared emphatically in Iskenderum on July 29, 1960, that any Syrian attempt to incorporate Hatay would lead to war.

The disintegration of the Baghdad Pact put an end to Turkish active efforts to promote a Middle East policy among her Arab neighbors suitable to the interests of NATO. The policy had been a dismal failure because neither Turkey nor her Western mentors understood the true nature of the profound social and political transformation occurring in Asia and Africa. It appears in retrospect now that the Baghdad pact helped quicken the rise of nationalism, socialism and of radical regimes in the Middle East. It also speeded up the emergence of Nasser as a leader of the Arab world, brought about the demise of Great Britain from the Middle East and prepared the ground for Soviet penetration.

The end of the Turkish-Western efforts to direct the course of Arab foreign policy eased somewhat the tensions in the area, and allowed the inter-Arab rivalries to come violently to the surface. These new conditions, emerging mainly after 1960, permitted Turkey to reshape more realistically her Middle East policy. The Nasser-Kassem rivalry gave a new twist to the Kurdish problem which was a matter of concern to Turkey too. Nasser appealed to the Kurds of Iraq in order to undermine Kassem's authority. Kassem, in turn, permitted Mullah Mustafa Barzani to return to Iraq and guaranteed some rights to Kurds in order to quieten the unrest at home, and mostly to stir up independence movements among the Kurdish minority of Syria. Turkey, in turn, allowed some arms to slip to the Kurdish insurgents in Iraq, who stiffened their resistance and put forth new demands, and eventually forced the Iraqi government to take retaliatory action against Barzani. The Iraqi air force bombed a few Turkish villages which were used as a haven by Kurdish insurgents. Iraq lost two planes, ambassadors were recalled but eventually in 1964, Turkey and Iraq patched up their quarrel and later Iraq agreed symbolically to pay indemnity to the Turkish villages whose houses had been destroyed in air attacks. Meanwhile, in 1961, Turkey recognized Syria soon after she left the union with Egypt. Nasser retaliated immediately by severing the Egyptian-Turkish diplomatic ties which were resumed fully only in 1965. Meanwhile, Jordan and Saudi Arabia challenged as conservative monarchies by the nationalist and socialist Arab countries headed by Egypt, began to seek Turkish counsel and support but without a basic change in their foreign policy orientation. It was in this transitional period in 1959-64, that Turkish-Israeli relations, although somewhat less active than in the past, appeared to be the major stumbling bloc to the improvement of Turkish-Arab relations.

Turkish relations with Israel, as mentioned before, stemmed first and above all from Turkey's commitment to the Western alliance, and then from strategic and economic considerations of strictly domestic order. Indeed, as far as trade was concerned, Turkey had generally a favorable balance only with Israel and

Syria. The Middle East trade of Turkey in 1963-66, amounted to 7-8 percent imports and 8 percent exports of her total foreign trade. The percentage figure however was misleading because in gross sum Turkey's imports from the Middle East superseded her exports. Turkey imported mostly oil from Saudi Arabia and Iraq. Indeed, some 86 percent of her imports were in oil products. The trade with Israel on the other hand covered a greater variety of products, and as mentioned before, was also favorable to Turkey. Moreover, the expansion of Turkish-Arab economic relations was jeopardized by lack of transportation facilities, trade agreements and representation, and the fact that Turkish and Arab economies produced the same kind of goods while trade with Israel benefitted from better organization and diversified production.

In sum, it appeared certain that Turkey's relations with Israel could not be altered without a change in Turkish-Western relations, and the offer of better economic and trade opportunities by the Arab countries.

Indeed, the Turkish-Arab and Turkish-Israeli relations after 1964, were conditioned first by the deterioration of the Turkish relations with the West caused by the Cyprus dispute, and second, by improved commercial opportunities in the Arab countries. The expansion of commercial relations with the Arab countries was a welcome development concomitant with the diversification of Turkey's industrial products, and the improvement in the packaging and marketing of food stuffs, which found new markets in the Arab countries. The Turkish economic relations with the Arab countries, although insignificant in comparison with her Western trade, improved even further after the Israeli-Arab War of 1967. It is, however, too far fetched to believe at this stage that the search for markets in the Arab countries will be a cause of friction between Turkey and Israel, despite the contention of an Israeli as told to this writer that "we, the Israelis fought the war of 1967, and the Turks are reaping the economic fruits."

The Cyprus dispute and the failure of the West to back Turkey produced a profound and multi-sided reaction among all Turks. The sight of thousands of Turkish Cypriot refugees flocking into safe quarters in order to escape the Greek, the picture of numerous Turkish houses destroyed, and the usurpation of land belonging to Turkish Cypriot peasants by well armed and trained

Greeks evoked a new understanding and created profound sympathy for the Palestine refugees. Israel on the other hand did not back Turkey on the Cyprus dispute causing thereby some consternation in official circles since much of Turkey's trouble with Arabs resulted from her recognition of Israel and relations with her. However, this incipient pro-Arab sentiment in 1963-64, failed to produce any visible results since the Arab countries sided with Archbishop Makarios, and Nasser shipped arms to Greek Cypriots, which were used against Turks. This situation, coupled with the nearly total lack of support in the United Nations debates in 1965, brutally forced Turkey to realize that her policy towards the Middle East and the new nations in general had isolated her from the rest of the world, despite the fact that she was favored by strategic, historical and cultural factors to achieve a leadership position among the third world countries. Thus, as might be expected, the first Turkish move was to break away from isolation. It materialized soon in the form of good will missions to the third world nations, and especially to the Middle East countries, to explain the Turkish stand on Cyprus. A delegation headed by Senator Sadi Koçaş, a man trusted by the military, who became Minister of State for a while in 1971, visited Iraq, Kuwait, Jordan, Syria and Lebanon. Already Turkey had participated in the second Afro-Asian conference held in Djakarta on April 10, 1964, while reassuring Israel of her friendly intentions by sending on a visit there the Minister of Rural Affairs on April 21, 1964. A little time later on June 17, 1964, Turkey established diplomatic relations with Malaya. At the end of 1964, in a gesture of friendship the Lebanese returned a state visit. The rapprochement to the third world countries and the courting of Muslim nations did not fail to produce results. The World Islamic Congress held in Somalia from December 27, 1964 to January 2, 1965, endorsed a resolution calling for a federation in Cyprus based on equal rights for Turks and Greeks. Turkey received new support on the Cyprus issue the following year at the Congress held in Mecca, which was attended by 60 delegations, 36 of which represented member states of the United Nations.

Meanwhile, Turkish-Soviet relations underwent considerable improvement after Cemal Feridun Erkin, the Foreign Minister, visited Moscow late in 1964. However, it would be erroneous to think that Turkish-Arab relations improved solely as the consequence of the thaw in Turkey's relations with the USSR. Turkey searched now for friends and support in the international arena not in order to promote the policies of the big powers as in the past, but merely to protect her own security and national interest. These were legitimate aims and consequently met with understanding and support. The Minister of Foreign Affairs declared on February 1, 1965, that the Turkish "policy on issues of common interests with the Arab world has been misunderstood and has given place to views which did not conform to reality" and promised to improve and correct Turkey's policy toward we Arabs.

The visit of Habib Bourgiba of Tunisia on March 25, 1965, had considerable impact on Turkish public opinion. The relations of Turkey with North African countries, because of some favorable historical background, have been generally excellent, despite an initial negative attitude towards the Algerian revolution on the part of the Turkish government, which caused profound public reaction in the country. During his visit, Bourgiba, as a moderate and as a North African, urged Turkey to understand the state of mind prevailing among Arabs who were still reacting to the recent colonial and imperial rule of the West. He called for justice for the Cypriot Turks and compared them with the Palestine refugees while criticizing some of Turkey's "modernist" reforms as a denial of her culture and history. The new Minister of Foreign Affairs, Hasan Işık, on the other hand, assured the Tunisian journalists that Turkey's relations with Israel were just normal and would not develop in a way detrimental to the Arabs. Meanwhile on June 9, 1965, a special representative of President Ben Bella arrived in Turkey with a special message concerning the Turkish participation in the Afro-Asian conference due to be held in Algeria that very year. The conference did not take place because of Ben Bella's ousting. However, the Turkish chief delegate Halük Bayulken, then Secretary General, and Foreign Minister in 1972, was able to go to Algeria. He referred to the Algerians as brotherly people and praised their liberation fight as a "struggle which we had also fought half a century ago under the leadership of Kemal Atatürk" and asked for support in the Cyprus case.

The Syrians, however, who a little earlier had vowed with their customary oratorical bravado to move onto Turkey if the latter invaded Cyprus, put in a nutshell the Arab condition for improved relations. "Our attitude" the Syrian Foreign Minister declared, "is related to Turkey's relations with Israel." But soon in 1965, the Turkish-Syrian talks on the division of Euphrates waters ended without agreement. Nevertheless, relations with the other Arab countries improved after Saudi Arabia and the UAR on June 16 and August 10, 1965 respectively, and Somalia on February 9, 1966, raised their diplomatic representation to ambassadorial level.

Meanwhile the elections of 1965 in Turkey brought to power a Justice Party government headed by Suleyman Demirel. A number of observers have stressed the fact that Demirel's relatively pro-Arab policy was undertaken in order to please his conservative rural constituency which supposedly had religious sympathies for the Arabs. This is a subjective judgement stemming from real lack of understanding of the Turkish process of decision making in foreign affairs. First, Turkish foreign policy is made essentially by a group of professionals in the Foreign Ministry and it is accepted as such in the Parliament with little debate. Second, the Turkish rapprochement to the Arabs was a logical step in 1964-67, undertaken in order to end isolation and seek support for the Cyprus policy among third world nations. Third, Demirel's government was accused at home of being identified with NATO and of enjoying the close confidence of the USA rather than being in favor of nonalignment. Fourth, and finally, paradoxical as it may sound, Turkish-Soviet relations flourished under Demirel's rule despite the vehement antagonism towards the Soviet Union and communism of the same conservative peasant masses which supposedly were instrumental in conditioning his policy towards the Arabs. Actually the Justice Party government merely conformed to a more or less general desire for a more independent foreign policy as expressed by Sadrettin Bilgiç, the chairman of the Party at the time, in Erzurum on October 18, 1964. (Demirel replaced Bilgiç as party chairman in December of 1964). Bilgiç declared that Turkey, while remaining loyal to the Western alliance, should follow a national and independent foreign policy by establishing friendly relations with the Muslim countries of the Middle East and the Afro-Asian bloc, and called for a more aggressive policy in Cyprus. However, despite these promising developments with respect to the Arab countries the relations between Turkey and Syria deteriorated in 1966, because of a Syrian land reform which led to the confiscation of properties owned by Turkish citizens. Turkey reacted by seizing the lands of Syrian subjects and closed the border. But undaunted by the Syrian-Turkish dispute, Iraqi leaders paid a visit to Turkey and pleased with the improvement in relations called for further contacts.

The same year, King Faisal of Arabia proposed an Islamic Pact which was rejected by Turkey. The proposal was to unite all Muslims around a common idea, to place Islam on solid foundations, to mobilize Muslims against atheism and communism, to create cultural union and to establish a Muslim Common Market. The Turkish government, and especially the opposition, pointed out that the acceptance of an Islamic Pact would lead to the abandonment of neutrality in the Middle East conflict and of secularism. Ismet İnönü, the leader of the opposition Republican Party asked meaningfully "what would happen if the Christian states signed a Christian pact?" (On the other hand it must be pointed out that the idea of an Israeli identity based on religious foundations, and later, Israel's own efforts to portray the Islamic nations as being united against herself because of common religious ties in obvious contradiction to the actual situation, played some role in turning the Turkish public opinion against her, since the basic attitude in Turkey, at least among the groups influential in policymaking, remains fundamentally secularist.)

The Turkish-Iraqi dialogue continued with the visit of Adnan Pachachi, Minister of State of Iraq, who arrived on February 7, 1966, to conclude a cultural agreement with Turkey. Consequently Arabic and Turkish languages were recognized mutually as being scientific languages, a new Turkish cultural center was opened in Iraq, and the chair of Turkish language and literature was reestablished at the University of Baghdad. But in order to forestall speculation that the country was moving towards a pro-Islamic policy, Premier Demirel found it necessary to state that Turkey would participate only in Islamic conferences of non-political character and consequently would not join Islamic Pacts as proposed by Saudi Arabia. Furthermore in 1966, relations with the UAR warmed to the extent that the Egyptian ambassador spoke over the Ankara radio praising Arab-Turkish relations, while the Secretary General of the Turkish Foreign Ministry who met with Nasser declared that Turkey's current policy in the Middle East will result in a "reliable group around us, markets for our goods and friends who can understand us at international meetings." Indeed, a credit agreement of six million dollars enabled Turkey to buy cotton, cement, phosphate from the UAR and sell her copper, tobacco, wool and livestock. Turkey already had trade agreements with Jordan, Iraq but also with Israel. Travel between Turkey and Arab countries also increased. For instance in 1965, 29,804 Turks traveled to Arab countries (21,393 of them went to pilgrimage to Mecca) while 62,723 Arabs came to Turkey, many of them were in transit over land routes to Europe. Premier Abdurrahman al-Bazzaz of Iraq and King Faisal of Arabia paid state visits to Turkey, while President Sunay visited Tunisia late in 1966, and Turkey exchanged ambassadors with Algeria. The visits produced strong support for Turkish position on Cyprus and open rejection of *enosis* on the part of the Arabs. It also produced trade and tourist agreements, profuse statements in favor of Palestinian refugees but still did not sway Turkey from her basically neutral position towards the Arab-Israeli conflict. In fact, in order to set the balance straight Shak Nisim, the head rabbi of Israel was invited to Istanbul by the *hahambaşı* (chief rabbi) of the city and declared publicly in 1966, that the "history of the Jewish community in Turkey was the best evidence of the religious tolerance and freedom prevailing in the country."

Mutual Turkish-Arab visits at high level continued in 1967. Dignitaries from Arab countries, notably the Iraqi leader Abdurrahman Arif, all pressed Turkey for concessions with respect both to NATO and Israel. On January 15, 1967, Foreign Minister I.S. Çağlayangil arrived in Cairo for one week visit and met with Nasser. The visit ended without the usual communique but upon return to Turkey the Minister declared that the entire range of Turkish-Arab relations were reviewed and that "unanimous agreement was reached about broadening and consolidating relations between the UAR and Turkey." Thus, despite obvious disagreement over some key issues, agreement had been reached to seek ways to improve Arab-Turkish relations. The following events showed that indeed this was the case. Eventually Turkey declared that she would not allow the NATO powers to use the military facilities in Turkey in any conflict involving the Middle East countries, that is the Arab nations. Al-Ahram, the government newspaper in Cairo, promptly labeled the declaration as a Turkish decision to side with the Arabs in the Israeli conflict.

The events following this declaration although they did not indicate a major change in the Turkish policy of neutrality towards the Arab-Israeli conflict, nevertheless showed a shift in favor of the Arabs. On May 23, 1967, the Ambassadors of the UAR, Syria and Iraq visited the Foreign Ministry and asked the government of Turkey to support the Arab stand in the brewing conflict in the area. The demand was followed by a similar call on the part of all Arab diplomats in Ankara while Arif, the President of Iraq urged President Sunay to support the Arab struggle. The Turkish government, however, failed to take the immediate steps desired by the Arab countries. Meanwhile the Arab consuls in Istanbul payed a visit to the *Cumhuriyet*, one of the most influential Turkish newspapers which had turned pro-Soviet and pro-leftist and supported all schemes designated to weaken Turkey's dependence on and alliance with the West. The consuls defended the Arab policy and asked that Turks support the Arab claim for control over the Gulf of Aqaba. Turkey rejected the demand since she favored freedom of navigation. Finally on May 29, 1967, the Turkish government made public its position through a declaration full of generalities in favor of peace and security, which failed to please the Arab countries. However, as the Arab-Israeli hostilities began in June, Turkish public opinion sided with the Arabs and the government cast aside its strict neutrality by adopting gradually a pro-Arab attitude, despite the insistence of the Republican Party that the government should preserve a strict neutrality in this conflict as it did before. The student body, following its leftist leaders, many of whom incidentally supported the Republican Party, came out strongly against Israel by asking the government to openly support the Arabs. The Turkish radical left regarded Israel as a colonialist country and supported the Arabs as the victims of imperialism.

The Israeli-Arab War of 1967, crystallized the Turkish attitude towards the conflict, not only because of public pressure, but also because of the Soviet effort to see the Russo-Turkish relations as part of the general political picture in the Middle East. In fact the Socialist bloc considered the Turkish moves in favor of the Arabs an endorsement of its own stand. After 1967, indeed, the

Turkish-Soviet communiques included a series of references to the Middle East, usually supporting the Arab viewpoint. Turkey strongly opposed any annexation of territory by Israel and refused to represent the U.S. interest in Iraq after relations between those two countries were severed in 1967. In fact, Turkey asked explicitly for the withdrawal of the Israeli troops and payment of indemnity for damages by voting for the USSR resolution in the United Nations. However, Turkey abstained from voting for the first paragraph of the same resolution which condemned Israel as an agressor. Later she co-authored with Pakistan the resolution rejecting the Israeli decision to annex Jerusalem. Turkey participated also, after considerable discussion and hesitation at home in the Muslim Summit Conference which debated and condemned the burning of the al-Aqsa mosque in Jerusalem in 1969. At the Rabat Summit Conference, Turkey, nevertheless, opposed a resolution which called for all participants to break diplomatic relations with Israel, and sided with Pakistan in rejecting Indian participation in that conference. Relations between Turkey and the UAR cooled off considerably because of this incident, despite hurried attempts by both sides to patch up the difference. Turkey's intensive diplomatic activity in the Middle East prompted the opposition Republican Party to criticize the government for having deviated from its basic policy of neutrality towards the Israeli-Arab conflict and the country's secularist standing.

Meanwhile, the Middle East policy of Turkey developed an additional dimension through the rise of radical leftist movements and their close identification with the Palestinian guerilla organizations. The Turkish radical left regarded the Palestinian guerilla organizations as part of a world-wide struggle against capitalism and imperialism, and especially against the United States and hence, her protégé, Israel. Some members of the Revolutionary Youth Federation actually received military training in al-Fatah camps in Syria and Jordan and engaged in guerilla fighting there. It was the members of this organization, who kidnapped and murdered the Israeli consul in Istanbul in 1971. It is estimated that several hundred Turks, mostly students, received training in Syria and Jordan. A few youths returning from these missions were arrested as the government realized belatedly that the training of guerillas, as proven by later events, was aimed ultimately at undermining the security and political regime of Turkey. Consequently, Turkey viewed the ceasefire proposed by the U.S. Secretary of State Rogers as a constructive step, a necessary cooling-off period, and wisely remained neutral during the clashes between Jordanian regular forces and guerilla organizations. This neutrality was intended primarily as an act of good faith towards Syria who was backing the guerillas. Nevertheless, by the end of 1970, Turkish-Arab relations entered a period of re-evaluation as the desire to maintain a neutral attitude towards the Arab-Israeli conflict prevailed. This development resulted in large measure from an improvement in the relations with the United States, a certain stagnation in Turkish-Soviet rapprochement, and the lethal challenge to the regime posed by the militant radical left in the country itself. Already the Turkish attitude towards some issues posed before the Islamic conferences proved that she opposed identification with the radical stand. For instance, Turkey participated in 1970 in such a conference but opposed the idea of establishing a permanent secretariat for Islamic nations. Later she opposed a proposition to sever all relations with Israel.

To sum it up, the Turkish-Arab relations in the early 1950's were adversely affected by Turkey's total identification with the policies of the West, notably England and then the United States. In 1964-70, these relations were normalized without affecting Turkey's basic commitment to NATO and her membership in a variety of European organizations. Turkish relations with Israel were maintained although on a somewhat reduced scale. On the other hand, better relations with Arab countries were helpful in improving Turkey's stand in the third world, and subsequently in undercutting in large measure the support which Greeks received from these quarters on the Cyprus issue. Moreover, improved relations with Arabs increased the flow of tourists and the volume of trade in favor of Turkey. A Turkish Chamber of Commerce created especially with the purpose of promoting trade with the Arabs reported in 1970, that the Turkish exports to Arab countries increased by about 38 percent over the previous year.

It must be stated emphatically, however, that Turkish policy-makers view with increasing alarm the Arab-Israeli conflict. They feel that the conflict is affecting directly their own security and peace in every possible way making it thus increasingly difficult to maintain a neutral stand. Turkey feels that a complete Israeli withdrawal from Arab territories occupied in 1967, will not only pave the way for true peace but will also effectively stop the Soviet penetration and the radicalization of the intelligentsia in the area. Turkey attaches more importance to its effects rather than to the Arab-Israeli conflict itself. Moreover, Turkey feels that her own security and the maintenance of good relations with the Arabs calls for a more active policy on her part in the Middle East provided that such a course of action is reconcilable with her commitment to NATO and the country's long range interests. The government of Nihat Erim, which was brought to power by the military in March 1971, occupied with internal disorder, has relegated the Turkish-Arab relations to a secondary rank in the foreign policy of the government despite declarations to the contrary. This reaction against further improvement of Turkish-Arab relations has resulted from a deep apprehension that foreign policy commitments entail involvement in the ideological movements in the area. Yet, it is clear that a policy oriented towards consolidating Turkey's position in the Middle East and protecting her multi-sided interests in the area calls for a more active participation in the affairs of the region. Indeed, the Turkish interest and involvement in the Middle East, after a short respite in 1971, was resumed in 1972 and 1973. An important event was the visit of the Turkish Foreign Minister Halük Bayülken to Syria in December of 1972, followed by Syrian Minister's visit in 1973, a country with which Turkey's relations remained rather cold. This visit which lasted for five days was used to discuss and settle issues stemming from the confiscation of property belonging to Turkish citizens. Relations with Iraq in 1972 and 1973 continued to develop at a speedy rate, especially after Turkey reduced substantially, and in fact eliminated the CENTO aid given to the Kurdish insugents in Iraq. On August 27, 1973, Iraqi Foreign Minister, Murtada al-Hadithi signed an agreement to build a 350 million dollar oil pipeline from Kirkuk to Dörtyol in Turkey as well as a gas line from Iraqi field to Turkish industrial centers. Turkish Arab relations improved further after the Arab-Israeli war of October 1973. Turkey did not permit the use of her military facilities to ship American materials to Israel. She did not permit the Russians to use her air space or highways for shipping aid to Syria and Iraq either. In other words Turkish policy in the Middle East, although showing considerable support for the Arabs, still maintained its neutrality. After the coming to power of the Ecevit government in January 1974, new interest in improving relations was shown both by the People's Republican Party, the chief coalition party, largely because of its general leftist social philosophy, and by the National Salvation Party, the minor coalition partner in the government because of its religious conservatism and pro Arab sentiments. However, a state visit by Necmeddin Erbakan, the deputy Premier and chairman of the National Salvation Party to Saudi Arabia in May 1974 in order to secure a large loan and lower price for oil did not produce any results. It seemed that politics, economic interests and religious sympathies did not mix, a lesson the Turkish religious conservatives found hard to understand or accept. Thus, in conclusion one may say that short of a drastic change in Turkey's basic foreign policy alignment Turkish-Arab relations will develop in the form of bilateral agreements dealing with trade and other technical matters rather than broad political commitments. It is evident on the other hand that if Turkey is to play a role in Middle East politics, and prompte her interest in the area and in the Third World in general while remaining faithful to her own political traditions of national independence, then, she must adopt a friendlier policy towards the Arab states. The logic of facts and history dictates Turkey to seek security and friends in her immediate area rather than rely on whimsical allies overseas —

THE CYPRUS CONFLICT AND TURKEY

SUAT BILGE
University of Ankara, Ankara

The island of Cyprus, an old Turkish land, is located approximately 40 miles from the southeastern coast of Anatolia. It is the third largest island on the Mediterranean covering an area of 3,572 miles.

According to the census of 1960, the island was inhabited by 577,615 people, 18.06 per cent of whom were Turkish Cypriots, and the rest Greek Cypriots and some minor groups. There is no distinct Cypriot nation. Greeks and Turks who came originally mostly from Greece and Turkey constitute the greatest proportion of the population. Turkish Cypriots are mostly the descendants of the soldiers of the army which conquered the island in 1571, and of the administrators and craftsmen from Anatolia, who were assigned to serve in Cyprus. The relative proportion of the ethnic groups on the island showed variations in the course of history. After 1750 the Turks constituted the majority. However, in 1878, that is, the year in which England took over the administration of the island, the number of Turks began to decrease. It fell eventually to twenty per cent because of migration after the English rule began to root itself in 1881, and deepen the island's political alienation from Turkey. The two major ethnic groups did not live in separate areas but in mixed settlements. There were also separate Turkish and Greek villages as well as mixed villages. Even in the mixed settlements the two ethnic groups were not integrated; each preserved its own distinct language, religion, culture and ethnic origin. The Turks followed closely the economic, social and political developments occurring in Turkey, despite the fact that they had their own administrative organization and political parties.

Cyprus was under Turkish sovereignty between 1571 and 1914. The Turkish Government entrusted the administration of the island to the British in 1878, who changed this status by acquiring the island in 1914, and by making it a crown colony. Britain governed Cyprus between 1914 and 1960. The independent Republic of Cyprus was founded in 1960 through the Zurich and London Agreements of the same year.

The Cyprus conflict broke out as a result of Greek desire to unite Cyprus with Greece, a policy known as ENOSIS, and because of the opposition of Turkish Cypriots and Turkey to this policy. In one word, Turks and Greeks cannot agree on the future of the island. Greeks look upon Cyprus as a Greek island. They hope to achieve ENOSIS by relying on the numerical majority of Greeks on the island. At times they have tried to fulfill their objective either under the guise of a drive against British imperialism or demands for the right of self determination.

Turks look upon the Greek demands as being part of a desire for territorial expansion and a revision of the present boundaries which, they fear, would upset the balance established by the Treaty of Lausanne in 1923. Actually the Turkish-Greek conflict in Cyprus should be placed within a broader historical context, and assessed in the light of Turkish-Greek relations to be developed in the future.

World public opinion fails to understnad fully the stand taken by Turkey against Greek demands for the annexation of Cyprus. Turkey is a descendant of the Ottoman Empire whose partition left large groups of Turks within the boundaries of all the neighboring countries. The number of such Turks exceeds by far the number of those living in Cyprus. Why, then, is the Turkish policy with regard to the Turks in Cyprus so inflexible as to affect her entire foreign policy, while she does not seem to take much interest in the Turks living in other neighboring countries? The most important answer is that the Turks on the island are deprived of their basic right to life. Greece, while attempting to win over world public opinion, initiated a campaign of terror which led to the murder of many innocent Turkish Cypriots. Turkey cannot be expected to witness this situation as a disinterested observer. Secondly, there is not yet a distinct Cypriot nation in Cyprus, and it cannot have distinct ethnic characteristic as in other neighboring countries. Consequently, the Turkish Cypriots are not a minority group. As mentioned before, the population of Cyprus is made up mainly of two communities. The Turkish community and Turkey have just as much right to decide the future of the island as the Greeks. Furthermore, the status of the island is an extension of the balance established in the region by the Treaty of Lausanne. Turkey cannot possibly stay aloof if and when this balance is changed. One must remember also that geographically Cyprus has a direct bearing upon Turkey's national defense. All these factors combine inevitably to force Turkey to take a firm stand against Enosis.

The year of 1954 marks the beginning of the conflict of Cyprus. We chose this year as the date for the conflict because the question of Cyprus was officially posed then as an international issue. Though conflicts associated with Cyprus appeared sporadically during the Ottoman and British rule, Greece brought the conflict of Cyprus before the United Nations General Assembly and made it an international problem for the first time in 1954. Greece charged that the people of Cyprus were not granted the right of self determination. From the very start it was clear that Greece was behind the demands of Greek Cypriots. This new Greek move was motivated by the desire to exploit the strong emotions against imperialism which prevailed in the world after the Second World War.

At the time the Cyprus conflict broke out, the memories of the recent past were still very much alive in Turkey. The unacceptable Soviet demands for bases on the Turkish Straits as well as for territory in the North had not been forgotten, despite the reassurance stemming from the Truman Doctrine of support against Communism in 1947, and the admission of Turkey into NATO in 1952. The formal renunciation by the Soviet Union on May 30, 1953, to her demands could not dispel the anxiety she had created in Turkey. Turks awaited convincing signs to confirm the new Soviet policy. The Hungarian crisis of 1956, and various other developments in the Middle East stretched this waiting period as late as 1959.

Turkey reported the conflict of Cyprus at the beginning from the viewpoint of the Western alliance, and refrained from acts that could disrupt her security as well as that of Greece and England, all allies and parties to the conflict. Foreign Minister Fuat Köprülü made several statements at the time, implicitly calling the attention of Greece to the negative effect which the emerging conflict might have upon the relations among the Allies. Later, when the conflict was officially brought into the international arena, Turkey did her utmost to confine it to its own limits. For instance, attempts made by youth organizations in Turkey and by Turkish Cypriots on the island to retaliate against Greek provocations were largely curtailed. The official circles expressed deep satisfaction when the discussion of the issue in the United Nations was postponed to the following year.

During the discussion of the Greek complaint in the Political Committee of the United Nations General Assembly, Selim Sarper, the Turkish permanent delegate, defined the conflict of Cyprus as having direct relevance to the peace and power balance in the Mediterranean, and claimed that provocations in this region would be detrimental to all parties. At the same time he expressed hope that the United Kingdom would grant gradual autonomy to the people of Cyprus. In the end, a proposal by New Zealand resolved the impasse: the United Nations Political Committee decided not to discuss the Greek complaint. The world press made it clear that the United Nations decision resulted largely from the opposition of the United States to the Greek policy. Aware of the potential harm to the southeastern flank of the NATO, the United States tried first to prevent a conflict over Cyprus between Turkey and Greece, then advised moderation, and attempted to mediate the conflict, and finally when everything failed, strove to keep the conflict within its own limits.

Prime Minister Adnan Menderes, in a statement to the Anatolian Agency, saw the U.N. resolution as bringing the Cyprus conflict to an end and recommended that utmost care to preserve the friendship between Turkey and Greece, which he described as an ally of Turkey.

The conflict, however, continued to brew. When the Greek request was turned down at the United Nations, Greece consented to negotiations with the parties to the conflict, namely with England and Turkey. The Greeks on the island followed the same course. But at the same time Greece, in order to mobilize public opinion in the United Nations and England and settle the conflict on her own terms resorted to terrorism. The latter gave the conflict international dimension. With the help of Greece, the Cypriote Greeks engaged in terroristic activities, first in 1955, against the British administration and then in 1956, against the Turkish community. Two motives stood behind the terroristic acts directed against the Turkish Cypriots: first, to deter them from serving in the security force responsible for the maintenance of order on the island and second, to force them to leave the island by creating panic among them. The terroristic activities against Turkish Cypriots gradually intensified escalating in the end into a kind of civil war between the two communities. Foreign Minister Fuat Köprülü disclosed in the National Assembly on June 13, 1956, that the EOKA, the underground Greek organization responsible for terroristic activities, such as the murder of the Turkish police officers and the plunder of Turkish villages, was under the command of Greek army officers. Terrorism on the island continued until the beginning of 1959, the year in which the Zurich and London Agreements were signed. However, the EOKA, the terrorist organization, was not liquidated. Instead, its members were recruited into the police force and the army of the newly created Republic, to be reactivated under different names toward the end of 1963.

England was inclined to treat the conflict of Cyprus as an internal problem as long as the island was under her rule. When the other parties to the conflict found this stand unacceptable, she tried to settle the conflict through negotiations with Turkey and Greece, and with the Turkish and Greek communities on the island. Later, realizing that she could not contain the conflict, England accepted the agreements reached by Turkey and Greece with the idea of prolonging her own stay in Cyprus a while longer.

Some circles claim that Turkey was dragged into the Cyprus conflict by England in order to help preserve British sovereignty over the island. The fact remains that Cyprus being an old Turkish land with a Turkish community on it, Turkey could have not possibly remained passive to a revision in the political status of the island. In fact no government in Turkey could be expected to remain passive when faced with the slaughter of Cypriote Turks. The opposition party eventually turned the disturbances on the island into a major issue during the following campaign for elections in 1957. Thus, the Cyprus conflict became a major domestic political issue and eventually transformed itself into a national cause.

Since the outbreak of the conflict Turkey has favored a settlement through negotiations between the states concerned with the issue and the two communities on the island. This approach stems from the belief that there is not any Cypriote nation but only Turkish and Greek people living on the island. These people are of the same ethnic origin as the Turks in Turkey and the Greeks in Greece. Therefore, the conflict can be settled only through negotiations between Turks and Greeks. Experience shows indeed that whenever a settlement is reached, it is achieved only through negotiations between Turks and Greeks. On the other hand, the conflict tends to take devious aspects and proliferate when the United Nations is involved.

The Cyprus conflict was discussed the first time at the London Conference after. On June 30, 1955, Prime Minister Anthony Eden informed the House of Commons that he had extended an invitation to Turkey and Greece to discuss a series of strategic matters relating to the Mediterranean, including the conflict of Cyprus. The agenda of the conference has not been pre-determined. The purpose of the conference was defined in vague terms possibly in order to soothe Greece which officially did not recognize Turkey as a party to the Cyprus dispute, and might have refused the invitation. Actually the entire purpose of the conference was to discuss the conflict. In the early stages of the conflict, Greece had refused to consider Turkey as a party to the issue, hoping to impose exclusively her demands on Britain. Consequently, Turkey had to direct her energies during an initial period in 1954-58, to have herself accepted as a party to the conflict by Greece and world public opinion. Turkey claimed all along that she had yielded her rights over the island through Article 16 of the Treaty of Lausanne only in favor of Britain.

Greece accepted the invitation with apprehensions because it would have implied implicit acceptance of Turkey as a party to the conflict and would have given the British a new rationale to stay in Cyprus in case Greece and Turkey could not reach an agreement. Finally, the fact that Greek Cypriots had not been invited to the conference gave Greece further cause for concern. Turkey, on her part, looked upon the proposed conference as an opportunity to become a party to the conflict and to make her views known publicly. Actually the British government might have resorted anyway to a multilateral conference, in order to prove that an easy and quick settlement to the conflict was not possible.

The London Conference took place between August 29-

September 7, 1955 without achieving success. It dispersed, supposedly in response to the riots against the Greeks in Istanbul on September 6-7, but actually because of the utter irreconciliable positions taken by the parties to the conflict. England proposed that Cyprus be granted local autonomy on condition that sovereignty over the island would rest with her, while Turkey and Greece participated in the defense. Greece insisted that Cyprus should be granted the right of self-determination. Turkey, rejecting both the proposal for local autonomy and self-determination, came out in favor of the *status quo*, and if that was not possible advocated the return of the island to herself. She also rejected the proposal that Greece participate in the defense of Cyprus.

Prime Minister Adnan Menderes in a speech on August 24, 1955 described Greek demands as representing an irredentistic policy. Indeed this charge becomes meaningful if relations between Turkey and Greece are considered in historical and strategic perspective. Immediately following her independence in 1827-29 Greece adopted an expansionist policy known as *Megalo Idea*; she occupied the island of Crete, and invaded Anatolia at the end of the First World War. Turkey consequently regards Cyprus and the Dodecanese Islands as part of a strategic ensemble whose change of status bears directly upon the relations between Turkey and Greece. In general, Turkey was not against self-determination, as she explained at the London Conference. She had conducted her War of Independence in 1919-1922, in conformity with this principle. But she believed that in the case of Cyprus there were other vital considerations which made it an exception to the general principle. For instance, the Turkish demand in the past that Turks in Western Thrace and Mosul be given the right of self-determination had been rejected both by Greece and England because of special factors mitigating against self-determination. Cyprus was in a special situation because of the relatively large number of Turks living on the island along with Greeks. Which one of them will exercise the right of self-determination? Furthermore, the island has a direct bearing upon the defenses of Turkey and the Eastern Mediterranean as a whole. Finally, the status of the island was determined by a treaty. It is evident that this status cannot be revised by unilateral action by one party without the consent of the others. Consequently, Turkey refrained from consenting to unqualified enforcement of a self determination which disregarded not only the existence of other factors and historical experience but was contrived as a means to achieve *enosis*, that is the unity of Cyprus with Greece.

The prevailing circumstances did not favor local autonomy either. At a time when Greek terrorists strove to annihilate the Turkish community, by murder and other acts of violence, and when the two communities seemed entirely apart, it was utterly unrealistic to demand local autonomy under a single government ruled by Greeks. A government composed both of Turks and Greeks could be established only if order and security were properly secured first.

The island of Cyprus is of vital importance to Turkish defense. The Second World War demonstrated that the ports of the Eastern Mediterranean had a basic role in Turkish defense and consequently the present day defense facilities support routes and capital investment in the area were planned accordingly. As defense strategy, Cyprus is an integral part of Turkish security and cannot be left entirely to the discretion of Greece. The defense of Cyprus will weaken her total defense capability since Greece's means are limited. Cyprus is far off the shores of Greece. Strategically it seems more appropriate for Greece to concentrate her limited power in Thrace where defense cooperation between Turkey and Greece can be more successfully achieved than in Cyprus. To leave the defense of Cyprus to Greece, which incidentally failed to defend even the island of Crete during the last war, would amount to leaving the island defenseless.

The opposition by England to self-determination, the violent reaction by Turkey and the rejection of the same principle by Cypriote Turks forced Greece to turn to the United Nations where she hoped to find a more favorable atmosphere. Following the London Conference in 1957, the conflict of Cyprus was debated twice in the United Nations. Greece tried to secure a recommendation from the General Assembly to the effect that the people of Cyprus be granted the right of self-determination. England pointed out during debates that the United Nations Charter did not entrust any state with a mandate to work for the dependence of a territory which belonged to another state, and urged Greece to refrain from assisting the terrorists in Cyprus.

Turkey stated that underneath the Greek insistence on self-determination lay the plan for union of Cyprus with Greece, and hoped that Greece would desist encouraging, organizing and supporting the terrorist activities, and would settle the issue peacefully that is through negotiations between the interested parties.

Faced with the contradictory demands of the parties to the conflict, the United Nations abstained from passing a resolution on the essentials of the issue. Instead, it accepted an Indian proposal recommending that the parties settle the conflict peacefully through negotiations according to the United Nations Charter. The Turkish delegation interpreted the United Nations recommendation as supporting her proposal for negotiations and as rejecting the Greek design for *enosis*.

The United Nations discussed the conflict of Cyprus once more in December, 1957, again upon the request of Greece. The latter insisted once more that the people of Cyprus be granted the right of self determination. She claimed that the insecurity and disorder, which actually had been created by her very own actions, would be eliminated only if the people of Cyprus were granted the right of self determination. Turkey accused Greece of being reluctant to engage in negotiations as suggested by the General Assembly at the beginning of the year. She emphasized the fact that the island was populated by two communities entirely different in language, religion, ethnic origin and national identity, and proposed that the conflict be settled by granting the right of self determination to both communities.

The vote in the Political Committee of the General Assembly favored the draft proposal submitted by Greece, which called for negotiations with the ultimate aim of enforcing self determination in Cyprus. However, the Greek proposal failed to muster the two-thirds majority vote in the General Assembly, thus leaving its own recommendation adopted earlier in February still in force. The Turkish delegation interpreted the vote as a rejection by the General Assembly of self determination in Cyprus as suggested by Greece. Turkey was primarily interested in pressing Greece into bi-lateral talks by preventing the adoption of a United Nations resolution which favored the Greek position. She felt that the conflict had to be taken first out of the United Nations.

Meanwhile NATO and the Council of Europe attempted to find a solution to the conflict. At the annual meeting of NATO in Paris on March 20, 1957, the Secretary General of the organization arranged a meeting among the Prime Ministers of the United Kingdom, Turkey and Greece but without success. In September and October of 1958, NATO again tried to act as mediator by calling a round table conference, but this attempt met also with failure because of the Greek opposition to such a meeting. Greece still hoped to secure a favorable resolution in the United Nations where the concept of self determination enjoyed great favor at that time. The resolution adopted by the Political Committee mentioned above, had its share in encouraging Greece to think that she will achieve her goal sooner or later. Consequently Greece went to the United Nations again in 1958. But this time, during deliberations, she reformulated her stand in the light of the Macmillan Plan and the idea of independence which now had received United Nations approval. She presented her claim to self determination of Cyprus as a plan for independence to be granted after an interim period of local autonomy.

England announced that the Macmillan Plan which envisaged a settlement through negotiations, and the cooperation of the two communities, would be put in effect. Thus, she looked upon the conflict not any longer as a domestic issue as she had claimed earlier. Turkey repeating her previous position, insisted that both self determination and independence would amount to *enosis*, and while suggesting that the Macmillan Plan should be given a trial, she pressed for a resolution recommending a settlement through negotiations between the parties concerned. The heated discussions in the Political Committee lasted eight days during which a series of proposals were submitted. Ultimately the Iranian proposal received a majority vote. Iran proposed that the conflict of Cyprus be definitely settled at a conference to be attended by the three states, parties to the conflict, and the representatives of Cyprus. But it was evident that the Iranian proposal which embodied the ideas put forth at the London Conference at a later date, could not muster a two-thirds majority in the General Assembly. Consequently a more general proposal drafted by Mexico was accepted. This proposal affirmed the United Nations confidence in the intention of the parties to make continuous efforts for a peaceful, democratic and just settlement of the conflict in accordance with the principles of the Charter.

The Turkish delegation deliberately refrained from interpreting the final recommendation of the General Assembly as backing Turkey's stand in order to avoid the possible adverse effect of such an interpretation upon her future bilateral negotiations with Greece. She was satisfied to state that success would be achieved only when the rights and interests of all the three states and the two communities involved in the Cyprus dispute were reconciled. Greece, thus unable to obtain a resolution from the United Nations dealing with the essentials of the conflict, turned to bilateral negotiation with Turkey. The attempts outlined above undertaken in the United Nations to settle the conflict of Cyprus were clearly related to procedure rather than to substance. It was obvious that the issue could be more basically dealt with only by the states directly concerned with the conflict.

The draft constitution known as Radcliffe, the blue print proposed by the Macmillan Plan, and the Zurich and London Agreements, all put forth as possible solutions to the conflict, deserve special but joint treatment because they are closely interconnected and derived from each other. Three proposals were mostly unsuccessful largely because of the nature of difficulties rooted in the Cyprus dispute. To repeat what was pointed out earlier, the two major communities do not have a common goal; the Greek community desires to unite Cyprus with Greece, while the Turkish community strives not to fall under Greek sovereignty. The two communities are entirely different from each other with respect to religion, language and culture and do not intermarry. Throughout their long history on the island they stayed as such. A marriage between a Greek and a Turk can take place only after religious conversion and a shift of membership from one community to another. Both of the communities are spread over the island in small clusters. Though separate Turkish and Greek villages constitute a majority, there are mixed villages as well. If a larger portion of the Turkish community were gathered in a certain region of the island, a settlement would have been easier to find. It was the geographical difficulty which led to the functional federation decided at the Zurich Conference.

Faced with persistent disorders on the island, England attempted to bring a local solution to the conflict at the London Conference in 1955, although the views of the parties over the conflict had not crystallized yet. Lord Radcliffe, a lawyer who drafted the constitution, paid a visit to Cyprus to investigate local conditions and to talk with the representatives of the two communities. According to the Radcliffe draft officially announced on December 19, 1956, the administration of the island was to be left to a local government but, matters pertaining to foreign affairs, defense and internal security were to stay within the exclusive jurisdiction of England. A legislature, an executive body, and courts, were to be established to conduct the matters left to the jurisdiction of Cypriots. The Radcliffe draft proposed a sort of autonomy for the Turkish community in matters within the jurisdiction of Cypriots. Thus Turkish Cypriots' requests to conduct their own affairs seemed accepted. Such requests were advanced since 1930, in a variety of ways, including the proposals of the Turkish Affairs Commission set up in 1949.

The autonomy granted to the Turkish Cypriots as a separate community was apparent in every aspect of the proposed self government; of the 36 legislators to be partly elected and partly appointed to the legislative body, six were to be Turkish Cypriots elected by the Turkish community from a list of candidates separately prepared for them. A two-thirds vote of the Turkish members in the legislature would be required to pass a bill on matters pertaining to the affairs of the Turkish community. Furthermore, either the President or the Vice President of the legislature was to be a Turk. The local government would include a minister responsible for the Turkish affairs which included personal status, religion, foundations, education and culture. The proposed Cypriot courts were to be constituted in equal numbers of both Turkish and Greek judges, while the Supreme Court would be composed of one Turkish, one Greek and one neutral President, etc. The Radcliffe draft was to take its final form after consultations with the Greek and Turkish Cypriots, Greece and Turkey. Turks participated in these discussions but the draft could not be revised because of apprehensions and suspicions. Turkish Cypriots and Turkey had feared at first that the self government proposed by Radcliffe would lead to ENOSIS. Turkish apprehensions calmed down following the proclamation of Prime Minister Eden in the House on March 14, 1956, to the effect that the conflict of Cyprus could not be settled without the consent of Turkey, and again, following Lennox-Boyd's statement that if

Cyprus as a whole were granted the right of self determination, the Turkish community specifically would be granted the same right. Pressed by the crisis in the Middle East, Turkey looked with some favor to a temporary settlement. The pronouncements by British statesmen, though indirectly suggestive, had not ruled out the possibility of partition of the island, and this had some appeal for Turkey.

The second ineffectual measure proposed to settle the Cyprus conflict was the Macmillan Plan. The conflict created a multitude of problems for the British administration on the island, and posed a serious threat to its military facilities there. Meanwhile the Greek terroristic acts, initially directed against the British, escalated to include the Turks, and intensified the clashes between the Turkish and Greek communities, and thus it made increasingly difficult their collaboration in the future. The opposition in England also played up the situation in Cyprus in order to embarrass the government. In the end the British government was forced to consider a new form of settlement.

The first British move was the recall at the end of 1957 of Field Marshal Harding, a sort of military governor on the island. A civilian governor, Sir Hugh Foot, took his place. The new governor met with the leaders of the Turkish and Greek Cypriot communities and discussed a settlement to the conflict. Early in 1958, he made a trip to London to submit to his government proposals based on his own assessment of the situation. After a series of studies and deliberations the cabinet came to a final decision about the form of government to be instituted in Cyprus. The decision was announced by Prime Minister Macmillan in the House of Commons on June 19, 1958.

The proposal of the government, known as the Macmillan Plan, envisaged a joint type of administration. Rather than determining the future of Cyprus in definitive terms, the plan advocated a transitional government for a period of seven years under British sovereignty. At the end of this period England would let Turkey and Greece participate in the government of the island if the latter two so wished. During the seven year transitional period, the tripartite administration was to consist of England, Turkey, Greece and Cypriote Turkish and Greek communities, but foreign affairs, defense and internal security matters were to be the sole responsibility of a Governor to be appointed by England.

The members of the two communities were to be allowed to obtain, according to their ethnic origin, either Turkish or Greek citizenship, while retaining British citizenship; in short, possess double citizenship. The two communities were to conduct their communal affairs through their respective legislative assemblies. A council presided over by the Governor and composed of the representatives of Turkey and Greece, and of four representatives for the Greek community and two representatives for the Turkish community was to deal with other matters falling outside the Governor's functions.

Turkey and Greece received the Macmillan Plan with misgivings. This negative reaction induced Prime Minister Macmillan to pay a visit to Athens and Ankara on August 7-9, in order to explain the Plan personally and secure an agreement. Greece opposed the plan because it recognized in principle the separate existence of the two communities; the partition of the island; and Turkey's status as a party to the conflict of Cyprus. Turkey on her part made it clear that she would agree to the Plan as a provisional form of settlement only if given a guarantee that partition would be the final form of settlement in the future.

The final stand adopted by Turkey in regard to the Macmillan Plan derived from two reasons. As mentioned before Turkey looked upon the conflict of Cyprus as likely to undermine NATO's solidarity and consequently abstained from acts that could have undermined this solidarity. Events in Syria and Lebanon were considered proof of Soviet penetration in the region and Turkey hoped to reach a quick settlement of the conflict before her own security became a subject to a concern more serious than that of Cyprus. At the same time Turkey felt that by renouncing her original demand for the return of the entire island in favor of partition, she had reached the utmost limits of her capacity of sacrifice.

The Turkish Grand National Assembly resolved on June 16, 1958 to inform all parliaments in the world that the conflict of Cyprus could be settled only by partition. The need for an immediate and definitive settlement because the situation had reached serious proportions; and the necessity for separate government for each community because the degree of mutual distrust and antagonism made it impossible for Cypriote Turks and Greeks to cooperate under a single government, were the two chief reasons which prompted the Assembly's decision. In fact, the proposal for the partition of the island was put forth for the first time by the Greek Foreign Minister Averof to the Turkish Ambassador in Athens. This fact was disclosed by Prime Minister Adnan Menderes in a message to the British Prime Minister on June 14, 1958. The message was met favorably by the British as disclosed by Lennox-Boyd to the Turkish Government during his visit to Istanbul. The Turkish Government accepted the idea of partition as a form of conciliation and impressed it upon the Turkish public opinion as such. The Greeks, however, denied that they had proposed such a solution. Consequently, Britain halted her efforts to reach a final understanding with Turkey based on the idea of partition. Ultimately the Macmillan Plan caused a feeling of disappointment in the Turkish government because of the retreat from an earlier promise of partition. This explains the prompt rejection of the Plan. Yet in time it became clear that the idea of partition could be reconciled with the idea of a tripartite administration embodied in the Macmillan Plan, and consequently the attitude of the Turkish Government underwent some changes as expressed in a statement made by Foreign Minister Fatin Rüştü Zorlu on July 5, 1958.

After returning from his visit to Athens and Ankara, Prime Minister Macmillan revised his Plan. The representatives of Turkey and Greece were to be excluded from the Council presided over by the Governor, supposedly in order to provide the representatives with more freedom in the performance of their duties. Thus the Plan lost its tripartite character as a result of the pressure applied by Greece. Furthermore, the idea of double citizenship for both Turkish and Greek Cypriots was eliminated because of the legal difficulties that it would have created. Yet these revisions resulting from their own pressure did not suffice to satisfy the Greeks who, therefore, rejected the Plan. Turkey eventually announced on August 25, 1958, that she would support the Macmillan Plan and noted that the British gave assurances that the Plan would not obstruct in the future the Turkish demand for the partition of the island. Having secured this guarantee Turkey did not see any harm in supporting a Plan that provided her with a chance to participate to some extent in the administration of Cyprus. The Macmillan Plan was officially implemented in October 1958. However, it failed to settle the Cyprus conflict not only because Greece and Greek Cypriots did not cooperate as envisaged by the Plan, but also because they increased their acts of terrorism on the island. The next stage in the conflict was the Zurich Agreement.

Greece was faced with the more or less similar British and Turkish positions on Cyprus and realized that she did not possess sufficient military and diplomatic means to achieve the desired end. Consequently Greece resorted to her initial method of obtaining a favorable solution through the U.N. although as indicated previously, the world organization did not agree to grant independence to Cyprus in the form desired by Greece. Instead it adopted a procedural recommendation affirming its faith in the continuous efforts of the parties to find a peaceful, democratic and just settlement in conformity with the Charter. With her proposal turned down once more in the U.N., Greece was left with no alternative but to enter into discussions with Turkey. Anyway the Greek view that Turkey was not a party to the conflict had been unrealistic all the time.

The settlement of the Cyprus conflict reached at Zurich resulted from negotiations thus started between Turkey and Greece. The Zurich Agreement emerged piecemeal in a series of principles from the negotiations undertaken by the foreign ministers of Turkey and Greece. The two ministers met for the first time in New York City immediately following the U.N. recommendation and determined the procedures to be followed in the forthcoming negotiations. Their following encounter dealing with essential issues took place on December 18, 1958, in Paris where they had convened to attend the semi-annual NATO meeting. When it became apparent that sufficient understanding had been reached on agreement principles the foreign ministers scheduled a meeting for their respective Prime Ministers on February 5-11, 1959.

The Zurich Agreement contained the principles agreed upon by the two prime ministers concerning the internal regime and international status of Cyprus. The provision which seemed certain to create difficulty was the one relating to the military contingents which Turkey and Greece could station in Cyprus. But after an understanding was reached on this seemingly difficult point, the consent of the sovereign power on the island, that is,

Great Britain, remained the only barrier. Consequently after the Zurich Conference, while the prime ministers of Turkey and Greece returned to their countries, the foreign ministers flew to London and obtained the British consent to the Agreement with the provision that her interest on the island, that is, the right to maintain her existing military bases, be safeguarded by inserting the proper clauses in the Agreement. Turkey and Greece acceded to this demand.

On February 19, 1959 at the London Conference, the parties to the conflict—England, Turkey and Greece—and the delegates of the Turkish and Greek Cypriots, officially adopted the principles previously agreed upon. Archbishop Makarios, the Greek Cypriots delegate to the Conference, attempted to raise objections to some of the provisions in the Agreement, though he had been fully informed and accepted them earlier, as disclosed by Prime Minister Karamanlis in an interview to *LeMonde* on December 29, 1967. He withdrew his objections, however, during the course of discussions and signed the final text of the Agreement. This very fact proves false the charges advanced later by Archbishop Makarios that he signed the Agreement under pressure. Indeed, he was fully aware of the provisions of the Agreement of which he was informed in advance and signed the Agreement after he consulted and obtained the approval of the large delegation he brought with him.

The principles adopted at the London Conference were released simultaneously by England, Turkey and Greece in their capitals in the form of the following four major Agreements:

1. Treaty of Establishment Concerning the Republic of Cyprus which transferred the sovereign powers of Britain to the Republic of Cyprus;

2. The Treaty of Guarantee which set forth the mechanism to preserve the independence, territorial integrity and the constitutional order of Cyprus;

3. The Treaty of Alliance between Cyprus, Turkey and Greece;

4. The Constitution of the Republic of Cyprus.

The overriding motive behind this form of settlement embodied in four agreements was the need to reconcile the rights and interests of the three states concerned with Cyprus, and of the two communities living on it. None of the basic demands advanced previously by the concerned parties were incorporated into the agreements. In other words neither the Greek and Greek Cypriot demand for ENOSIS, that is, the union of the island with Greece, nor the Turkish and Turkish Cypriot demand for partition were fulfilled. In short, the Agreements envisaged the establishment of an independent republic based on the partnership of the two communities, and maintaining close ties with Turkey and Greece. The individual affairs of each community and the affairs common to all were regulated separately. The Turkish and Greek communities would each elect a Community Chamber to conduct its own affairs. The difference in culture, language and religion between the two communities made this separtion necessary.

Affairs involving both communities were to be conducted by a government patterned after a presidential system. The head of the government, the President, would be Greek, and the Vice President a Turk. The ten member Council of Ministers was to be composed of seven Greeks and three Turks. Similarly, the fifty member legislative body, the Chamber of Representatives, was to consist of seventy per cent Greek and the remaining thirty per cent Turkish members. The legislators were to be elected separately by each community. In judicial matters, cases involving members of both communities were to be decided in mixed courts, while cases arising between members of one community were to be tried in their respective communal court.

The constitutional order of the Republic was guaranteed by England, Greece and Turkey. Furthermore, the constitution and the Treaty of Guarantee ruled out both the union of the Republic with another state and its partition. A variety of legal provisions and a mixed Constitutional Court were devised as instruments to prevent dominating each other. The defense of the Republic was entrusted, within the framework of the Military Treaty of Alliance, to a joint force provided by Cyprus, Greece and Turkey. England would preserve her military base on the island and have full sovereign rights over them.

According to the Treaty of Alliance, Turkey was to participate in the joint force with a contingent of 650 men. This meant that Turkey had, if need arose, the means to assure the defense of Cyprus and indirectly of Turkey. The Treaty of Guarantee provided Turkey further with the right to take action necessary to preserve the constitutional order in Cyprus.

Turkish Cypriots, safeguarded by special provisions, were to participate as partners in the administration of the joint affairs of the Republic while preserving their communal rights. The Vice President, as mentioned above, was to be a member of the Turkish community. He would have veto rights in matters of foreign affairs, defense and internal security and the right to return other matters for review. He would have access to the Constitutional Court in cases of discriminatory treatment against the Turkish community. The latter would be represented in the Council of Ministers by three Turkish ministers. Thirty per cent of the civil service and the security forces, and forty per cent of the armed forces, were to be composed of Turkish Cypriots. A majority vote of the Turkish representatives in the Chamber of Representatives was required for bills concerning elections, taxes and municipal matters. All these provisions aimed at one main objective: to prevent the Turkish community from being dominated by the Greek community which it distrusted. Because administration of communal affairs were separated, matters pertaining to culture, education, religion and personal status were to be conducted by the Turkish Community Chamber. Turkish was to be one of the two official languages of the Republic.

Greece derived equal rights under these Agreements as did Turkey and thus materialized a considerable part of her ambitions in Cyprus. It is vitally significant to state that though not absolute, the gains of Greece were made possible only with the consent of Turkey. Subsequently Turkish cooperation with Greece was renewed and the latter was assured of Turkey's support in her defense.

The Greek Cypriots actually gained the most from these settlements. The fact is that these Agreements ended the sovereignty exercised by a foreign power that is England over the Greek Cypriots and simultaneously placed the government of the island in their hands on the simple condition that they honor the rights of the Turkish Cypriots. Anyway, the Greek Cypriots' ambition to impose their unconditional and total rule on the island had been inconsistent with the realities of the island. That they tried to materialize sporadically their goal but failed to do so.

Following the London Conference a provisional government was set up in Cyprus and two commissions of mixed ethnic composition, began the preliminary task of drawing up the international treaties and the Constitution of Cyprus in conformity with the principles adopted at London. The work of both Commissions lasted over a year due largely to the Greek Cypriot attempts to alter some of the previously accepted basic principles. They renounced their efforts when the Turks refused to retreat, and eventually the Agreements were signed and the independent Republic of Cyprus was proclaimed on August 16, 1960.

The Turkish government considered the Zurich Agreement a document which reconciled to the utmost possible limits the rights and interests of all the states and communities involved in the Cyprus conflict. The Turks hoped that the agreement would open new vistas for cooperation between the two communities and, therefore, between Turkey and Greece. The opposition in Turkey, however, did not share the optimism of the government as it made it clear in the National Assembly during the discussions concerning the ratification of the Agreement. The opposition leader, Ismet Inönü, claimed that the Zurich Agreement did not contain adequate safeguards to forestall, among other things, *enosis*, and explained that Turkey might be forced to take unilateral action in case the Agreement was violated. He asked, therefore, the Assembly to reject the Agreement unless a definitive guarantee were secured from England. Foreign minister Zorlu replied that *enosis* and partition of the island were forbidden in the same article of the Agreement, that there were equal safeguards against both courses of action, and that a violation of the Agreement would place Greece and Turkey in the same situation. He indicated that the possibility of unilateral action could be an advantage for Turkey because it would grant it a certain degree of freedom of action. Another major objection raised in the Turkish parliament was the failure of the Agreement to provide Turkey and Greece with military bases on the island. The foreign minister responded that military bases in Cyprus for both countries would work to the advantage of Greece if the distance between the island and Turkey and Greece were considered.

The major shortcoming of the Agreement was its failure to equip the Constitution of Cyprus with a federal structure as necessitated by the presence of two separate communities. Turkey had advanced a proposal for federation during the preliminary negotiations leading to the Zurich Agreement, but withdrew her objections upon a pledge given by Greek Prime Minister Karamanlis. One may criticize the withdrawal by Turkey of her proposal for a federal structure simply in response to a personal pledge. However, this personal guarantee was bolstered up by an actual guarantee, namely, the presence of a Turkish military unit on the island. In other words, the functional federation as constituted would be given a trial first, but if it proved unsuccessful, Turkey thought that with the help of her contingent on the island, she could still protect the rights of Turkish Cypriots. This was the basic reasoning underlying the agreement between Turkey and Greece. However, change of government both in Turkey and Greece in the following years hampered the full implementation of this agreement.

The other major reason underneath the Turkish satisfaction with a functional federation was closely connected with the developments in international politics, especially the improvement of relations between East and West. Turkey at this stage was attempting to change her rigid, pro-Western policy into a more flexible posture in order to harmonize it with developments in world politics. A settlement of the Cyprus conflict could allow her considerable freedom to search for new foreign policy options. Already by the time the Cyprus dispute appeared headed towards a settlement, Turkey began to look towards the normalization of her relations with the Soviet Union. It was announced to this end in April 1960, that Premier Menderes would pay a state visit to Moscow. The visit was undermined by a violent change of government in Turkey in the spring of that year.

The Zurich Agreement, concluded after strenuous efforts, and the Constitution of Cyprus, concluded after exhaustive work, were soon subject to violations by Greek Cypriot leaders. The initial violations concerned the boundaries of Turkish municipalities, the percentage of Turkish participation in public services, financial appropriations for the Turkish community, and the composition of the armed forces. It was generally assumed that these initial disagreements ensued from difficulties involved in trying to bring together the Turkish and Greek communities which only recently had moved from armed confrontation under a joint government. However, events proved that these conflicts were incited purposely by Greek leaders in a calculated move to retrieve from Turks their rights granted by the Agreement under the pretext that these rights were disproportionate. The ulterior motive behind all these efforts was the desire to prepare the ground and unite the island with Greece, if and when conditions permitted it.

The inside story of one of the chief disagreements, namely, the establishment of separate Turkish municipalities can best illustrate the point. The need for separate municipalities for Turks and Greeks in one city may be traced to the Greek Cypriot's terroristic activities and drive for *enosis* in the past. The municipalities and their municipal councils staffed overwhelmingly by Greeks were used as instruments for *enosis* rather than service. Prompted by such political considerations, the municipalities either performed haphazard services for Turkish Cypriots or deprived them of such services causing thereby acute dissatisfaction. Faced with this most uncomfortable situation Turks were forced to establish their own municipalities in Nicosia and other cities in 1958. England, then the sovereign power on the island, recognized the establishment of separate Turkish municipalities. The same municipalities were present in Cyprus at the time the Constitution was drafted and were recognized as such. The boundary demarcation for Turkish municipalities gave Greeks opportunity to create a series of difficulties, despite the fact that the boundaries of these municipalities coincided with those of the Turkish communities. The demarcation process consisted of placing on paper what existed in fact. However, the Greeks looked upon the demarcation as nothing less than yielding territory to Turks, and did their best to obstruct it. After the Constitution of Cyprus went into force, the Council of Ministers following the opinion of its Greek members who formed a majority, moved to include the issue of Turkish municipalities on the agenda of general and joint subjects in utter violation of the Constitution. Consequently the Turkish community appealed to the Constitutional Court which ruled in favor of Turks. The leaders of the Greek community however not only refrained from implementing the Court ruling, but actually forced the neutral head of the Court, Professor Fasthoff of Germany to resign.

Obviously the disagreement over municipalities derived not from differences in the interpretation of the Constitution but from political reasons. The enforcement of the constitutional provisions concerning municipalities was not a difficult matter since, as mentioned before, the Turkish municipalities had already been in existence and had *de facto* boundaries.

As might be expected, President Makarios proposed constitutional changes on November 30, 1963. His proposals sent to the Turkish community and to the states concerned, outlined in thirteen points a series of amendments connected with the rights of the Cypriot Turks such as the veto right, voting in the Chamber of Representatives, merger of municipalities, the ethnic proportion of civil servants, and the liquidation of mixed Courts. The adoption of his proposals would have reduced the status of the Turkish community on the island from one of a community with equal rights to one of a minority subject to the mercy of the majority. Consequently in a prompt statement issued on December 6, 1963, the Turkish government rejected the proposal put forth by President Makarios. In the view of the Turkish government the disagreements in Cyprus could have been resolved by recourse to some practical measures within the framework of the existing treaties and the Constitution. The Greek Cypriot leaders, however, hoped to revise the existing constitutional arrangements with a series of *faits accomplis*. In a statement before the Grand National Assembly on April 3, 1963, Foreign Minister Feridun Cemal Erkin pointed out that the Greek Cypriots tried to achieve their objectives by taking advantage of the internal difficulties Turkey faced at the time. Personally we believe that this calculation by the Greek Cypriot leaders proved to be very detrimental for the island's future. In contrast to Greek penchant to exploit domestic trouble, Turkey, always viewing future relations has refrained from taking advantage of the internal difficulties in Greece.

The proposals of President Makarios to abolish the rights of the Turks and the rejection of these proposals by Turkey led to strained relations between the two communities. An attempt by Greek security guards to search a car carrying Turkish passengers from Kirnea to Nicosia on the night of December 21, 1963, and the murder of a Turkish woman during the skirmish that followed the passengers' refusal to agree to the search created panic within the Turkish community. The murder which otherwise could have passed for an ordinary police case became an outlet for the political tension which had been accumulating and triggered bloody strife between the two communities. Despite official announcement that the incident would be investigated, the members of the two communities fought each other at several places the next days. The toll of three day's fighting amounted to 24 dead and 40 wounded among Turks. In a speech before the National Assembly on December 24, 1963, Foreign Minister Erkin described the incident as an attempt by Greek Cypriots to gain by force what they failed to gain through legal means. As events unfolded the Turkish government was forced to invoke the Treaty of Guarantee. First Turkey, England and Greece issued a joint statement on December 24, 1963, asking the two communities to cease fire. President Makarios remained vague in his response for stopping the fire which kept coming from the Greek side. Therefore, invoking the right of unilateral action conferred on her by the Treaty of Guarantee, Turkey ordered on December 25, 1963, her military contingent on the island to take defensive positions while her Air Force undertook warning flights over the island. Turkish action was followed up by the joint action of the other two guarantor states, England and Greece, which acting in concord with Turkey notified the Government of Cyprus of their decision to take joint action for restoring order on the island. A joint force consisting of the English, Turkish and Greek contingents on the island was established. The joint force confined its efforts only to the maintenance of the *status quo*, because the Greek contingent, despite the joint declaration, was reluctant to work towards the restoraction of the arrangement as provided by the Zurich Agreement. Thus opened a new stage in the conflict of Cyprus after the regime established by the Zurich Agreement through endless difficulties was destroyed. The relations between Turkey and Greece to which each of the two ethnic communities in Cyprus were tied respectively became strained anew. A local conflict was artificially blown out of proportion contrary to the realities of the situation, due in large measure to the foreign policy pursued by President Makarios, a policy which facilitated in the end Soviet intervention in the conflict.

The tripartite force hastily organized to reinstitute order and security on the island, engaged in limited activity. England consequently proposed to the parties involved in the conflict to convene in London on order to search for a lasting settlement of the strife. The parties concerned met for the third time in a conference in London on January 15, 1964. The speech of Foreign

Minister Erkin on January 11, 1964, of Rauf Denktaş, the head of the Turkish Cypriot delegation, as well as of Kiprianu, the head of the Greek Cypriot delegation, both on January 12, 1964, expressing their respective views, were far from being conciliatory. Turks hoped to increase the constitutional safeguards while Greeks hoped to eliminate all safeguards so as to facilitate *enosis*.

The delegations apparently overwhelmed by the pressure of recent developments seemed determined to incriminate each other and demand an explanation rather than to seek an agreement. Turkey and Turkish Cypriots claimed that the Zurich Agreement fell short of providing actual protection to the Turkish community and demanded new and concrete safeguards to be embodied in a federal government and a population exchange to bring the Turkish community together. The Greek Cypriots on the other hand claimed that the situation prevailing in Cyprus was the inevitable outcome of the Constitution and of the Agreement which had given free rein to Turkish interference in the island's affairs. In order to alleviate the situation, therefore, they proposed the revision of the Constitution and the abrogation of the Agreements, including the Treaty of Guarantee. The Greek delegation seemed inclined to postpone the debate because of the forthcoming general elections in Greece. The English delegate tried to find a common ground between the contradictory views of the other delegations but failed to come up with a compromise solution.

During the London Conference the United States initiated negotiations to replace the tripartite force with a NATO force which would preserve order and security on Cyprus until a definitive settlement was found. Greeks, with their eyes set on the U.N. where the cause of independence enjoyed popularity, withheld their consent to projects of this nature insisting that any peace force assigned to Cyprus should be placed under the authority of the United Nations. Greeks also rejected the proposal for a mediator, to be chosen from a European country, who would work for a definitive settlement of the conflict. Failing to reach an agreement through negotiations, the London Conference broke up on January 31, 1964. The Turks consented to refer the conflict to U.N. partly because a settlement seemed impossible among the guarantor states and mostly to restore security on the island with the help of a peace force even if placed under U.N. authority.

The Security Council began to discuss the issue on February 26, 1964. The representatives of Turkey, Greece and Cyprus were invited to attend the discussions. Now they had a chance to express openly in the Security Council what they discussed behind closed doors at the London Conference. In a novel addition to their previous stand, Greek Cypriots now moved to declare Turkish right of intervention in Cyprus null and void, and tried to persuade the Security Council to approve the abrogation of the treaties conferring this right on Turkey. Turkey, of course, maintained that the treaties were still valid. At the end of prolonged discussions and attempts by Secretary General U Thant to mediate, the Security Council voted on March 4, 1964, on a proposal drafted, after consultations with the delegations of Turkey and Cyprus, by its five temporary members.

The eight-paragraph resolution, which made no reference to the opposing views expressed by the two sides on treaties concerning Cyprus, asked the parties involved in the conflict to refrain from acts which could aggravate further the conflict. It recommended also the establishment of a peace force, and resolved to assign a mediator to the conflict.

Regarding the formation of a U.N. peace force, Paragraph 4 reads:

> [The Security Council] Recommends the creation with the consent of the Government of Cyprus of a United Nations Peace Force in Cyprus. The composition and size of the force shall be established by the Secretary General in consultation with the Governments of Cyprus, Greece and Turkey and the United Kingdom. The commander of the force shall be appointed by the Secretary General and report to him. The Secretary General shall keep the governments providing the force fully informed and shall report periodically to the Security Council on its operations.

According to Paragraph 7, the mediator was to be appointed in the following manner:

> [The Security Council] Recommends further that the Secretary General designate, in agreement with the Government of Cyprus and the Governments of Greece, Turkey and the United Kingdom, a mediator, who shall use his best endeavors with the representatives of the communities and also with the aforesaid four governments for the purpose of promoting a peaceful solution and an agreed settlement of the problem confronting Cyprus, in accordance with the Charter of the

United Nations, having in mind the well-being of the people of Cyprus as a whole and the preservation of international peace and security. The mediator shall report periodically to the Secretary General on his efforts.

The Resolution in essence attempted to establish a peace force which could prevent clashes between the Turkish and Greek communities on the island, and to assign a mediator who could work toward a settlement of the conflict. Turkey greeted the Security Council Resolution with high hopes. The peace force would help bring back security and order on the island while the mediator would seek new avenues to settle the conflict. However, neither of these hopes were fulfilled. The speech delivered by Prime Minister Ismet Inönü on May 5-6, 1964, before the Grand National Assembly reflected the strong feeling of disappointment born out of this failure. More important, the Turkish confidence in the U.N. was shaken.

Since the birth of the Republic, during Ataturk's lifetime and between the two World Wars, Turkey had unselfishly devoted her energies to promoting international cooperation and establishing collective security systems. Motivated by the same traditional zeal for international cooperation, she did not hesitate following the Second World War to place all her heart in U.N. Now, however, Prime Minister Ismet Inönü, the architect of this policy, was forced to painfully realize, on a subject of direct concern to Turkey, the shortcomings of U.N. In spite of the Security Council Resolution the United Nations Peace Keeping Force could not be organized promptly. The first Turkish disillusionment began to take shape then. Once the Force was organized it did not prove capable of restoring security and order on the island simply because it lacked power and authority. Fighting, ransom taking and the murder of Turks were every day incidents. In addition to over 200 dead, 25,000 Turkish Cypriots were forced to leave their homes and become refugees. Under these circumstances the Government of Turkey had no alternative but to make a definite decision. In military terms she had ample power to achieve a settlement in Cyprus according to her own wishes. Experts reviewing the conflict, and the international political atmosphere, advised the government that a total response to the Greek action was feasible. The Turkish government took the ultimate decision for action early in June, 1964. This decision was implicitly disclosed by Foreign Minister Erkin in a statement on June 5, 1964, where he stated that Turkey would inevitably move onto Cyprus if the Greeks continued their attacks.

However, the Turkish action on Cyprus could not be expected to be confined to Cyprus and would, sooner or later, evolve into a conflict between Turkey and Greece, the two members of the southeastern flank of NATO. This possibility created deep anxiety in the government of the United States. Consequently, President Johnson addressed a letter to Prime Minister Inönü inviting him to Washington. Because it falls outside the scope of our topic, we shall not dwell here on this letter, drafted hastily by a low-ranking officer, which proved to be extremely detrimental to the relations between Turkey and the United States, and destroyed almost in one stroke the confidence in NATO. (See section on U.S.-Turkish relations). The Turkish government preferred to weigh the purpose of the letter rather than be carried away by its wording. During his visit to Ankara on June 11, 1964, Assistant Secretary of State George Ball reassured the Turkish Government that the purpose of the letter was to find an immediate and definitive settlement to the Cyprus conflict in a way most suitable to the best interests of Turkey and Greece. Consequently, Prime Minister Ismet Inönü agreed to take a trip to Washington on June 21, 1964. The Government of the United States had invited Greek Prime Minister Papandreau to Washington, too.

The meetings between President Johnson and the State Department officials, and Prime Minister Inönü and his delegation, took place on June 22-23, 1964. The Turkish delegation explained its position and the United States officials outlined immediate measures deemed necessary to settle the conflict. Prime Minister Inönü's visit to Washington was followed immediately by Prime Minister Papandreau's visit, thereby creating the impression that President Johnson intended to act as a mediator between the two Prime Ministers. Yet, these speculations proved groundless from the beginning since President Johnson, after holding separate meetings with each of the Prime Ministers, failed to call a tripartite meeting because of the Greek Prime Minister's reluctance to attend. It was clear that a top level meeting could not be called at this stage.

The joint *communique* issued on June 24, 1964, at the end of the American-Turkish bilateral talks, reaffirmed the validity and the binding nature of the international treaties, and expressed the hope that a settlement to the conflict in Cyprus could be found as soon as possible through negotiations and conciliation. On his way back from Washington, Prime Minister İnönü stopped briefly in New York, London and Paris and explained the Turkish stand to Secretary General U Thant, Sir Alec Hume and President De Gaulle.

The Washington talks began to be translated into action early in July. A meeting between the delegates of Turkey, Greece and England was organized formally through the initiative of U.N. mediator Sakari Tuomioja, but actually by the former Secretary of State Dean Acheson, who had attended the talks in Washington, D.C.

Sakari Tuomioja, a diplomat from Finland, had been appointed to serve as mediator in the Cyprus conflict on March 25, 1964, in accordance with the Security Council Resolution of March 4, and the full consent of the parties to the conflict. His visits to Ankara in April, and again in June to Athens and London, and to Cyprus earlier where he met with the leaders of both of the communities, convinced him that the views expressed by each party were quite far apart from each other. Therefore, he could not produce proposals likely to bring all of the parties together. Meanwhile, events deteriorated and Mr. Tuomioja responded with understanding to the initiative of the United States to open negotiations between the parties. The efforts for mediation of the Finnish diplomat's efforts, his neutral attitude won unconditional confidence in the official circles in Ankara during his very first visit to the Turkish capital.

The talks, originally planned on a tripartite basis, turned out to be bilateral because of the Greek refusal for direct participation. At the Geneva talks Turkey was represented by Professor Nihad Erim, the Premier of Turkey in 1971-1972. The talks between Erim, Tuomioja and Dean Acheson started on July 9, 1964. The definitive form of the proposed settlement, at first known as the Acheson Plan, envisaged the partition of the island between Greece and Turkey. According to this new proposal a section of Cyprus in the northeast on the Karpas Peninsula was to be ceded to Turkey. Cypriote Turks living outside the boundaries of this area were to have an autonomous government in two or three regions where they congregated. While General T. Sunalp was appraising the suitability of the area to be ceded, to the military needs of Turkey, Cyprus became once more the scene of strife. Fighting broke out in Erenköy and Mansura and necessitated the intervention of the Turkish air force on August 8-9, 1964.

The Acheson Plan was subjected to some alternations during the second round of talks following the flare-up in Cyprus mentioned above. Instead of an area to be ceded to Turkey as previously envisaged, the Acheson Plan now proposed to lease an area of fifty square kilometers to Turkey for a duration of fifty years. Turkey did not find the revised plan acceptable. Dean Acheson and Nihat Erim returned to their respective countries for more directives early in September, but did not resume their talks. The Acheson Plan produced no results. In a statement made before the National Assembly on September 3, 1964, Prime Minister İnönü stated that Turkey withheld her consent to lease a piece of territory simply because the proposed settlement did not have permanence, despite the fact that the search had been all along for a definitive and permanent settlement of the conflict. This meant that no settlement could yet be found through the efforts of the United Nations. Neither the United States pledge given during the talks at Washington to aid the Turkish Cypriots in Cyprus, who had become refugees in their own country, nor the American determination to bring the conflict to a swift settlement, were fulfilled. The change in the United States attitude was prompted possibly by the Greek opposition to the plan. In any case this change of attitude began to have repercussions on the Turkish-American relations and speeded up the anti-American and anti-NATO feelings in Turkey.

After the failure of the United States attempts at mediation, the conflict was put once again before the United Nations. Following the death of Tuomioja on September 10, 1964, Galo Plaza was appointed mediator on September 16, 1964. He visited Ankara, Athens and London in October and November, 1964 and February, 1965, and met in Cyprus with the leaders of the two communities. Thus informed of the position of all parties, he submitted a report on March 26, 1965. The Report met with a violent reaction in Turkey. In a statement issued on April 1, 1965, the Turkish Foreign Ministry announced that

Turkey no longer considered Galo Plaza acceptable as mediator.

Turkey was compelled to reject the U.N. mediator because Plaza had arbitrarily trespassed his mandate by proposing in his report under the title of "Certain Directions" a series of proposals without the consent of Turkey, despite the Security Council Resolution of March 4, 1964, which had clearly specified that the mediator would work for a settlement to which all parties would consent. Indeed, Plaza undermined the confidence of Turkey by violating his own pledge given to Turkish Foreign Minister Hasan Işik at a meeting on February 25, 1965, to the effect that his report would include not a conclusion but simply a new section emphasizing the need for a conference between the parties. This pledge was secured as response to a reminder by the Turkish Government during Plaza's visit to Ankara in February that the first goal of his mediation efforts was to bring together the parties in a conference. Turkey was compelled to reject a mediator who attempted to force her into a *fait accompli* by stating his own views on the essence of the conflict without first obtaining the consent of all parties.

The Turkish reaction was caused by other self assumed liberties of the mediator. He outlined in his report the mediation attempts undertaken so far, the history of the conflict, and the positions of the conflicting parties. In Chapter IV, Plaza stated his own observations on the past and future tasks of the mediator. He noted that as far as the functions of the mediator were concerned, certain parties, that is the Greeks upheld the idea that the role of the mediator was to submit proposals on the essence of the conflict, while other parties, the Turks were opposed to such a view. Plaza pointed out that he sided with the first position in order to be able to lead the parties to a settlement. Turkey had not agreed to such an interpretation of the mediation and consequently regarded Plaza as having trespassed the mandate assigned to him by the Security Council. In fact this was not a matter of procedure only. Greek Cypriots had taken the Government of Cyprus into their own hands through a series of arbitrary acts in defiance of the Zurich Agreement. The Greek Cypriots were willing to stay away from negotiations as long as possible and assume *de facto* control of the entire island. In this they were strongly encouraged by Greece. Galo Plaza, by bowing to the Greek Cypriot argument that negotiations would not lead to a settlement, was indirectly supporting their position despite the fact that his primary function was to bring together the parties.

Plaza set forth in the same chapter certain directives necessary to reach a settlement. In doing this he adhered to the Greek Cypriot position that the Constitution and the treaties were responsible for the conflict. Basing his action on the alleged desire of the Security Council for a new form of settlement, he attempted to visualize such a settlement in complete disregard for the old Agreements. A proper approach would be to propose revision of those provisions which were not functioning properly, while remaining within the framework of the basic principles set forth in the original instruments. Although Plaza stated that he benefitted greatly from the work of the late Tuomioja in his endeavors to settle the conflict, he displayed an approach far different from that of his predecessor. In his talks during his visit to Ankara in June 1964, Tuomioja made it clear that he considered the Constitution, which had been made the target for unilateral and illegal revision by Greeks, and the international agreements and treaties sought to be abrogated again by the Greeks, still valid and in force. The publication of Tuomioja's papers might prove immensely useful in bringing to light the truth of the matter.

The report submitted by Galo Plaza thus included suggestions on the essence of a settlement which were not acceptable to Turkey. In the opinion of Plaza, Cyprus would have the right to *enosis*, that is, union with Greece, a right that could be implemented through a referendum as a result of the unconditional independence Cyprus would possess if the treaties were abrogated. Foreseeing a probable reaction from Turkey, however, he admonished against the union of Cyprus with Greece by a unilateral action until after the Turkish reaction withered away. He was informed in clear cut terms by officials during his visit to Ankara that neither of these suggestions were acceptable to Turkey. Knowing that all these proposals were not acceptable to Turkey, Plaza still insisted in including them in his report, in full contradiction to the Security Council Resolution.

Moreover, Galo Plaza ignored the Turkish proposal for a federal system of government and insisted upon his own view in favor of a unitary system on grounds that there was no geographical basis for establishing a federation. He rejected the idea of geographical separation of the two communities through population exchange because, he argued, this would violate human rights. He was briefed that in the past an exchange of population took place between Greece and Turkey which helped solve a multitude of problems between the two countries, and that the differences of religion, language, cultural and ethnic origins between the two communities would be best served on the island by a federal system of government. The culminating argument showing Plaza's partiality was in paragraph 161 of his report. He previously proposed certain mandatory safeguards to in order to protect the rights of the Turkish Cypriots. In this paragraph he suggested that the Turks should be granted the right to emigrate to Turkey if they didn't find the safeguards sufficiently strong. One cannot be sure whether Plaza was even aware of the fact that this proposal, if implemented, would have amounted to nothing less than uprooting the entire Turkish population of Cyprus, and giving the island to Greeks, whereas a federal form of government necessitated only a limited population exchange.

Secretary General U Thant did not accept Turkish withdrawal of consent to Galo Plaza as mediator in the conflict of Cyprus.

Turkey was adamant. The government had the backing of the opposition. At the end, realizing that he could not function as a mediator after losing the confidence of one of the parties, Plaza resigned early in 1966, shortly after the General Assembly ended its debate on the conflict.

The publication of Galo Plaza's report induced the Greek Cypriots to entrust again the conflict to the U.N. General Assembly in the Fall of 1965. Turkey expressed the same wish. The conflict was subjected to a lengthy discussion in the Political Committee and the General Assembly. The Greek Cypriots, counting on the votes of the nonaligned countries, were intent on obtaining a resolution which would abrogate the treaties supposedly limiting the independence of Cyprus, and would forbid Turkey from undertaking action in Cyprus to maintain constitutional order there. Turkey on her part sought a resolution which would recommend negotiations between parties with a view to assuring a settlement.

The discussions in the U.N. did not produce many new suggestions. The parties repeated their previous views and recriminations. Turkey confined her argument chiefly to defending her legitimate rights on the island and tried to make it clear that she could not condone the violation of the Zurich Agreement. A novelty in the discussions was the position taken by the Soviet Union. Foreign Minister Gromyko, after stating the traditional Soviet opposition to military bases in foreign countries, made allusion to the possbility of a form of settlement based on the existence and rights of two communities in Cyprus. This was a position in line with his stand disclosed originally in his statement issued earlier in 1965.

The draft recommendation sponsored by 32 member states, mostly nonaligned and African countries, was adopted in the General Assembly by a vote of 47 for, 6 against, and 51 abstentions on December 18, 1965.

The recommendation referred first to the Security Council resolutions; to the declaration by the nonaligned countries issued at their Cairo meeting in 1964; the Report by Galo Plaza; and the statement by the Greek Cypriot government pledging respect for the rights of the minorities, and stated that in conformity with the Charter of the United Nations the Republic of Cyprus would have the right to full independence and sovereignty and be free from outside interference or intervention. In order to achieve this right, all states were asked to respect the sovereignty, unity and territorial integrity of the Republic of Cyprus and to refrain from intervening in the affairs of the Republic.

Though there was no explicit reference in the General Assembly recommendation to Turkey, it was implicitly addressed to Turkey for it was she who had opposed the violation of the Zurich Agreements by the Cypriot government. Turkey made it known that she would not accept this recommendation. Therefore, though a recommendation was formally adopted by the General Assembly, it did not produce the intended results. As pointed out, Turkey and a majority of the U.N. members, which could have contributed to its implementation, did not support the recommendation. We shall not dwell here on the procedural confusion which paved the way for the adoption of the recommendation, or on the fact that the draft proposal supporting the Turkish position was not submitted to a vote. These are mere details. Vital to remember, however, is the fact that the General

Assembly recommendation was not taken into consideration by the Security Council.

The General Assembly recommendation was received in Turkey with ample attention. At the time of the discussions in the U.N. a change of government had occurred. The new government and the foreign minister, belonging to the Justice Party, were charged with failure. In response, the new government stated that the previous government had failed to take prompt and effective action. A majority of the editorials and columnists in the press expressed pessimistic opinions professing that the cause of Cyprus had been lost forever, despite a statement by the Foreign Minister upholding the Turkish rights in Cyprus.

The recommendation by the U.N. General Assembly and the public discussion that developed in Turkey following the recommendation may be held responsible for the partial change in Turkish foreign policy. One of the primary changes was related to Turkey's relations with the Soviet Union. As mentioned before, due to the change of government in Turkey in the Spring of 1960, Prime Minister Menderes could not undertake the planned trip to Moscow. Later the leaders of the Soviet Union reiterated their desire to establish friendly ties with Turkey's new rulers. These entreaties were received with caution by Turkey. Yet, prompted by the general reassessment taking place in international politics at the time, it was decided that a visit to Moscow by Foreign Minister Erkin in March 1964, following the invitation of USSR, would produce beneficial effects upon the relations between the two countries. The outbreak of the conflict of Cyprus and the negative attitude of the Soviet Union on the subject initially had adverse effects on the preplanned visit. After the outbreak of fighting in Cyprus toward the end of 1963, Turkey informed the Soviet Union of the recent developments, explained her position on the issue, and expected the Soviet Union to condemn the bloodshed caused by the Greeks at least on humanitarian grounds. The Soviet Union in response, ignored the course of events but advised against outside interference in Cyprus. The Soviet Union was concerned with the prospect of seeing the island turned into a NATO base rather than with the inhumane treatment inflicted upon the Turkish community. She went as far as to supply indirectly the Greek Cypriots with arms. It was this attitude of the Soviet Union which delayed the preplanned visit of Foreign Minister F.C. Erkin to Moscow to a further date.

As the possibility and hope of settlement in Cyprus dimmed, Turkey began to change her own assessment of the conflict. Turkey had hoped initially to settle the conflict within the framework of her alliances, particularly of NATO, and to his end she had patiently waited for the fulfillment of the promise of her allies. When she realized, however, that her expectations fell far short of fulfillment, she tried on one hand to bolster her military preparedness, and on the other to pursue a multidimensional foreign policy to win diplomatic support. This new reassessment and the ensuing policy inevitably called for a reconsideration of the relations with the Soviet Union. All these led ultimately to Foreign Minister Erkin's visit to Moscow in November, 1964. Following the visit, the Soviet Union changed partially her attitude on Cyprus. The visit also marked the beginning of a series of state visits between the officials of the two countries followed up by joint *communiques* in which Cyprus figured predominantly. In addition to the references in the joint *communiques*, the Soviet position on the Cyprus issue found formal expression chiefly in a statement by Foreign Minister Gromyko to the *Izvestia* on January 21, 1965. Gromyko stated that the Cyprus conflict could be solved by taking into consideration the legitimate rights of the Turkish and Greek communities and by respecting the independence and territorial integrity of the Republic of Cyprus. Though he suggested that the conflict had to be settled chiefly by the communities themselves, he went on to say that a federal form of government could be a possible way for settlement. One need not go into details of the statement and the extent to which it coincided with the Turkish position on Cyprus. The political significance of the statement stemmed from the recognition accorded by the USSR to the Turkish Cypriote community and its rights with which Turkey was vitally concerned. This statement, coming from the Soviet Union, was a blow to the aspirations of the Greek Cypriots and of Greece. The statement, moreover, came at a time when Turkey was turned down by her allies and was consequently acclaimed with far more enthusiasm than would have been the case otherwise. Actually it would be misleading to evaluate the normalization of relations between the Soviet Union and Turkey merely in terms of the change in the

Soviet attitude on Cyprus without due respect to the general trends in international relations of the times. Yet, one can safely assume that the conflict of Cyprus acted as a catalyst in the general reassessment of the Turkish foreign policy and the normalization of the relations with the Soviet Union was its byproduct.

The second imprint left by the Cyprus conflict on Turkey's foreign policy concerned Turkish-American relations. True, the United States was one of the six countries which voted against the draft proposal in the General Assembly. However, this vote in favor of Turkey was insufficient to undo the unfavorable impression created by President Johnson's letter of June 5, 1964, addressed to Prime Minister İnönü. During the general debate in the Turkish National Assembly immediately after the General Assembly issued its recommendation, the United States was accused of having prevented Turkey from moving onto Cyprus. All this increased the disappointment felt against that country. Besides, once Turkey made it clear that she would refrain from direct action, the United States gradually slowed down her efforts to find a definite settlement, and ultimately helped the Greeks, at least indirectly by mere inaction. It is premature to indulge here in an argument concerning the effects of President Johnson's letter on the planned Turkish action in Cyprus. Whatever the truth on this matter, one may nonetheless say that the attitude adopted by the United States on the conflict of Cyprus shook the confidence of Turkey in her and in NATO. The attitude of the United States became subject to discussion in certain leftist circles in Turkey which were intent on creating hostility against this Atlantic power. Anyway the changes in international politics and the emergence of a more flexible attitude in the intrabloc relations might have weakened the hope placed by Turkey in the United States, NATO, and the Western concepts in general. The bitterness and disappointment caused by the failure to take action against the Greek community murdering the Turkish Cypriots swelled out of proportion and was converted into anti-Americanism by certain circles outside of the government. In the end Turkey was forced to reassess her bilateral relations with the United States and her multilateral relations within NATO.

The third impact the General Assembly recommendation on Turkish foreign policy was related to her relations with the Arab and African states. Turkey, based on historical bonds, had always hoped to establish friendly relations with the Arab countries. These relations failed to reach the desired level mainly because of the disagreements between the Arab states among themselves and the differences of view concerning the source of foreign threat faced by Turkey and the Arab countries. The detente between blocs encouraged Turkey to attempt to better her relations with the Arab countries. Turkey also engaged in efforts to win friendship among African states which had voted for the draft proposal in the U.N. by dispatching good-will teams and opening diplomatic representation led in these countries.

The recommendation adopted by the U.N. General Assembly did not prove to be nearly as effectual in bringing a settlement to the conflict of Cyprus as the Greek Cypriots had hoped. Once Turkey withheld her consent, the recommendation could not be implemented. Archbishop Makarios insisted that the international treaties and agreements were abrogated but he had no way of enforcing his claim. If Turkey consented to withdraw her military contingent stationed in Cyprus, then this would have supported Makarios' claim. Still, he refused to enter into talks with Turkey to secure even such an end. He also refused to attend the round table conference proposed after the General Assembly recommendation by Fazil Küçük, the leader of the Turkish Cypriot community.

Turkey which had favored the idea of settling the conflict by negotiations in the past, did not seem too enthusiastic this time to take the initiative for negotiations. On the other hand, relations between Turkey and Greece became increasingly strained. The deterioration of military and economic cooperation, which advanced toward a point of no return was most evident in the measures taken by Turkey with respect to Greek citizens living in Turkey. Holding on to her old position that it was Turkey and Greece which created the Republic of Cyprus, that this Republic was made up of two communities and that it was Greece which backed the Greek Cypriots who violated the Zurich Agreement Turkey regarded the Turkish-Greek bilateral relations as part of the conflict of Cyprus. Under these circumstances Greece, which initially pursued a policy in line with that of Makarios, was driven to enter into talks with Turkey over the conflict of Cyprus in May, 1966. A statement issued in Ankara and Athens on

May 18, 1966, announced the decision of Turkish and Greek Governments to enter into negotiations in order to settle the conflict of Cyprus through understanding and to improve the strained relations between them. The procedure to be followed during the negotiations was set by Foreign Minister Ishan Sabri Çaglayangil of Turkey and Foreign Minister Y. Thumbas of Greece when they met at the NATO meeting in Brussels early in June, 1966. The talks were to start at the ambassadorial level and work toward an agreement. The announcements made it clear that the talks were not to be conducted on the basis of any definite form of settlement. Just as the talks began, Turkey issued a declaration of four principles concerning the settlement of the conflict, as follows: first, nonviolability of the Zurich Agreement by unilateral action, which implied a categorical rejection of all the acts carried out by the Greeks until then; nonabandonment of the Turkish community to the domination of the Greek community, which implied that the rights of the Turkish community had to be protected; third, non-unilateral *enosis* which implied that Turkey would not consent to the union of the whole of Cyprus with Greece without concessions to herself; and fourth, the maintenance of the balance established between Turkey and Greece by the Treaty of Lausanne, which implied that the preservation of the present political balance in the region was imperative. The talks were conducted in confidential sessions between the delegates of the two countries in June and July. The brief announcements released occasionally explained that after a close scrutiny of various froms of settlement, the talks explored the possibility of a settlement on which both of the sides could agree. The talks failed to discover a point of mutual agreement; yet, it was found advisable at the end of 1966 to hold bilateral talks between the foreign ministers of the two countries when they met at international conferences. The changes of government in Greece interrupted the talks now and then but without effect on the commitment to hold bilateral talks.

The military junta which took over the government in Greece in April, 1967, expressed the desire to hold negotiations with Turkey in order to settle the conflict of Cyprus. Turkey, which had advocated negotiations between the parties as the best way for a settlement, accepted the Greek request. A statement issued on September 7, 1967, announced that the prime minister of

Turkey and Greece would meet at Keşan and Dedeağaç on September 9-10, in order to review the whole spectrum of Turkish-Greek relations, including the conflict of Cyprus.

Headlines in the press just before the start of the Turco-Greek negotiations spread the news that Greece was going to ask for *enosis* in exchange for a military base on the island accorded to Turkey, and the recognition of the Turkish Cypriot minority rights. The Turkish prime minister and foreign minister declared that proposals of this nature which would be tantamount to unilateral *enosis* were bound to be rejected, therefore, the Turkish delegation was not optimistic when the talks opened. The two Prime Ministers accompanied by their aides met on September 9th at Keşan. Because the meeting had been organized upon the request of Greece, Greek Prime Minister Kollias disclosed first his proposals at this meeting. Later, on September 10 in Dedeağaç, Prime Minister Suleyman Demirel presented the counter proposals of Turkey. The meetings were held in closed sessions. According to the statements of Prime Minister Demirel issued at a press conference on September 12, Turkey proposed a number of settlement options within the framework of the four principles outlined above, rather than impose one single form of settlement. Despite the common view expressed by parties at the outset of the talks that a settlement of the conflict of Cyprus would serve the mutual interests of both countries, no agreement was forthcoming. The two prime ministers did not meet again despite the joint *communique* issued at Dedeağaç on September 10, 1967, embodying the desire of the two sides to strive for bringing their views closer. All this meant that the bilateral talks carried on for more than a year at different places and levels did not produce any results.

In their search for a victory at all costs, and faced with failure to achieve *enosis* through negotiations, the Greek leaders stirred purposely conflicts on the island and engaged in other acts which ultimately culminated in a serious threat of war between Greece and Turkey. On November 14, 1967, in a show of force members of the Greek police force entered in armored trucks the Turkish section of Böğaziçi (Ayios Theodoros), a mixed village. Firing started in the afternoon the next day when the same group tried to reenter the village at the same point but met the Turks' resistance. The fighting spread to the Turkish village of Geçitkale

(Kophinou). Equipped with heavy arms, armored trucks, and deploying a force of approximately ten times the number of Turkish Cypriots, the Greeks commanded by Grivas captured the Turkish section of Bŏgaziçi by seven, and Geçitkale by eight o'clock in the evening. An hour and a quarter later, a cease-fire agreement was reached. Meanwhile, twenty-nine Turkish Cypriots were killed and the homes and belongings of the Turks living in the two villages were destroyed. While the Turkish Council of Ministers was in session reviewing the situation, the Greek ambassador in Cyprus phoned the Turkish ambassador there to inform him that the Greek forces had evacuated the villages. The evacuation and the repatriation of the prisoners of war were completed soon. However, the Greek forces reentered the two villages on November 16 and 17, and established a check point at Bŏgaziçi. But on Novermber 19, Grivas, commander of the Greek forces, left the island. Indeed, the Greeks evacuated the villages promptly when confronted with an imminent Turkish air intervention, and finally withdrew, first, General Grivas, and later a majority of the Greek forces from the island when faced with an all out Turkish intervention. The Greek forces numbering about 10,000 people, in excess of her allotment under the Zurich Agreement, had been smuggled into the island over the past year in order to bolster the Greek Cypriote army. All this was actually the result of determined action on the part of Turkey.

The attack on the two villages incited a considerable degree of excitement in Turkey which had repeatedly declared her decision to oppose such acts. The desire to settle the conflict through the use of armed forces rather than limited response seemed to have taken hold of the country overnight. In a decision taken on November 17th, 1967, the National Assembly authorized the government to use armed force in Cyprus. Military preparations were speeded up. In a note submitted on November 18, Turkey asked Greece to withdraw Grivas and the Greek forces from Cyprus. If the request were not fulfilled, Turkey threatened to dispatch an equal number of forces to the island, and asked for the reparation of the damage caused to the Turkish Cypriots during the attack.

The Turkish resolve to secure her rights in Cyprus this time on her own mobilized her NATO allies into action. The United States, England and Canada came out with a tripartite proposal urging the withdrawal of the Greek forces from Cyprus, the strengthening of the authority of the U.N. Peace-Keeping Force, and the compensation of the loss and damage suffered by Turkish villages. Turkey found herself in the uneasy position of having to choose diplomatic means or force in order to compel Greece to yield to her demands. She chose the diplomatic avenue while maintaining military preparedness. Suddenly there was an influx of mediators coming to Turkey. President Johnson's personal representative Cyrus Vance, Secretary General U. Thant's representative Rose-Bennett, and NATO Secretary General Manlio Brosio came to Turkey. The chief mediator was Vance. At first Greece responded with vague answers. In the end, under the pretext of yielding to the call of Secretary General U Thant, Greece agreed to withdraw her forces from the island which was the most essential Turkish demand. Actually Greece felt that she could not afford an armed confrontation with Turkey. The Greek Cypriot leader Makarios had been excluded from these talks. When approached for his consent, he declared that he would be a party only after the withdrawal of all military forces from Cyprus. This was a move designed to force the withdrawal of the Turkish contingent which had been stationed in Cyprus in conformity with the Zurich Agreement. He tried to free himself from the threat of a Turkish intervention, but his demand remained a symbolic one. Eventually Greece and Turkey yielded to the call of Secretary General U Thant of December 3, 1967. Turkey started to rescind her military measures, while Greece began to withdraw her forces stationed in Cyprus in violation of the Zurich Agreements.

The barely averted war made it obvious once more that the conflict of Cyprus could not be settled through impromptu acts. Consequently talks between Turkey and Greece were resumed when foreign ministers Çağlayangil and Pipinellis met in Brussels at the end of the year. The withdrawal of a major portion of the Greek forces dramatized the Turkish determination not to accept a forced settlement in Cyprus, and compelled Greece to accept, no matter how reluctantly, the fact that the conflict of Cyprus could not be settled without the consent of Turkey to be secured through negotiations. A new phase was about to open in the history of the Cyprus conflict.

The attempts by Archbishop Makarios to impose unconditional Greek rule over the whole of Cyprus by ignoring the Turkish community on the island, and the determination of Turkey to oppose such rule, instead of preserving territorial integrity opened the way to a new set of negotiations and a *de facto* partition of the island. One major outcome of this policy became evident toward the end of 1967. On December 28, 1967, the Turkish Cypriots announced the creation of the "Provisional Turkish Administration" to conduct the affairs of their community. Indeed, after the consistent violation of the Zurich Agreements by Greek Cypriots since the end of 1963, the Turkish Cypriots drifted away from the central government. Under the conditions prevailing then, the government needs among Turks were met by a "General Committee" established in May 1964, which made *ad hoc* decisions to tackle problems as they emerged. But the persistence of the conflict compelled the Turkish community to establish a more general type of administration. The Provisional Turkish Administration was the outcome of these factors. The basic principles regulating the work of this body was expressed in 19 articles. The newly established administration was to have a legislature, an executive, and independent courts. Attempts were made to merge into the newly created government the bodies and committees established under the Constitution of 1960. It was announced that the Provisional Administration would function until the Constitution of 1960 were reinstated. Sources in Turkey presented the new administration to world public opinion as an administrative reorganization in Cyprus. This indeed was the reality. Turkish Cypriots could no longer be expected to live haphazardly with no administrative order of their own. Greek Cypriots and foreign sources interpreted the new administration as of a separate government headed toward partition. Thus Makarios had to face the logical consequences of his policy aimed at keeping the Turkish Cypriots outside the administration of Cyprus, a policy which he followed incessantly and untiringly from the very beginning. Now he faced the dilemma whether to accept the Provisional Turkish Administration or to enter into talks with the Turkish community about reinstating the Constitution of 1960, which he had one-sidedly abrogated. Worried that the newly created administration might further entrench itself if he chose the first alternative, he chose the second.

The reaction of the Greek Cypriot Government to the Provisional Turkish Administration following the announcement of its establishment was not violent. The Greek government was content to issue a declaration addressed to the foreign missions in Cyprus asking them not to enter into contacts with the Turkish Administration. In time this declaration lost much of its force and applicability.

The diplomatic contacts between Ankara and Athens which had begun early in 1968, after the tension created by the crisis of Boğaziçi and Geçitkale, and the establishment of the Turkish Administration subsided, produced an agreement to seek a negotiated settlement to the conflict. Newspapers spread the word that Turkish Foreign Minister Çağlayangil and Greek Foreign Minister Pipinellis met secretly in Switzerland around the middle of February 1968. Eventually the President of the Turkish Communal Chamber, and the representative of the Greek Cypriot community, met for the first time in Beirut early in June to begin a lengthy series of talks. The meeting in Beirut determined the procedure and the frame of reference of the forthcoming talks. The talks were to be held consecutively in the homes of the two representatives in Nicosia. Reportedly the two representatives would turn their attention to those aspects of the conflict related to the Constitution while at the same time examining closely the measures necessary to improve relations between the two communities.

The talks began on June 24, 1968 in Nicosia and as reported, revolved around those features of the Constitution of 1960, which aroused Greek misgivings, such as the Vice-President's veto and other powers the use of a single list of candidates at general elections, the voting procedure in the Chamber of Representatives, the merger of the municipalities, the ratio of employment of Turks in the civil service, the unification of courts, and regional autonomy demanded by Turkish Cypriots. The two representatives probed into the possibility of compromising the views of the two communities but these preliminary talks did not produce results. In addition to demands for the revision of the Constitution of 1960, Greek Cypriots put forth claims that aimed at converting the 1960 Constitution, based on the concept of a functional federation, into one promoting a unitary system of government. Essentially these were the very revisions which Makarios tried to achieve by force back in 1963. The Greeks this time, possibly for tactical reasons, came up with demands which went even further than their past claims.

The representative of the Turkish community demanded full autonomy in communal affairs in exchange for agreeing to the revision of the constitutional provisions which provided safeguards for the Turks' rights. If full autonomy were accepted the Turkish participation in joint administration would be reduced. But this in turn would loosen the bonds between the two communities and all Turkish affairs would be excluded from joint administration and be placed in the hands of the Turkish Cypriots. The press reported in early July that talks reached an impasse caused by the sharp discrepancy between the claims of the two communities. The Greek Cypriots knew well in advance that they would have to yield to some of the Turkish demands if they wanted to secure Turkish concession to their own demands. In fact the Greeks had conceded in principle to the Turkish demand for autonomy at the start of the talks. Nonetheless there was disagreement between the two parties on the extent of autonomy, and consequently this became the main issue of the talks. The Turkish community agreed to revise the Constitution of 1960 as demanded by Greeks provided that their own demand for autonomy was met. Clusters of Turkish villages would form a region which would have autonomy to be decided through a referendum. The Turkish regions to emerge in this fashion would administer their own affairs through their own organizations and would be responsible to a higher authority. The Greeks could establish the same type of organization. All this meant that in addition to a central government responsible for the administration of common affairs, Turks and Greeks would have their specific administrative organization dealing with the affairs of their respective communities. Cooperation between the communal administrations and the central government were to be achieved through mixed committees and the ministries in the central government. The Greek Cypriots were prepared to concede autonomy at village level, which was more reminiscent of local government than autonomy. In fact, the Turkish Cypriots had conducted customarily their own affairs through elected village head-men. So they could not accept the already existing form of local government as "autonomy", and in exchange agree to revise the Constitution, thus nullifying the rights of the entire community. Greek Cypriots were suspicious that the Turkish demand for autonomy would create a state within the state and lead to the island's partition while Turks first wanted autonomy before agreeing to revise the Constitution of 1960. In short, though the two communities formally continued their talks into 1974, they had in fact already entered an impasse in August, 1969. The Greeks were determined to preserve an independent island. But due to their numerical majority this was likely to lead ultimately to the establishment of an all-Greek state with an all-Greek government. The regional autonomy sought by Turks on the other hand possibly carried the seeds of Cyprus' *de facto* partition. But as long as Greeks did not seek unity with Greece, this regional autonomy would have actually helped preserve the independence of Cyprus by assuring the survival of the two communities and by improving cooperation between them. While bi-communal talks took place, the foreign ministers of Turkey and Greece tried in their encounters at international meetings to spur the sides to reach a final agreement but were not succesful. The only apparent result of the marathon talks occurring in the last three years seems to have been the desire by both parties just to continue to talk.

World public opinion seems to be well informed about the Greek policy in Cyprus. This policy has always been *enosis* except for periods when a possible Turkish intervention was imminent, and when Greek Cypriot leaders were disheartened with Greece. On the other hand the Cyprus policy of the Turkish governments towards Cyprus and the Cypriot community showed considerable variation. Turks have defended the following positions in succession: the maintenance of the *status quo* and, if that was not possible, the return of the island to Turkey; the proposals included in the Radcliffe draft; the partition of the island between Turkey and Greece; the tripartite form of government between England, Turkey and Greece envisaged by the Macmillan Plan; the Zurich Agreement which established a type of joint government; the proposal to establish an independent federal form of government; the granting of a military base to Turkey on the island which ultimately would lead to partition; and finally the demand for regional autonomy for Turkish Cypriots.

The fact that Turks didn't have a definite Cyprus policy and their proposals have undergone many changes has been subject to criticism both in and outside of Turkey. The opposition parties have criticized this wavering as early as 1956, when the government first dropped its claim for the maintenance of the *status quo* and the return of the island to Turkey in favor of partition, and then again in 1959, when the government changed its attitude in favor of the Zurich Agreement and abandoned the demand for partition. These policy shifts became the subject of recriminations after the Cyprus conflict became the central theme of debate among Turkish political parties. Adnan Menderes, the Premier at the time, in a speech in Bursa on May 3, 1957, insisted that even if the views accepted at the London Conference of 1955 and the proposal for partition seemed divergent in appearance, the essence of the Turkish position had not changed. He claimed that he had originally asked for the return of the island to Turkey in order to give to the Turkish Cypriots a government of their own, and to protect the security of Turkey. These purposes would have been served simultaneously through partition which would have allowed both the Turkish Cypriots to live under Turkish rule, and would have guaranteed the security of Turkey by extending her sovereignty over Cyprus. Foreign Minister Fatin Rüştü Zorlu replied to Ismet İnönü, the head of the opposition, who criticized the shift of policy from partition of the Zurich Agreement by pointing out that the government had at its disposal several alternatives to achieve the same definite and unchanging goals. The best of these alternatives was to protect the national interest through the consent of the other parties involved in the conflict and that was exactly what had been achieved through the Zurich Agreement. At a later date, pressed to account for his own shift from a stand in favor of a federal system to the first Acheson Plan, İnönü, now Prime Minister, explained before the National Assembly on September 3, 1964, that the Turkish government was persuaded to enter into talks because of the prospects of a definitive settlement embodied in the Plan. As mentioned before, the Plan, included the secession of a certain portion of Cyprus to Turkey, as a safeguard for the life and security of the Turkish Cypriots, and as a military and administrative base for Turkey. Prime Minister Suleyman Demirel in a press conference held on September 12, 1967, immediately after the Turkish-Greek talks at Keşan and Dedeağaç, explained another change of position. He claimed that the essential goal was to preserve the rights of the Turkish community and of Turkey. But this could not be secured through rigid formulas. He claimed that the defense of a single form of settlement would amount to dictating one's own wish, and leave the other party no alternative but either accede to or reject the proposal. With this in mind the Prime Minister said that Turkey would seek a solution to the conflict within the framework of four principles: the non-violability of the Zurich Agreement by unilateral action; the non-abandonment of the Turkish community to the rule of the Greek community; the rejection of unilateral *enosis*; and the preservation of the balance established by the Treaty of Lausanne. Moreover at the start of the bicommunal talks in Beirut in June of 1968, Rauf Denktaş, the President of the Turkish Communal Chamber, put forth a new proposal, namely, regional autonomy for the Turkish community as a form of safeguard to protect the rights of the Turkish Cypriots.

A quick review of the positions advanced by Turkey so far indicated that all these had two essential objectives: first, to protect the rights of the Turkish Cypriots and, second, to safeguard the territorial security of Turkey. There has not been any change in these basic objectives adopted by Turkey since 1955.

Today a body of well over 100,000 Turkish Cypriots live on Cyprus. These people have resisted since the start of the conflict terrorism, aggression, restrictions of freedom and economic blocade. They have thus fully demonstrated their determination to stay in Cyprus. Despite all kinds of pressure the Cypriot Turks have refused to sell their property to Greeks who offered them prices well above the real value of the property, and did not emigrate from the island expect in a few isolated cases. On the contrary, they have clung even more vigorously to their land, and eventually established their own Turkish administration. Under most difficult conditions they continued to live under their own flag in regions whose borders have been delineated fully. The existence of the Turkish community in Cyprus is an accepted fact which cannot be ignored in any possible form of settlement. Occasionally proposals were put forth to move the Turkish population of Cyprus to a smaller Greek island, or to Turkey. Such proposals cannot be carried out because of two basic reasons. First, as explained above, the Turkish Cypriots do not wish to leave the land where they and their ancestors have lived for centuries. Second, the attempt to change the status of the Turkish Cypriots from a community to a minority group merely because their number is smaller than that of the Greeks, and move them to another land, would constitute a gross violation of the most elementary human rights. Cyprus is not only an old Turkish land, but the Turkish Cypriots—through the Zurich Agreement—have been rightfully entitled to have a say in the future of Cyprus.

The Republic of Cyprus was founded on the principle of partnership between the Turkish and Greek communities. One cannot expect the Turkish Cypriots to migrate and settle elsewhere by surrendering their partnership rights. The Turks would not consent to this solution. However, for the sake of a peaceful end to the conflict, a small scale resettlement within the island may be undertaken in order to gather the Turkish Cypriots now dispersed all over the island. Such a limited resettlement would take place in three or four regions. This solution could assure the coexistence of the two communities and achieve a definitive settlement.

Cyprus is situated exactly across the main line of Turkish defense in the South. It has a commanding position over the Turkish supply lines and defense installations which are now shared with NATO. The security of Turkey is closely intertwined with Cyprus. Turkey therefore cannot remain aloof to the future of Cyprus. This is the reason for which Turkey favored the retention of the British rule in Cyprus, a powerful ally when the conflict first broke out. Turkey has been opposed to Greece which is also an ally—to take the place of the British for two reasons. First, Greece does not possess adequate military capabilities to defend Cyprus, and is located at a long distance from the island. This may result possibly in the occupation of Cyprus by a power unfriendly to Turkey. Second, Greece has not renounced the *Megalo idea*, or a Greater Greece. Even though Greece doesn't have the capability to carry out this grandiose ambition. Greeks still cherish this idea. It would be a historical folly on the part of Turkey to leave the destiny of the islands entirely in the hands of Greece even though she is Turkey's ally today. The strategic position of Cyprus in the defense of Turkey excludes also the possibility of a settlement through a complete demilitarization of the island. Demilitarization in time of peace is not a permanent guarantee that the island will not be used eventually by a hostile power against Turkey. Demilitarization actually enhances the possibility of Cyprus being taken over and used against Turkey.

The security concern of Turkey toward Cyprus has not diminished despite the improvement in Turkish-Soviet relations since 1964. Without suggesting that the Soviet Union has immediate designs against Turkey, one would agree that the chances of a new threat from the North in case of a shift in international relations are rather high. The geopolitical situation of Turkey and the outlook of the countries encircling her in the North are such as to force Turkey to keep secure her southern defenses. Consequently Cyprus maintains its vital importance. The Soviet penetration into the Middle East and her naval power in the Mediterranean have enhanced the strategic importance of Cyprus as far as Turkey is concerned. On the other hand, the position of the Soviet Union in the Middle East and her presence in the Mediterranean are dependent to a large extent on maintaining normal relations with Turkey. If these relations change, the Soviet position in the area may be negatively affected. One may therefore assume that Cyprus will continue to maintain its strategic importance for the defense of Turkey for a long time to come. On the other hand, one must agree that the conflict of Cyprus has had a certain influence on Turkish foreign policy. It has affected first of all the Turkish-Greek relations. The political, military and economic cooperation between the two countries has deteriorated since Turkey made cooperation with Greece conditional upon a settlement of the conflict. The worsening of Turkish-Greek relations, in turn, has affected the military situation in the southeastern flank of NATO. As pointed out previously, the conflict of Cyprus had negative impact upon Turkey's bilateral relations with the United States and upon her general attitude towards NATO. Anti-Americanism in Turkey developed faster and on a broader scale than normally expected. Efforts are under way to this day to contain such movements within their natural limits. The Cyprus conflict has led to Turkish reassessment of NATO's value. Following the outbreak of the conflict, a more flexible concept of national defense was formulated and the drive to get out, or at least to decrease participation in the military arrangements connected with NATO, such as MLF gained momentum. Moreover, the Cyprus conflict speeded up the normalization of Turkish-Soviet Union relations, especially in the economic field.

As might be expected, Turkey, like any other state, is concerned above all with her own security and is intent on achieving economic development. Cyprus occupies a special position in Turkey's general foreign policy objectives. Yet this special position does not affect Turkey's basic foreign policy goals—even when Turkish public opinion became overly excited because of the Greek attacks on Turkish Cypriots, the government acted with restraint and refrained from acts which could have brought about a change in the fundamental objectives of its general foreign policy. Prime Minister Adnan Menderes, in a speech before the National Assembly on December 28, 1956, stated most explicitly this position: " ... at a time when the world is in so much ferment the island of Cyprus is not the single issue confronting the Turkish state. Turkey is not the kind of state to devote all her material and moral potential to the Cyprus issue." After the Greeks renewed the attacks against the Turks in Cyprus toward the end of 1963 and through 1964, Turkey, despite her obvious military superiority over Greece and Cyprus, did its best to cooperate with the U.N. Peace Keeping Force on the island, and deployed her own military force in an extremely restrained manner. Again, during the crisis of November 1967, Turkey waited patiently until the very last minute for the outcome of diplomatic endeavors, despite the completion of preparations for military intervention in Cyprus. The fact that Turkey does not lose sight of her fundamental objectives, namely, maintenance of national security and achievement of economic development, may explain her restrained attitude. This should not be construed to mean that Turkey will never go into action if the rights of the Turkish Cypriots are at stake. If at some future date the Turkish Cypriots are again attacked and their rights are violated, and if the U.N. Peace Keeping Force and diplomatic attempts fail to bring an end to this situation, Turkey, no matter how attached to her fundamental foreign policy objectives, might be forced into action. Only the other parties to the conflict can prevent such a course.[1]

---

1) This article was prepared and updated in 1972. For a discussion on recent events in Cyprus, see next article — ed.

WAR ON CYPRUS: THE TRAGEDY OF ENOSIS

KEMAL H. KARPAT

University of Wisconsin, Madison, Wisconsin

On July 15, 1974, a strong unit of the Greek Cypriot National Guard, under the command of officers from the Greek mainland, attacked the palace of President Archbishop Makarios in Nicosia and nearly destroyed it. Makarios, according to early reports, was killed although in reality, the Archbishop was able to escape through a back door and take refuge in Paphos, and from there go to England. Soon the head of EOKA-B, Nikos Sampson, was made president of Cyprus with the obvious purpose of declaring Enosis, unity with Greece. This act, if carried out, would have put an end to the independence of Cyprus and would have led to the possible annihilation of the Turkish Cypriot community. Five days after the Greek Cypriot putsch, Turkey, based on the Treaty of Guarantee of 1960, landed troops and occupied a section in the northern part of the island. A new and decisive, and maybe final act was added to the unending Cyprus tragedy.

The involved situation in Cyprus would appear as natural to an impartial observer who knows both Greeks and Turks, their ways of reasoning and especially their vital interest in the dispute. Essentially Cyprus is an extension of the foreign policy of Greece and Turkey in the Eastern Mediterranean. It is also an inseparable element in the balance of power between the two countries established at the end of the Greek-Turkish war of 1919-22, and the Lausanne Treaty of 1923. It is a new and powerful factor in a two-century old historical-cultural confrontation between an aggressive but weak Greece bent on transforming the Mediterranean and Aegean seas into an Hellenic *mare nostrum*, and a quiet but alert Turkey, well aware of her adversary's ability to display cunning friendship and bellicose postures but also engage in quick action when circumstances permit. Indeed, the annexation of Cyprus would allow Greece to control the southern coast of Turkey, including the important ports of Mersin and Iskendurun which are the export outlets of south-eastern Turkey. It would also permit Greece to play an important role in the politics of the

Middle East as a whole, especially after ultimately acquiring the two British bases on Cyprus, once the island is securely annexed. Great Britain on the other hand, wants to hold on to her two bases on Cyprus, the last strongholds of her once unlimited dominance of the area, in order to play some role in the politics of the Middle East and the destiny of the Suez Canal only a couple of hundred miles south. England would like to keep Cyprus as it is, dependent on her, since this situation guarantees the safety of her bases. Turkey is intent on preventing, at all costs, the annexation of Cyprus to Greece because it would complete her encirclement by sea and open the way to new Greek territorial claims. The scope and nature of Greek claims and plans was evident in the oil crisis which erupted in March 1974, and nearly caused war between Turkey and Greece. The Greeks apparently struck oil in the Aegean Sea. Subsequently Greece claimed that the entire Aegean—being surrounded by Greek islands—should be considered part of the territorial waters of Greece. She claimed, consequently, that Turkey had no right to explore the sea bed despite the fact that Turkey had continuous borders with the Aegean Sea and the Turkish territorial shelf extends well beyond the Greek islands. Turkey, in order to assert her right and in defiance of Greek claims, moved in a drilling craft under the protection of war vessels, and carried out some work in the disputed area. The oil issue was not solved but deferred for discussion to the UN Maritime Law Conference held in Caracas in June, 1974. No concrete results came out of the Caracas discussion and the issue, short of a war, may be settled together with the Cyprus dispute.

Thus, in the ultimate analysis, both Greece and Turkey have vital interests in Cyprus and neither is willing to forgo her influence in the island. The two communities, that is the Greek and Turkish Cypriot communities, serve as leverage for Greece and Turkey to promote their foreign policy goals in Cyprus. There is, however, a major difference between Turkish and Greek views concerning the role of their respective communities and the future of Cyprus. The maintenance of the status quo, that is, of an independent Cyprus totally free of danger of annexation, serves Turkey's interests well because it keeps her southern coast free of potential blockade and attack while the same status quo prevents Greece from expanding her influence and power into the Eastern

Mediterranean. The Cypriot Turkish community in a way guarantees Turkey a foothold on the island. Greece has, on the other hand, a fundamental interest both in preventing the emergence of Cypriot national identity and in allowing Cyprus to follow a foreign policy different from her own. The Cypriot Greek community therefore is kept constantly in action and compelled by Greece to follow a policy suitable to the interests or viewpoint of Athens even if that brings her to the brink of war with Turkey. As shall be indicated later, the Greek junta's direct interference in Greek Cypriot affairs in July, 1974, which went as far as to oust the elected head of the government, was due precisely to Archbishop Makarios' efforts to liberate himself somewhat from the tutelage of Athens and to chart a non-aligned foreign policy for Cyprus.

The decision of Greece to annex Cyprus and thus provoke massive Turkish retaliation apparently was based on a prior decision to risk ending the Turkish-Greek friendship established by Venizelos and Ataturk in 1924, and to revert to an ancient but disaster causing dream, the *Megalo Idea*, of a greater Greece. The friendship that began in 1924 put an end to the Greek-Turkish confrontation which had started after the establishment of the Greek national state in 1822/9, and had lasted until the Greek armies which invaded Anatolia in 1919-22, suffered a disastrous defeat and retreated, leaving death and ruin in their wake. Yet, this friendship and cooperation coming not from sentiment but rational decision, was far more beneficial to Greece than to Turkey for it provided her with security, as well as a series of economic benefits.

The decision to risk the Greek-Turkish friendship seems to have been taken by the Greek ruling junta in 1967, regardless of the fact that both countries were part of NATO. At this time, Greece was forced through an ultimatum delivered by Turkey, to retire her troops from Cyprus, brought there illegally, supposedly to stop a Turkish invasion but actually to destroy the community and autonomy of the Turkish Cypriots. The junta was humiliated and forced to back down because it was not prepared for a full scale military showdown with Turkey. Though the Greek military government suffered a massive moral defeat in 1967, it did not abandon its plans to annex Cyprus and thus achieve what civilian government had failed to do and incidentally assure itself of overwhelming popular support and a lifetime mandate for governmental power. From 1967 onwards, the junta worked astutely to create a situation whereby Turkish intervention in Cyprus would be decisively prevented and the local resistance of the Cypriot Turks liquidated in a few hours. Up to this point the government in Greece and Makarios saw eye to eye since both were firmly committed to ultimately achieve Enosis. However, events among the Turkish and Greek Cypriots and in Greece followed a course quite different from the one envisaged both by Makarios and his mentors on the mainland.

The Greek attacks on Turkish Cypriot communities in 1963/4, and 1967, in sheer violation of the Constitution, drove out some 20-30,000 Turks from their villages and forced them to take refuge in Nicosia, Baf (Paphos), Larnaca and Famagusta, as well as in a few villages north of Nicosia. Thus, the Turkish community was forced to concentrate itself in a few areas, thereby achieving control over substantial territory in the northern part of the island. The area north of Nicosia extending to four miles from the sea shore was in the hands of Cypriot Turks. Kyrenia was totally dominated by the Turkish Cypriots controlling the St. Hilarion castle as was the Serdarli area, the old section of Famagusta, and areas in the Karpaz peninsula north of the city. There were also several areas in the south held by Cypriot Turks. Thus, the Turkish Cypriot community was no longer spread all over the island in the form of hundreds of settlements but had developed into a major area in the north and another six or seven major areas around an urban nucleus, as well as a number of villages. The Greek Cypriots tried to undo this spontaneous regrouping of the Turkish Cypriots; first, by imposing an economic and military blockade around the Turkish communities, and second, by using the intercommunal talks to wrest major concessions while trying at the same time to undermine the resistance of the Turkish Cypriots by prolonging these talks indefinitely. Moreover, the Greek Cypriot administration used every conceivable means to rid itself of its adversaries. It encouraged the Cypriot Turks to migrate to any country they desired by buying their land at as much as ten times the market price and paying their airfare to the place of destination. The Turkish Cypriots responded to all these pressures by consolidating their internal organization and by strengthening their determination to resist.

Indeed, about the middle of 1972, the Turkish Cypriot community had established all the administrative offices—a ministerial cabinet, postal services, military and para-military organizations, a radio broadcasting station, etc.—necessary to conduct its affairs as an independent entity. There was after 1968/9, also a limited degree of economic development among Turkish Cypriots due to infusion of capital from Turkey as well as demand for agricultural commodities from abroad which enabled Turkish Cypriot peasants to cultivate their land rather extensively.

The Greek Cypriots allowed all this to happen, first, because they had no means to stop the Turks, and, second, because economically they were the ultimate beneficiaries. Thus, the economic aid from Turkey given to the Turkish Cypriot community was spent for food and materials purchased largely from Greek entrepreneurs who sold it at good profit. The agricultural commodities produced by the Turkish Cypriots were marketed abroad by Greek middlemen. Greek entrepreneurs employed thousands of Turkish workers, notably in port areas, often by paying them half of the wages of the Greek workers (who were organized in trade unions) and, often without contributing to the social security chest. Ironical as it may appear, even some of the food for the Turkish regiment stationed in Cyprus according to the Treaty of Guarantee, was purchased in the Greek sector. The Turkish Cypriots, although exploited and constantly under the threat of losing their jobs in the Greek sector, either because of communal trouble or for lack of employment, and reduced to the status of second class citizens, tolerated the situation merely for lack of better alternatives. Very few Cypriot Turks decided to leave their homes despite constant efforts by the Greek Cypriot government to encourage their emigration. The powerful attachment of the Turkish Cypriots to their ancestral land and their fearless determination to hold on to their abode, and especially the moral support of Turkey, prevented their migration. In fact, the morale among Turkish Cypriots and their determination not to bow to Greek pressures remained very high. Consequently the Greek Cypriots, while continuing to benefit from economic opportunities inadvertently provided to them by the Cypriot Turks readied themselves militarily to liquidate the Turkish community when and if the situation warranted it. For instance, early in 1972, the Greek Cypriots bought from the Czechs, arms worth

2.5 million dollars for the National Guard, not to speak of other shipments from Greece and Arab countries. The idea was to launch an attack and within a few hours, liquidate the Cypriot Turks' resistance, and, then, face a possible invasion from the mainland of Turkey. The rapid liquidation of the Cypriot Turkish resistance was a key element in the military preparations of Greece. The officers from Greece commanding the Cypriot National Guard calculated that without some secure support from Cypriot Turks inside the island, Turkey would be deterred from landing troops, lest it suffer big losses in men and material. These calculations proved only partly correct largely because the Greek military underestimated the military potential of Turkey and of the Turkish Cypriot units. Anyway, in anticipation of an eventual showdown, and with the full concurrence of Archbishop Makarios, a large number of officers and troops (some 5,000) from Greece were brought into Cyprus in direct violation of the treaty of 1960, either as commanders or specialized units of the National Guard, the latter consisting of about 22,000 people, was established in violation of the Constitution. The Police Tactical Reserve Force was also controlled by Greek army officers. The Turkish Cypriot Force, or Mujahids as they called themselves, numbered altogether some 8,000 soldiers and was stationed in several places. This army equipped only with light weapons was essentially a defense force whereas the Cypriot Greek forces, armed with relatively heavy guns, including tanks, had excellent offensive and defensive capabilities. Yet, the overwhelming Greek military, economic and political superiority in Cyprus was undermined by developments within the Greek community in Cyprus and especially by the souring relations between President Makarios and the junta in Greece.

The military coup in Greece in 1967, and especially the inability of Greece to provide adequate protection for Greek Cypriots and her withdrawal of troops as answer to the Turkish ultimatum in 1967, gradually shook the confidence of Archbishop Makarios in the military junta. Moreover, Archbishop Makarios and General Ioannides, the head of the intelligence section of the Greek army, and the man who eventually ousted Premier Papadopolous in November, 1973, did not get along well. Some friction had developed between them as early as 1963, when Ioannidis was the commander of the Greek regiment stationed on Cyprus. Moreover, some observers claim that the coming to power of the military in Greece in 1967, had thwarted Archbishop Makarios' ambition of playing a key role in Greece's internal politics, chiefly by annexing Cyprus to the "motherland", his lifetime goal. Anyway, after 1968, and especially after 1971/2, the Archbishop and his government, which did not include any Turkish Cypriots, began to emphasize the non-aligned status of Cyprus and to establish even closer relations than before with the third world countries. This reorientation towards non-alignment demanded the pursuance of a leftist policy which displeased the rightist dictatorship ruling Greece. The foreign policy devised by Makarios secured for Cyprus a good position among the non-aligned nations and in the United Nations, and bettered her relations with the USSR. As a consequence of all this, the Greek Cypriot government was able to secure loans from various international organizations, expand its international trade, invest in tourist facilities and even bring in some industry. Thus, the budget of Cyprus came to be balanced not by production and trade, but by a variety of loans and invisible income, including the subsidies paid by the Turkish government to Cypriot Turks. For instance the expenditure budget for 1973 was raised from LC 36 (the Cypriot pound is more or less equivalent to the British pound) to LC 43.6 million. An overwhelming part of this expenditure, something in the neighborhood of 90 percent was spent only for the benefit of the Greek Cypriots. The same year in 1973 the European Economic Community agreed to lower tariffs 70 percent for industrial and 40 percent for agricultural products from Cyprus by 1977, a measure which would have consolidated further the economic situation of the Cypriot Greeks. (One must add here some 20 million dollars spent yearly by the UNPKFC, practically all of it in the Greek sector.) There is no doubt that after 1970, the economy of Cyprus began to boom and the beneficiaries were almost exclusively the Greek Cypriots and their associates in mainland Greece and Europe. As the Greek Cypriot upper class, which benefitted from these conditions, grew in size and wealth, it gradually seemed to lose its interest in union with Greece, especially after the military junta instituted some controls over Greek business and launched a national-social policy of development. A union with Greece would have greatly hindered the freedom of trade and action of the Cypriot Greek upper class, at least for the time being. The workers' leaders, especially those in the trade union controlled by AKEL, the communist party of Cyprus, were opposed to union with Greece from the very beginning, despite the ambigous stand of the rank and file members on this issue. Thus, the deteriorating relations with the junta in Greece, the great benefits and prestige derived from recognition as an independent country, the subtle pressure of the upper class business group and of the workers' leaders in favor of independence, compelled Archbishop Makarios to chart a more independent policy towards Greece. As early as February 1972, the conflict with Athens had reached a dangerous point, especially after the Holy Synod, expressing Athene's views, asked Makarios to resign as President because that position violated canonical law. The New York Times reported on February 21, 1972, that the junta in Greece had decided to remove Makarios from power but were dissuaded by the United States from doing so. Soon Athens expressed the view that it would be satisfied not to press for the ouster of Makarios if men enjoying "mutual confidence" were brought into his government. Eventually a new Greek Cypriot government was formed. Soon however, the conflict between Athens and Archbishop Makarios became more complex as General Grivas and his terrorist EOKA organization began to take drastic action, often with elements of tragi-comedy in it. For instance, in March, 1972, three bishops from Paphos, Kitium and Kyrenia acting in collusion with Grivas and Athens defrocked Makarios of his religious position only to be defrocked in turn by another Synod assembled by Makarios. The supporters of Grivas stole ammunition from the National Guard arsenal and killed a number of Makarios' men such as George Photieu and Adonis Pissouris, just to have their own men killed in revenge, and bombed police stations and cities; on April 7, 1973, for instance, 33 bombs exploded in 3 cities. Arrests and kidnappings, demonstrations and counter-demonstrations by EOKA and Makarios partisans continued throughout the spring of 1972, leaving Cyprus and especially the Turkish community in a state of tension and insecurity. During his troubles with Grivas, who was actually carrying out the instructions of Athens to achieve Enosis, Archbishop Makarios showed some signs of compromise in the inter-communal talks conducted by Glafcos Clerides and

Rauf Denktas. But, as the internal troubles died down temporarily due to Grivas' death of natural causes, the Archbishop reverted to his old attitude of ignoring the Turkish Cypriot community. For instance, though on February 28, 1973, Rauf Denktaş was installed officially as the vice-president of Cyprus, the Greek Cypriot administration refused to issue him a passport to attend a meeting in Rome.

After George Papadopolous was ousted and Generals Gizikis and Ioannides became the strongmen of Greece, in November 1973, they apparently decided to act more decisively towards Makarios. Incidentally, both men had served in Cyprus with the Greek contingent. Archbishop Makarios, meanwhile, began to show interest in closer ties with the Soviet Union, possibly in the hope of using the Soviets to counterbalance the Turkish threat and the Greek junta as well as to increase his own freedom of action possibly to the detriment of the British, and implicitly of the United States. This was in fact a turning point in the relations of Cypriot Greeks with Greece because the independence sought by Archbishop Makarios would have deprived Greece of her influence in Cyprus and would have dealt a mortal blow to her power ambitions in Eastern Mediterranean. Turkey, on the other hand, although apprehensive about the Greek Cypriots' rapprochement to the Soviets and of Archbishop Makarios' ultimate goals, regarded all these developments as likely to consolidate the status-quo in Cyprus and strengthen the position of the Turkish Cypriot community. Inevitably, the independent policy of Archbishop Makarios would lead to a fundamental change in the relations of Greece with Cyprus. Consequently Greece was bound to react strongly to this situation, especially since the ruling junta, faced with growing opposition in the country and criticism from abroad, could not survive the loss of its influence in the island. On the contrary, if the military junta could achieve the union of Cyprus with Greece this would raise their prestige and popularity, and assure them of government power for at least several years to come. The showdown between the Greek junta and Makarios was precipitated by the Archbishop's refusal to follow instructions from Athens, and possibly commit himself to a timetable for Enosis as drawn up by the military junta. In an interview with the correspondent of Le Monde on September 18, 1974, Makarios declared that he had a secret talk with General

Ioannides who proposed to liquidate Turkish Cypriot resistance prior to achieving Enosis. The Archbishop, according to his own account, turned down the proposal. The displeasure of the Greek junta with Makarios was obvious. Yet, the Greek government was not prepared to act before making certain that Turkey would not intervene. The possibility of Turkey's intervention based on her treaty rights to safeguard the constitutional order and the safety of Cypriot Turks had been and remained the chief deterrent to Enosis. The Greek junta assessed the possibility of Turkish intervention and apparently came to the conclusion that the odds against intervention were greater than those in favor. In the past ten years Turkey had used the threat of intervention so many times without actually carrying it out as to make it appear as a bluff. Moreover, the crucial attitude of the United States towards Turkish intervention appeared to be negative. Twice in 1964 and 1967, when Turkey decided to intervene, the United States opposed her vigorously and caused serious deterioration in Turkish-American relations. The United States' opposition to Turkish intervention stemmed supposedly from a real concern that it would cause a war between Greece and Turkey and undermine the NATO position in the Mediterranean. Yet the United States' stand against intervention worked in favor of Greece because it nullified the only deterrent likely to prevent Greece from carrying out her Enosis plans. At any rate, the junta in Greece seemed to have reached the conclusion that the United States would not allow Turkey to land troops on the island. One may assume that the granting of new facilities to the American Navy, the use of some seven bases by American personnel in Greece and the fervent pro-Greek attitude of the American ambassador in Athens were some of the factors supporting the Greek junta's belief that the United States would continue to oppose and if necessary even use force to prevent Turkish landings on Cyprus. After all these hypothetical questions were answered, seemingly to their own liking, the junta went ahead to fulfill its Enosis plans.

The tragic events of July 15, 1974 in Cyprus were preceded by an exchange of letters between President Makarios and the Greek junta. The President asked the junta to pull out from Cyprus the officers from the mainland commanding the National Guard. Moreover, he told them bluntly that he was the elected president of Cyprus and not the appointed official of the Government of Athens. This was an unusual and unexpected behavior from someone long regarded as a docile agent of Athens. A short time after this exchange of letters, Archbishop Makarios made public the existence of a plan devised by the military junta in Greece to assassinate him and give the presidency to their own man. Already the terrorist EOKA-B organization which followed the instructions of Athens, had resumed its campaign of assassination against the followers of Archbishop Makarios, while bombing and setting on fire several police stations, especially in the south, its stronghold. Thus, on the eve of the coup the Greek Cypriot community was divided into two: the majority, comprising various governmental groups as well as leftist organizations headed by Archbishop Makarios, and the minority, or the rightists headed by EOKA-B. The latter, after the death of General Grivas, its first commander, was headed by Nikos Sampson, the head of the assassination squad, who personally and in cold blood, killed many Britishers and many more Turkish men, women, and children indiscriminately. Turkey and Cypriot Turks followed the escalating conflict among Cypriot Greek factions with concern but not undue alarm, since such internal strife among Greeks had become routine. Consequently, the bombing of the presidential palace and the alleged death of Makarios by the Cypriot National Guard commanded by Greek officers on July 15, 1974, came as a complete surprise to them. The Premier of Turkey was scheduled to deliver that day a series of talks to the poppy-growing farmers in south-western Turkey. He was informed of the coup while delivering a talk to an audience in Afyonkarahisar and had to cut short his visit and return hurriedly to Ankara. In Cyprus, after the initial coup was carried out and Archbishop Makarios was erroneously declared dead, the National Guard in association with EOKA-B began to liquidate the sympathizers of Makarios in the National Guard, police and the government. According to some reports some 2-4,000 supporters of Makarios were thus liquidated. The Turkish Cypriot community was not harmed yet, however. Soon, in the afternoon of the day of the coup, Nikos Sampson was declared President of Cyprus. Later he stated in total defiance of the responsibility one seeks even in a makeshift president, that the junta appointed him because four others preceding him on the list could not be found. The apprehension among Turkish Cypriots grew, despite Sampson's promise to resume intercommunal talks and safeguard their rights, since his past record was a sure indication that Enosis would be declared soon, and the Turkish community would be subdued or liquidated by the force of arms. Turkey, meanwhile, declared that she would not accept a fait accompli and would enforce the existing international agreements in order to maintain the independence of Cyprus. The United States in turn warned both Turkey and Greece not to compromise the independence of Cyprus while the United States' ambassador in Ankara, William B. Macomber, who had been called to Washington, reportedly in order to protest the Turkish decision to lift the ban on poppy cultivation, returned hurriedly to his post in Ankara. Greece, on the other hand, nonchalantly labeled the events in Cyprus an "internal affair" and warned Turkey not to interfere or intervene. Meanwhile the United States seemed ready to accept the situation in Cyprus as an accomplished fact and concentrated her efforts mainly on preventing an armed confrontation between Greece and Turkey. The United States apparently wanted to preserve the quiet in the Eastern Mediterranean to prevent Soviet interference in the affairs of Cyprus and to maintain the good will of the Greek government and thus assure the safety of its own bases on Crete and the Greek mainland. Great Britain, the other signatory of the Treaty of Guarantee, first reacted strongly against the coup and seemed determined to take some action but soon appeared satisfied to ask for the removal of the Greek officers from Cyprus and restore the status-quo. Great Britain issued a rather strong statement in favor of Makarios still recognizing him as the legitimate President of Cyprus. The Nixon administration, meanwhile, seemed to back Sampson rather than Makarios. Under continuous Turkish pressure, Great Britain found it expedient to invite Premier Bülent Ecevit to London presumably to hold talks for taking a joint action in Cyprus. The talks which were soon joined by US Undersecretary of State, Joseph Sisco, appeared designated to stall possible Turkish intervention in Cyprus and ease the tension. The Soviet Union, on the other hand, began to attack NATO as preventing the United Nations from intervening in Cyprus, and seemed ready to support Turkey if she wished to use her treaty rights and intervene to restore the pre-coup constitutional order in Cyprus. World opinion both in the West and the third world nations, turned strongly against Nikos Sampson, Greece and the military junta. Greece found herself alone.

The United States now found itself in the unenviable situation of being not only the supporter of the Greek junta but potentially the biggest loser in the Cyprus drama. It was clear that Makarios could not be brought back to the Presidency without outside intervention. To charge the United Nations with intervention would have involved the Soviet Union in the Cyprus affair, something the United States had struggled to avoid for years. Moreover, to prevent Turkey from intervening under treaty rights would now turn Turks against the United States and NATO, and the United States' interests in the Middle East greatly outweighed that of Greece. Turkey controlled the Straits and had a common frontier with the USSR as well as with Syria and Iraq. A slight move by Turkey towards the Soviet bloc would have drastically altered the balance of power in the Mediterranean and would have enhanced greatly the Arab position towards Israel by removing pressure on the northern frontiers of Syria and Iraq and by securing for them direct land communication with the USSR. It was at this point and as a consequence of all these calculations, that the United States, although still intent on preventing a Greek-Turkish war, began to adopt a neutral attitude towards the Cyprus crisis. Meanwhile the talks in London continued but it was obvious that Great Britain was interested mostly in confining the Cyprus conflict and preserving her own position there. Greece on the other hand, sure that she had weathered the worst of the Cyprus crisis, agreed to nothing, except to gradually recall the officers from the island according to her own time table. Consequently, the Turkish Premier returned to Ankara on July 19, 1974, while the world seemed reconciled to another international *fait accompli* in which Turkey was the loser. This was actually the quiet before the storm. The night of July 19, was spent in frantic talks between Ankara-Washington-London and Athens. All knew that Turkey had decided to land troops on Cyprus. The United States ambassador in Athens, Henry J. Tasca, who had been a close friend and supporter of the Greek junta, asked Secretary of State Henry Kissinger to use the sixth fleet to block the Turkish landing. Kissinger reportedly refused because this would have totally undermined Turkish-American relations and would have made the United States appear as the supporter of the Sampson group in Cyprus. Some claim also that the United States was becoming unhappy with the Greek officers largely as a consequence of public opinion and looked upon Turkish action in Cyprus as a move likely to discredit and eventually oust the junta from power. Besides Turkey was determined to pursue her plans at all cost based on her treaty rights.

Early in the morning of July 20, 1974, Turkish marines landed on the beaches of Kyrenia while paratroopers landed on the plain north of Nicosia with the intention of connecting with the marines to march on to Nicosia, which is located some sixteen miles south of Kyrenia. Turkey claimed that her action was justified by article 412 of the Treaty of Guarantee of 1960, which entitled her to safeguard the independence, territorial integrity and security of Cyprus and to protect the Turkish Cypriot community. Within a few hours of the Turkish landing, the Cypriot National Guard attacked Turkish Cypriot villages and enclaves and occupied them with the exception of the vital area around Nicosia and Famagusta and a few villages. Meanwhile, Turkish troops, after breaking through unexpected heavy fire and stiff resistance, occupied Kyrenia and the area around it and prepared to push inland. Greece, in turn, decreed general mobilization with the intention of attacking and forcing Turkey to withdraw her troops from Cyprus. Greece was actually unprepared for such an action. The Turkish forces, in view of the proximity of their bases to Cyprus—some 60-150 miles—had established full control over the sea and air space around the island, while Greek forces were jeopardized by the distance—some 4-600 miles—that separated them from Cyprus. Eventually the United Nations Security Council called for a cease-fire; Greece and Cypriot Greeks complied immediately, while Turkey did so two days later on July 23rd. During the landing and immediately afterwards, the Soviet Union strongly backed Turkey and apparently even promised to provide help if she desired it. The fighting in Cyprus, involving the armed forces of Turkey, the National Guard and the Greek officers commanding it, and the Greek and Turkish Cypriot communities, continued. Famagusta was bombed by the Turkish air force as were some targets around Nicosia. Eventually the cease-fire was implemented while the number of soldiers in the UN peace-keeping force in Cyprus was raised from 2800 to 5,000 men. Great Britain, Greece and Turkey decided to hold truce talks in Geneva on July 25, 1974.

Meanwhile drastic political changes of far reaching consequences occurred in Greece and Cyprus. The Chief of the Greek junta called upon former Premier Constantin Caramanlis, living in self-imposed exile in Paris, to return to Greece and to form a national government capable of facing the grave crisis confronting the country. This was, in fact, the end of the military government and the beginning of Greece's return to a civilian government and the restoration of civil liberties. The process of democratization in Greece thus engendered by the Turkish action in Cyprus culminated in a decisive victory by Caramanlis—he received 54% of the votes cast in the national elections held on Novermber 17, 1974. In Cyprus itself, Sampson resigned and was replaced by Glafcos Clerides, the head of the Greek Cypriot community.

During the Geneva talks, Turkey, acting from a position of strength, proposed to establish the cease-fire along the territorial lines prevailing on July 26, that is including territory occupied by Turkish troops after the initial cease-fire, and also to solve all basic questions concerning the status of Cyprus. Turkey claimed that the Turkish community in Cyprus was now a separate entity by itself. Consequently she proposed to establish the new constitutional order in Cyprus based on two autonomous—one Turkish the other Greek—communal units. The Turkish Cypriots would have the northern part of the island and the Greeks the southern part, but would be united under one federal government. Turkey declared that this arrangement would safeguard the integrity and independence of Cyprus since she had no intention of partitioning Cyprus or annexing the Turkish Cypriot unit. Greece and the Greek Cypriots rejected the idea of a federation based on two geographically separated units as leading eventually to the partition of Cyprus. Eventually the truce talks in Geneva ended on July 30, with the understanding that substantial talks would be held on August 8. The following days were spent in drawing the cease-fire lines between the Turkish troops and the units of the National Guard. Nevertheless, fighting continued sporadically in northern Cyprus as Turkish forces, partly in retaliation for attacks, occupied new territory while the Greeks shelled the encircled Turkish enclave in Famagusta and rounded up some 6,000 Turks and crowded them into a stadium in Lymassol. Meanwhile news of atrocities committed by Greeks filled the Turkish newspapers and increased further the tensions.

The talks in Geneva between Greece, Turkey and Great Britain and the representatives of the two Cypriot communities opened in August. Turkey insisted on a new arrangement based on two autonomous units while Greece agreed to recognize a degree of autonomy for various Turkish enclaves spread on the island but not to geographical federation. In other words, Greece was willing to accept a federation based on a system of cantons, a solution which she had rejected continuously in the past. Turkey pressed for quick decisions in Geneva while Greece and Greek Cypriots stalled for time. The United States came forth with a statement supporting the Turkish demand for greater autonomy but opposed the use of force. A request for 36 hours by Clerides to go to Cyprus to consult his ministers on the federation plan was rejected by Turkey as a device used to gain time. Consequently, on August 14, fighting resumed in Cyprus. Turkish troops, now fully in control of the situation quickly overran the resistance of the National Guard and occupied first Famagusta, in the East and then Omorfo and Lefka in the West. This last town of about 2,500 people was inhabited solely by Turkish Cypriots but had been occupied by the Cypriot National Guard in July. The net result of this new fighting was the division of the island into two. The Turkish forces controlled the northern part of Cyprus and were poised for further advance south. The area under Turkish control constituted about 35 percent of the entire island. During the fighting some 120,000 Greeks and 45,000 Turks were displaced. Some found refuge on the British bases or were camped in various areas in the south. Thus, a new problem, that of the refugees, hardened the endless Cyprus tragedy. Greece on the other hand, while openly declaring that she was unprepared for a war with Turkey, pulled her troops out of NATO. This move, in view of the United States' interest in keeping its bases in Greece, appeared designed to put pressure on Americans to force Turkey to withdraw her troops from Cyprus. The pressure made itself felt further as Greeks in Greece and various Greek Communities in the United States, under the joint urging of the Greek Orthodox churches and Greek intellectuals, demonstrated against the United States. Secretary Kissinger was blamed for condoning the Turkish action in Cyprus because he decided that Turkey was more important than Greece for the complex United States' interests and policies in the Mediterranean and the Middle East. Apparently the Greek sympathizers believed naively that the United States would sacrifice her interests and use her military might to promote the ambitions of Greece against Turkey. The fact is well established that the United States tried but did not succeed in persuading Turkey not to intervene in Cyprus. The United States was not prepared, and anyone with a minimum sense of reality could not expect her, to use force against Turkey.

The attitude of the Soviet Union towards Turkey underwent quick change. Initially the Soviets supported the Turkish action in Cyprus because it definitely prevented Enosis and thus preserved the status of Cyprus as an independent state which could maintain relations with the USSR as in the past. However, the Soviet Union reacted negatively to the Turkish demand for a federation composed of two autonomous units and to further military advance into the interior of the island. Eventually the Soviet Union proposed an international conference to be attended by all interested parties and members of the United Nations Security Council to settle the issue. Greece accepted the offer reluctantly while the United States and Turkey rejected it because it would involve the USSR in the Cyprus dispute and render it more complex and unsolvable.

The eventual solution to the Cyprus crisis was complicated by additional developments. The United States Congress under the pressure of various pro-Greek groups and congressmen of Greek origin and other Byzantine machinations decided, against the opposition of President Ford and Secretary Kissinger, to cut off military aid to Turkey after December 10, 1974, unless substantial progress towards a peaceful solution in Cyprus was achieved. This move, unparalleled in recent diplomatic history, aimed at forcing Turkey to withdraw her troops from Cyprus. Indeed, one can hardly conceive of a situation where the security of an important ally, namely Turkey, is sacrificed in favor of a small and non-aligned group, namely the Greek Cypriot community of Cyprus. Anyway, this action apparently, instead of intimidating the Turks, actually strengthened their determination to hold on to the territory acquired in Cyprus and to secure a full autonomy, and if necessary, form an independent, separate state—for the Cypriot Turks. Furthermore, Premier Bülent Ecevit who had adopted a moderate view on Cyprus in comparison with other Turkish political leaders, resigned chiefly because of conflict with his coalition partner, the National Salvation Party. Consequently, the planned visit of Secretary Kissinger to Ankara in November 1974, to discuss the Cyprus issue had to be cancelled for lack of a responsible counterpart. Meanwhile, the United Nations General Assembly passed a resolution in November 1974, accepted also by Turkey, where it called on all parties to respect the sovereignty, independence and territorial integrity of Cyprus, to withdraw all foreign armed forces and to allow for the return of refugees to their homes. It also commended the negotiations underway between Rauf Denktaş and Glafcos Clerides the heads of the Turkish and Greek Cypriot communities respectively. Indeed, the two held a series of talks and reached agreement on a number of humanitarian issues such as the exchange of prisoners and the like.

The basic dispute in Cyprus appears unsolved, despite some rumors to the effect that Turkey and Greece had reached full agreement in secret talks held between their Foreign Ministers during the UN General Assembly meeting in New York during October of 1974. Today, at the end of 1974, the situation of Cyprus and the position of the parties involved in the dispute is drastically different from the one prevailing at the beginning of the year. The key change has occurred in the position of Turkey and the Cypriot Turks. The northern part of Cyprus is under the effective control of the Turkish armed forces and of the Cypriot Turks. The overwhelming majority of the population in this area is Turkish. There are now about 35,000 well armed Turkish troops in this sector compared to some 20,000 Greek National Guard troops in the south. There is now a military balance between the Greek and Turkish Cypriots, unlike the past when the Greek Cypriots had an overwhelming military advantage. Short of massive aid from abroad and actual support on the battlefield, Greece cannot land easily troops on Cyprus and is even less likely to win a military victory. The guerilla warfare long publicized as a potential Greek response to Turkish refusal to compromise or withdraw, does not have much chance for success simply because the physical and political conditions for a successful guerilla warfare in Cyprus are lacking.

Premier Caramanlis and his foreign minister Dimitri Bissios, both of whom, incidentally, were the architects of the original Greek-Turkish agreement which resulted in the creation of an independent Cyprus in 1959/60, are democratic minded and reasonable leaders who can see the grave long-range consequences of the Cyprus dispute for the well-being of Greece. They know by experience that Turkey is willing to compromise on a number of issues, including territory in Cyprus, but will not agree to a return to the situation prevailing in Cyprus before July 1974. On the other hand, Archbishop Makarios, who carries the heaviest burden of responsibility for all the misfortunes which have befallen Greek and Turkish Cypriots, after recuperating from the moral blow he received from his own allies, the departed military junta, is preparing to resume power in Cyprus. Glafcos Clerides, the interim President, despite his success in bilateral talks with Rauf Denktaş, and despite his wide acceptance by the international comity of nations interested in settling peacefully the dispute, will be forced to resign in order to allow Makarios to act again as President. At the end of talks in Athens prior to his departure for Cyprus, Makarios declared that he is prepared to "offer" regional autonomy to Turkish Cypriots but will not agree to the division of Cyprus into two parts or to an exchange of population as demanded by Turkey and Cypriot Turks. Meanwhile most of the Turkish Cypriots moved and settled in the Turkish sector in the North. Only about 8000 Turks are left in the Greek sector. A *de facto* partition has taken place. All this may forecast additional troubles for all the Cypriots, Turkey and Greece, and other concerned parties. Yet, Turkey which holds now practically all the cards in her hands, may not engage in another round of fruitless talks with the Archbishop and may in fact choose to impose a unilateral solution on the Cyprus dispute. Any government in Turkey agreeing to an unacceptable compromise in Cyprus will be toppled in a matter of days. If pressured heavily, Turkey will resort to drastic actions and utilize to the maximum as leverage, her vital position in the Middle East and her military potential. If she decides to reassess her relations with NATO, this will not be used as pressure upon the

West, but will lead to a basic shift in her foreign policy alignment. Yet, in the complex tangle of Cyprus there is one point which Greece, and especially Archbishop Makarios blinded by his anti-Turkish and anti-Islamic prejudice, apparently cannot discern. Turkey is publicly and privately committed to maintaining the independence of Cyprus. This is a position which still assures the Greek community in Cyprus not only survival, security and peace, but also, because of its numerical superiority, promises it implicitly, important political functions as long as the autonomy of the Turkish Cypriot community is assured. Needless to say this position assures also the independence and integrity of Cyprus as a whole and the opportunities to work for a genuine sense of Cypriot identity and nationhood. Meanwhile, neither Greece nor Archbishop Makarios have rejected categorically Enosis. They still cling to the illusion that somehow and somewhere, regardless of the price and the suffering, they will achieve Enosis and incidentally put an end to the independence of Cyprus. At this juncture, the final decision as well as responsibility for the future of Cyprus and its people rests with Greece. Only time can tell whether the new democratic government of Greece will live up to expectations and reach a rational decision about Cyprus, not based on irredentist aspirations but on concrete political factors.

EXTERNAL FINANCING OF THE TURKISH ECONOMY AND ITS FOREIGN POLICY IMPLICATIONS

BARAN TUNCER

Department of Political Science
University of Ankara

During the post Second World War era, international transfer of capital through official channels has become an integral part of the international political scene. Immediately after the War large sums of capital were transferred to Western Europe from the U.S. for the reconstruction of the economies of the allied nations devastated by the War. The U.S. provided no less than twenty billion dollars to Europe under the various relief programs and the Marshall Plan, through 1952. After these countries were back on their feet economically, underdeveloped countries became the major recipients of official transfers of capital. This was an unprecedented development in view of the experience in the nineteenth and early twentieth centuries when the major international capital transfers took the form of direct private investments in the resource rich colonies. At the peak of these investments, the capital transfer from England was roughly seven per cent of that country's gross national product. The era between the two World Wars was a period of crisis in the field of international financing, when transfers declined sharply and a number of countries defaulted their obligations.

During the twelve year period from 1956 to 1967, net capital transfers—gross disbursements less capital repayments—from Western economies to underdeveloped countries averaged 8.7 billion dollars annually. Some sixty two per cent of this total was in the form of official transfers, the remaining thirty eight per cent representing private capital, and the United States was the main source supplying some fifty one per cent of the total. Net flows from the centrally planned countries was not very significant, averaging less than 350 million dollars annually between 1960-1967.

A number of reasons have been given for such an increase in the bilateral official transfers, often loosely referred to as "assistance" or "aid" from the more to the less developed countries. These terms sometimes give the impression that all transfers are outright grants to the underdeveloped countries. In fact only some sixty percent of all recent official transfers are in the nature of grants or grant-like contributions. Today few people think that humanitarian motives are behind these programs. Some point to the economic-commercial interests of the industrialized world in aid giving. Aid is said to promote trade and provide an outlet for the manufactured goods of the so-called donor countries in two ways: first, the receiving country is expected, and often compelled to shop from the country which made the capital transfer; and second, it is assumed that the overall growth of markets in an underdeveloped country as a result of general economic development will provide larger markets for the products of the industrialized countries.

Significant as they may sound, it would be unrealistic to explain the whole foreign aid phenomenon with these arguments alone. There are at least two common sense observations suggesting that there are some stronger motives behind the action of the aid giving countries. One observation is that the volume of foreign trade—both exports and imports—is relatively small in the gross national product of the largest aid-giving country, namely the United States. Thus the idea of trade promotion is not entirely convincing to explain U.S. foreign aid policy. The other observation is that the aid programs in both the market-oriented Western countries and in centrally planned economies have grown in recent decades parallel to some specific developments in the international political scene. Indeed, economic aid became a major instrument of foreign policy in the Cold War between the industrialized countries of the West led by the United States and the Soviet bloc. Geographical areas deemed to be most valuable became at one time or another the main recipients of assistance. Immediately after the Second World War, Europe was considered the most strategic area in the Cold War. Soon afterwards the battleground shifted to the countries neighboring the Soviet Union. In the 1950's those countries in Asia that gained independence from colonial rule were regarded as threatened either by radical ideologies or imperialism and were provided economic aid accordingly. In the sixties, Latin America and Africa attracted major attention. Thus, economic aid programs shifted geographically over the globe throughout the last twenty-five years according to the relative political importance attached by the Big Powers to various regions and specific countries. All this strongly indicates that bilateral capital transfers between governments had often dominant political motives and orientation.

The political motives behind the assistance programs need to be further assessed because of their relevance to Turkey's foreign policy. First of all a distinction must be made between military and economic assistance. The first programs involve the transfer of military hardware and know-how, and are clearly directed towards the achievement of certain political objectives. However, the case for economic assistance is more complex. In order to evaluate the political implications of economic assistance, a further distinction has to be made both between the general long-range and short-range political objectives of the donor on one hand, and between the effects of this policy in influencing the domestic and foreign policies of the recipient countries on the other.

The long-range political objective of the aid programs is to promote in the receiving country a type of economic and political development which is harmonious with the long-range interests of the aid-giving country. The consensus of the market-oriented Western economies is that their long-run interest lies in the promotion of institutions which rely heavily on private ownership and private initiative on a more equitable distribution of the fruits of development so as to subdue class conflict, as well as on the adoption of democratic institutions and procedures which broaden the basis for participation in the government decision making with a respect for civil liberties. In short, the long-term objective of the aid-giving countries in the West is to avoid far reaching political and military crises and revolutions which could produce abroad regimes hostile to their own socio-political and economic system. By the same token, the long-range objective of the Soviet economic assistance programs is to encourage the establishment of socialist-type institutions in underdeveloped countries, and to weaken the economic relations between these countries and the industrialized countries of the West.

The short-range political objectives involved in international economic assistance programs are far more diversified and often defy clear cut generalizations. Basically short-term political objectives dominate the present assistance programs. As already pointed out the maintenance of the socio-political status quo or changing the regimes of certain countries was the short-term objective in the so-called Cold War between Western and Eastern powers. The pressures exerted on the recipient country ranged from asking for understanding and support for the donor's policies, to restrictions placed on trading with, or even the use of any boat or vehicle carrying commodities to a country in the opposing camp. Another short-range political objective pursued by donor countries through their economic assistance programs is to maintain and protect certain military bases and installations located in the aid-receiving country. In many instances the aid-giving countries have made the maintenance of such bases a precondition to continuous economic assistance. Another short-term objective of the donor countries has been to secure the support and the alignment of the recipient country in international organizations, mainly the United Nations. A similar type of protection has also been extended to the private investments made by the citizens of the donor in the recipient countries. For example, the Foreign Assistance Act of the United States provides that assistance will be withheld from any country that nationalizes or expropriates the property of U.S. citizens without adequate compensation.

These are some of the more obvious short-term political objectives involved in the present aid programs. However, there is another group of short-term objectives which are also political in nature but aim at affecting the internal policies of the aid-receiving countries. For example, U.S. aid has been used extensively in the past to support leaders or governments which were friendly to American interests and policies regardless of the fact whether these governments enjoyed limited popular support and gained power through undemocratic processes.

The international economic aid to Turkey will be evaluated within the political framework described above. Turkey has received economic and military assistance, mainly from the United States, since the end of the Second World War and her dependence on external financing has continued until the present day. During the sixties Turkey ranked sixth among the major recipients of economic assistance after India, Pakistan, South Vietnam, Brazil and South Korea. On a per capita assistance basis she ranked seventeenth with a little less than six dollars per capita assistance from abroad annually.

Turkey's close cooperation with the Western countries in political, material and economic fields after the Second World War represents a significant reversal in her earlier policies in 1923-1946. The Turkish Republic established under Kemal Ataturk's leadership and guidance attempted to adopt the institutions and the values of the West with a view to expediting the process of modernization and economic development. This policy, however, was not carried out by depending on the Western powers, either militarily or economically. On the contrary, the government strained its resources in order to repay the debts inherited from the Ottoman Empire, and to buy the services owned and operated by foreigners. This was clearly a reaction to the foreign domination of Turkey's economy in the nineteenth century. The memory of the concessions given by the Sultans to foreigners and foreign operations in terms of extra territorial rights through capitulations and the Foreign Debt Administration established in the country after the Sultans had defaulted on their debts to European powers was powerfully alive. It is also important to note that the period between the two World Wars was a time when transfers of international capital were at a low ebb. Private transfers declined sharply and official transfers were nil. This was an era of distrust among would be lenders and receivers. Nevertheless, regardless of the availability of capital supplies the policy of the Turkish government was not to rely on foreign resources. Turkey's desire to be self-sufficient also manifested itself in her decision to establish a number of basic industries and consumer goods plants according to an industrial plan devised in the thirties. The world economic crisis in particular made the leaders of the country not only reluctant to depend on external resources for development but also to be wary of the fluctuations in international trade.

A number of factors were instrumental in Turkey's decision to establish closer ties with the Western countries after the Second World War. Probably the most important factor was the pressure of the Soviet Union, which manifested itself in the form of demands for territory and control of the Turkish Straits. The Russians first refused to extend the non-aggression treaty of 1925, and demanded that the provinces of Kars and Ardahan in north-eastern Turkey be ceded to them along with bases on the Straits. The Turkish government flatly refused to comply with these demands. However, the Soviet demands had the effect of narrowing the options available for Turkey in terms of choosing a side in the forthcoming Cold War. It should be remembered that this was a period when there was not yet a "Third World" but only two opposing blocs. Consequently a policy of neutrality at this time for a country like Turkey situated in such a geopolitically important area was not very realistic.

A second factor which contributed to Turkey's willingness to alter her position of non-alignment and seek closer links with the West was because the War had ended in a clear victory for the Western democracies, and the future seemed to be on their side and their political system. The significant change in the meaning and leadership of the West also had a share in Turkey's foreign policy alignment. "West" did not mean only England, France or Germany any more which were remembered as "exploiters", but included also the United States. From the Turkish viewpoint the United States was not only strong economically and militarily but was also geographically located at considerable distance from her borders. Finally, the U.S. did not have a history of colonial domination of the less developed nations.

Turkey quickly established a number of formal links with the Western community. In 1947 she began receiving military aid under the Truman Doctrine whose main objective was to strengthen militarily and economically Greece and Turkey against Soviet pressures. In 1948 Turkey became a member of the newly established Organization for European Economic Cooperation (OEEC) and in 1950 she joined the Council of Europe. Turkey's participation in these purely European and North Atlantic organizations was of primary importance for her future economic and political relations and policies. By being a member in OEEC Turkey was automatically included in the Marshall Plan which was designed to provide U.S. financial support for the economic recovery of Western Europe. During the implementation of the Marshall Plan from 1948 to 1952, Turkey received 225 million dollars in economic assistance, a little over two-thirds of which was in grants, and 305 million dollars as military grants.

Meanwhile Turkey's main foreign policy objective was to be a full member of the North Atlantic Treaty Organization (NATO), and she succeeded in 1952 in becoming a full member. Turkey's sending a brigade to the United Nations Forces in Korea and its distinguished service there played an important role in her acceptance into NATO.

On the domestic front, a very significant event took place when the Democratic party government came to power in 1950, by defeating İnönü's Republican People's Party at the polls. The new government was at least equally anxious to tie Turkey politically and economically to the West, and particularly to the United States. The Democrats had also in mind an economic system modeled according to the ones in the Western countries, that is, relying heavily on private initiative as well as foreign private investment. Under the Democratic Party rule which lasted for a decade from 1950 until 1960, when it ended with a military takeover, Turkey's reliance on economic and military assistance from abroad became an integral part of her foreign as well as domestic policy. The United States transferred large sums of economic and military assistance under the Mutual Security Act. In the 1950's, the United States' economic assistance to Turkey averaged a little over 100 million dollars annually, some two-thirds of which was in grants. The annual military assistance was nearly 200 million dollars. During this period Turkey remained a faithful ally by following the United States foreign policy and by supporting it in international organizations mainly in the United Nations, and by maintaining an antagonistic attitude against her northern neighbor. The foreign policy objectives were the chief motives behind the United States financial support of Turkey and Turkey did what was expected of her. The development aspect of the foreign assistance was not considered important yet. However, after an impressive economic start which lasted through 1953, mainly due to the expansion in the acreage of arable land, and successive years of good harvest, and good prices for farm exports because of the Korean War, the economic situation in Turkey deteriorated rapidly. Despite the indications of serious economic problems, the government pursued ambitious but uncoordinated development policies. It is interesting to note at this juncture that as early as 1954, the World Bank had issued serious warnings about the probable adverse outcome of the Turkish governments' economic policies. Displeased by the criticism that the Turkish economy could not support additional borrowing, the government severed its relations with the World Bank. Between 1950 and 1954, the World Bank had already made six loan agreements with Turkey. The commitments on these loans continued but the Bank did not make another loan to Turkey until 1966, even though, beginning in 1962, the Bank extended some development loans through its affiliate, the International Development Agency. Although Turkey continued to receive sizable sums in grants and loans from the United States during these years her balance of payments deteriorated. The government tried to cope with the situation by resorting to short-term borrowing and to credits from European sources. In 1958 Turkey found herself in the midst of serious economic crisis since she was unable to make payments on the services of her outstanding debts without seriously hampering the functioning of the economy. Rescue arrived in the form of the joint effort by her creditors to reschedule Turkey's debt as well as a new aid package of some 223 million dollars. The United States pledged 200 million dollars, Germany fifty million, and the United Kingdom ten million dollars. The remaining was made up by short-term loans from the European Payments Union and International Monetary Fund as well as small loans from ten other Western European countries. In exchange, Turkey accepted a stabilization program including the devaluation of the Turkish currency by some 300 per cent, and ceilings on the Central Bank credits.

The policy of the Turkish governments concerning the external borrowing during the 1950's was to borrow as much as possible without paying due attention to the consequences. Turkey had committed herself fully to the Western alliance and the dependence on Western resources was considered to be in line with the overall policies of the government. As pointed out above, the major contributor of capital to Turkey, the United States, appeared outwardly satisfied so long as Turkey fulfilled her role as a faithful ally and followed closely the foreign policy expected by the United States and allowed the use of strategic military bases located on her soil. Turkey played this role with minor variations until well into the mid-sixties, despite an important change of the government in 1960, and a series of civilian coalition governments which ruled the country from 1962 to 1965.

The military takeover in 1960 was a reaction at least partially to the mismanagement of the economy by the Democratic Party.

The army was aware of the damage done by the short-sighted and uncoordinated economic policies of the previous government. It also attached special importance to speeding up the rate of economic development. Consequently the military government established a State Planning Organization and initiated an era of economic planning by launching the First Five Year Development Plan in 1963. Planning brought a new perspective to Turkey's long-range requirements of external resource transfers. Attempts were made to better coordinate the administration of aid both internally and externally. In order to assure a steady flow of external financing for her development plans Turkey first applied to NATO in 1961 and asked for a NATO-sponsored aid Consortium. When NATO authorities declined to sponsor such an undertaking, Turkey turned to the Organization for Economic Cooperation and Development (OECD).

The Consortium for Turkey was formally established in July 1962 and originally had nine members. Later membership was increased to include the following thirteen countries: Austria, Belgium, Canada, France, Germany, Italy, Luxembourg, the Netherlands, Norway, Sweden, Switzerland, the United Kingdom and the United States. Turkey's reason for having such a Consortium was obvious. Besides guaranteeing a steady supply of external assistance for development, the government thought that a long-term commitment and a combined effort by her allies were necessary to reach the targets set forth in the Plan. This view was later criticized on the grounds that it weakened Turkey's position to bargain for more assistance on better terms. It was also argued that the Consortium was a step backward as far as Turkey's foreign policy was concerned because it invited a collective control over Turkey's economic policies reminiscent of the Ottoman Debt Administration of the past, and handicapped the pursuit of an independent policy.

The donor countries wanted to participate in the Consortium because this was a time when aid programs were enjoying public support. The governments of the participating countries must have also hoped that the Consortium would provide them with an opportunity to supervise developments in the Turkish economy so as to prevent a repetition of the unfortunate experience in the 1950's. So long as these countries were prepared to assist Turkey on account of her strategic position in the Western alliance and had some commercial interests in the Turkish economy, the Consortium was a worthy undertaking. The United States had an additional reason for supporting the establishment of the Consortium. She wanted the West European countries, particularly Germany, to make a relatively large economic commitment to Turkey's foreign aid requirements. The Consortium was also attractive to OECD which had just changed its old name OEEC to include "development" among its objectives. Turkey thus offered a good opportunity to OECD to demonstrate its desire for contributing to the cause of development.

After a rather shaky start the Consortium has operated smoothly since 1965 once the interested parties learned the problems and the realities involved in such an undertaking. It became obvious from the beginning that the donors were willing to contribute to the financing of the Five Year Development Plan, but they were not prepared to commit themselves to more than one year at a time. This was disappointing to Turkey. However, the cumulative pledges by the members of the Consortium came very close to the amounts asked by the Turkish governments. During the seven year period from 1963 to 1970 the Consortium pledges amounted to 2,076 million dollars against 2,114 million dollars requested by Turkey. This corresponds to an average annual assistance of 296 million dollars.

Meanwhile the United States economic assistance to Turkey continued within the framework of the Consortium. It averaged 135 million dollars annually even though the level of economic aid during the last three years was considerably below 100 million dollars. Also the amount of grants in the assistance was gradually lowered to approximately fifteen per cent of the total in recent years. However, military grants during the 1960's continued at an annual level of well over 100 million dollars.

In order to finance some large scale projects, the Turkish government resorted to other financial arrangements besides the assistance provided by the Consortium. The first attempt was to bring together a number of countries and some international organizations to finance a large portion of the Keban hydroelectric dam in Eastern Turkey. This technique is often referred to as "syndicate financing". The Keban syndicate includes the World Bank, the European Investment Bank, and the governments of the United States, Germany, France and Italy which pledged a total of 135 million dollars. The work started at the dam site in 1966. In a similar syndicate the European Investment Bank, the United Kingdom, Germany, France, Italy and Japan agreed to loan Turkey seventy six million dollars to finance the building of a bridge across the Bosphorous connecting Europe to Asia.

The most significant change in Turkey's foreign policy in the 1960's occurred in her relations with the Soviet Union. After nearly two decades of hostility and antagonism, the governments of the two countries agreed to seek an improvement in their relations, and this was reflected in their economic relations as well. The reasons paving the way for this rapprochement as far as Turkey was concerned were manysided. The most important reason probably was the deep disappointment, both among the population and official circles caused by the attitude of the United States on the Cyprus crisis in general and the reflection of this attitude in the rather abrupt letter sent by President Johnson to the Turkish premier in 1964. Turkey's desire to pursue a somewhat more independent foreign policy while still maintaining her strong ties with the West became evident after this. The rapprochement with the Soviet Union following the above developments manifested itself in terms of increased trade and Russian credit to Turkey to finance a number of industrial projects. According to an agreement reached in 1967 the Soviet Union extended Turkey credit for 200 million dollars towards the building of some factories, including a large iron and steel complex. Later the Russians increased the amount of credits, pledging a total of 361 million dollars by the end of 1970.

By the close of the decade another event which would have far-reaching implications for Turkish economic and foreign policies was in the making. Indeed, Turkey's decision to join the European Economic Community, better known as the Common Market, was an important economic and political event. Turkey had originally applied for membership as early as 1959, but it was not until December 1964 that an association agreement was reached between Turkey and the Common Market Six, somewhat resembling a similar agreement it reached with Greece. The agreement provided for Turkey's participation in the Common Market in three stages. A five-year preparatory period was envisaged as a prelude to enable Turkey to strengthen her economy. After that, upon mutual agreement, Turkey was to enter a transitional period lasting twelve years. In 1970 Turkey and her European partners agreed that Turkey had successfully completed the first stage and was ready to enter the transitional period during which she would gradually lower and then remove all restrictions imposed on imports from the Common Market countries. A special twenty-two year transitional period applies for a number of commodities.

Turkey's decision to enter the Common Market was obviously more political than economic. Turkey was already a member in various European organizations but she was obviously concerned about being left out in an eventual integration of the European communities, particularly in view of the fact that Greece had already made the necessary moves to join the Common Market. Naturally the decision to enter the Common Market drew criticism at home from many groups. Aside from ideological reasons, the major criticism was caused by apprehension that the small and relatively weak Turkish industry could not withstand the pressure and competition of its powerful European partners.

It is also interesting to note that the Common Market countries pledged financial credits to Turkey both for the preparatory and transitional stages and one may guess how much this pledge influenced the decision of the Turkish authorities to expedite the entry process. For the preparatory period, that is, for a period of five years, the European Economic Community extended to Turkey a total of 175 million dollars. For the second stage, a total of 220 million dollars worth of credits was agreed upon, to be dispersed over a five and a half year period.

The external financing of the Turkish economy has been analyzed so far within the framework of foreign policy. We can turn now to the economics of external financing.

It has been customary to explain the need for external financing in underdeveloped countries in terms of so-called "gaps" of two types. One gap originates in the difference between the necessary savings required to maintain a relatively high level of economic growth and the domestic savings actually realized. It is maintained that the low level of per capita incomes in underdeveloped countries do not permit domestic savings to increase to the levels necessitated by high level of investments. Thus, external resource transfers are seen as an instrument to close the gap between domestic savings and required investments.

The second type of gap exists because of the increased investments which often necessitate the import by the underdeveloped country of machinery and equipment from abroad. Unless foreign exchange is available to import capital goods, efforts to increase domestic savings cannot automatically result in increased fixed capital investments. As long as an underdeveloped country is unable to increase its foreign exchange earnings, external resource transfers act as a means for closing the foreign exchange gap.

The two following tables are intended to show the size and the relevant importance of external financing in the Turkish economy based on data supplied by the Ministry of Finance and the State Planning Organization.

Table I

External Financing Requirements and External Resources
(in million dollars)

	1950-54 Annual Average	1955-59 Annual Average	1960-64 Annual Average	1965-69 Annual Average
1. External Financing Requirements (Total	166.2	186.4	291.2	282.0
a. Current Account Deficit	136.6	105.0	192.0	150.2
b. Debt Payments	29.6	81.4	99.2	121.8
2. External Resources	180.0	244.0	291.0	318.8
a. Private Transfers	74.4	94.4	48.2	35.2
b. Public Transfers	105.6	149.6	242.8	283.6
3. Balance (Short-term credits, reserve movements, net errors and omissions) (2-1)	13.8	57.6	−0.2	36.8

The first row in Table 1 gives the size of the annual external financing requirements in terms of five year averages from 1950 to 1963. As can be seen from the table, the size of the financing requirement is determined by the deficit in the current account of the balance of payments and the payments on the amortization of the existing foreign debt. The table reveals that the absolute size of the external financing requirements rose to approximately 300 million dollars in the early 1960's and has remained at that level. A more dramatic and continuous increase is observed on debt payments. More than 40 per cent of the total financing requirements originated from the payments—excluding the interest paid—on the existing debt.

The external resources to which Turkey had access during the last twenty years is shown in the second row of the same table. By definition the resources are equal to the requirements in size in an *ex-post* sense. The nature of the difference between the requirements and resources is shown in the balance. External resources are further subdivided between the private and public transfers. During the last two decades the volume of private transfers gradually declined while the public transfers grew. Private transfers—consisting mainly of foreign private investments—were only about 10 per cent of the total transfers in the latter part of the 1960's, whereas they were no less than forty per cent of the total throughout the 1950's. In the 1950's private transfers were mainly in the form of suppliers' credits, that is, credits given by the foreign firms to distributors or sellers in Turkey. These relatively short-term, high-interest credits were a major cause in precipitating the financial crisis of 1958, mentioned above.

Public transfers consisted mainly of bilateral grants and credits on concessionary terms with long payment period and low interest. Only a small portion of the public transfers came from the multilateral agencies such as the World Bank and the United Nations. Bilateral public transfers were made almost exclusively by United States Government grants and credits. Since 1964 the economic assistance provided to Turkey by the Western world came through the Consortium. The United States continued to be the main supplier of credits while the Federal Republic of Germany was second. Contrary to the experience of the 1950's the transfers through consortium channels took the form of development loans, carrying a little less than four per cent interest with over twenty years of maturity and some period of grace. Another characteristic of the assistance rendered to Turkey in the 1960's was the fact that some 30 per cent of these credits were tied to individual projects, and nearly all of the assistance was tied to the country, that is, purchases had to be made from the country extending the credit. This, of course, increases the cost of borrowing.

Table 2 shows the relative importance of external resource transfers within the Turkish economy. Expressed in the fixed

Table 2

Relative Importance of External Resource Transfers
(in percentages)

	1950-54	1955-59	1960-64	1965-69
External Resources/ Gross National Product	4.69	5.02	4.92	3.98
External Resources/ Investments	27.99	32.16	31.63	21.49
External Resources/ Foreign Exchange Earnings	45.00	68.00	69.07	50.60

prices of 1961, the relative size of these transfers remained around five per cent of Turkey's gross national product from 1950 through 1964, and was about four per cent since 1965. The table also compares the size of external resource transfers with the gross fixed investments, as well as with Turkey's total foreign exchange earnings. The ratio between these transfers and the foreign exchange earnings has been strikingly high. It started from a level of forty five per cent in the early 1950's, went up to nearly seventy per cent in the first half of the 1960's, and was approximately fifty per cent in more recent years. It should be remembered that the transfers made under the military assistance programs are not included in Turkey's balance of payments. As a result, their estimates and ratios are downwardly biased. If one included the military transfers into the accounts—which have been consistently over 100 million dollars annually—it would be clear that the relative size of the real transfers was higher.

The foregoing reveals two important facts concerning the external financing of the Turkish economy. First, external resource transfers have been relatively large in the last two decades in terms of Turkey's own resources, particularly when compared with the overall foreign exchange earnings. Second, resource transfers maintained their high levels in recent years also, and declined only slightly in relative terms.

This last point brings up the Turkish government's policies regarding its dependence on external resources. The government's view of foreign assistance has been explicitly stated in Turkey's five year development plans. One specific goal of Turkish planning which began with the first five year plan in 1963, the second in 1969, and the third expected in 1973, has been to reduce and eventually eliminate Turkey's need for concessionary assistance. The First Plan suggested that the target date for this so-called state of "viability" be at the end of three five year plans. The Second Plan made it more specific by stating that no new loans on concessionary terms would be required after 1972.

As indicated above, the Turkish economy must fulfill two conditions if self reliance and viability are to be achieved. Domestic savings need to be increased to the levels required by the planned increases in gross national product and exployment. The annual foreign exchange earnings also have to reach optimum levels in order to meet the economy's demand for imports as well as to provide for the payment of foreign debt. Granted that domestic savings did increase from a level of less than fifteen per cent of gross national product in the early 1960's to nearly twenty per cent in 1970, studies indicate that the domestic savings/gross national product ratio needs to go up approximately twenty five per cent for Turkey to achieve self reliance in savings.

Difficult as it may be for Turkey to mobilize domestic savings at this level during the next decade, closing the foreign exchange gap poses even a more formidable challenge. Despite unexpected increases in the remittances from the Turkish workers in Western Europe, the foreign exchange deficit has still remained at a relatively high level. Particularly in view of the projected imports, foreign debt payments and military needs, the closing of the foreign exchange gap should take even more commendable effort than closing the savings gap. At any rate, the target of the Turkish government to achieve economic self reliance by the mid 1970's does not seem possible in view of the growth targets as well as other objectives.

To conclude, one may say that since the end of the Second World War the economic development of the underdeveloped world has become a major issue in international relations. The governments and leaders in underdeveloped countries have committed themselves to improving the living standards of their citizens. Due to the inadequacy of domestic resources, the need to transfer resources from other countries has intensified. The Cold War and ideological disputes between the market oriented Western bloc countries and the centrally planned Eastern bloc nations have caused the wealthier countries to become more receptive to the demands of the less developed world. The leading countries of both capitalist and socialist camps have used assistance programs as an instrument to reach their main political objectives, namely, to win and maintain alliances in the underdeveloped countries. Two decades of aid giving has undoubtedly contributed to the development efforts in these countries but it has also burdened some of them with heavy debt and, probably more important than that, with a state of dependence on external resources. Also, indiscriminate aid giving, mainly with political purposes, has at times contributed to economic inertia and to a lack of willingness to implement much needed reforms in many underdeveloped countries.

As noted earlier, Turkey has been a major recipient of economic assistance, undoubtedly due to her extremely strategic location. Turkey's willingness to establish close political, military and economic ties with the West corresponded to the United States foreign policy objective of preventing the Soviet Union from advancing into the Mediterranean and the Near East. The United States was willing to provide relatively small economic and military assistance to Turkey in order to have her on her side and to maintain access to the then strategic military bases on Turkish soil.

The purpose of this analysis is not to evaluate the impact of these assistance programs on the Turkish economy. However, it can safely be stated that foreign economic assistance eased the financial difficulties as well as the insufficiency of foreign exchange which at times reached a level of crisis. What is more important from the point of view of this study is the nature and the extent of economic dependency on the foreign policy of Turkey. Needless to say the stronger this dependency is the more limited the foreign policy options open to the government of Turkey. It is obvious that the possibility of pursuing a flexible short and long-range foreign policy suited to the best interests of the country is severely curtailed in the extreme cases of dependency. A few countries were rather successful in the past in playing the interests of the powerful creditors or donors against each other and thus receiving funds without making full foreign policy commitments. However, countries like Turkey which have depended heavily on one country alone or a group of countries within the same block for foreign aid have not had much room for maneuvering their foreign policy.

The information given in the previous pages reveals the extent of Turkey's dependence on external resources. The transfer of external resources has been between four and five percent of Turkey's gross national product, and was well over fifty percent of Turkey's foreign exchange earnings annually, not taking into account the military grants. A drastic reduction in the amount of these transfers could seriously impair the functioning of the economy, at least, in the short run. It would also dictate a lower rate of growth and employment. Discontinuation of resource transfers requires careful consideration of the potential problems likely to arise from it and certainly calls for cautious planning and gradual phasing out. But as long as external transfers are forthcoming, many governments are reluctant to take the necessary steps to achieve a "viable" economy, despite their pronounced intentions to do so.

Turkey has accumulated a large foreign debt on account of her heavy borrowing abroad. The Turkish outstanding foreign debt as of December 1970 was 2.5 billion dollars, payable through the year 2018. This amount does not include approximately 900 million dollars interest. The servicing of this debt will exceed 200 million dollars annually in the next several years. This shows that even if resource transfers for current needs are reduced drastically, Turkey's obligation on the existing debts remains quite high, amounting to no less than one-third of her current export earnings.

Management of foreign debt has become an important instrument of the aid diplomacy. Turkey is not the only country, of course, which has a debt repayment problem. No fewer than ten other countries have even more severe debt servicing problems. The usual practice is for the creditors to carefully follow the debt servicing capacity of the recipients, and at times rearrange their scheduling of payments, especially in case of serious difficulties. Thus the management of the existing debt is similar to aid-giving as far as the achievement of short and long-range foreign policy objectives is concerned. From the recipient's point of view this situation adds new weight to their problems originating in dependence on external resources. Two such rescheduling exercises were performed on the Turkish debts. One of them was in 1959 and the second took place in 1965.

As noted earlier, the foreign policy implications of external borrowing were not fully understood in Turkey in the 1950's, when both donor and recipient were interested mainly in establishing closer political links. The Turkish government was happy to be closely associated with the Western powers while receiving assistance, while the United States government was pleased to have a staunch ally in a strategic area. But after 1964, following the Cyprus crisis, the implication of such a dependence was felt by the Turkish government and it has given place to extensive debate among intellectuals. Since then Turkey has tried to diversify her economic relations, to expand her commercial ties and render more flexible her foreign policy by establishing better communication with the Eastern bloc and non-aligned countries.

In conclusion it should be reemphasized that the present state of heavy dependence on external resource transfers seriously limits Turkey's ability to pursue a more flexible foreign policy suited to her interests, and narrows her options. If the government considers the attainment of such flexibility a high priority, then the factors which contribute to Turkey's dependence on external transfers will have to be carefully identified and measures taken to remove them, if not in the short run, at least in a foreseeable future.

PRESIDENTS, PRIME MINISTERS AND FOREIGN MINISTERS OF TURKEY — 1938-1974

	PRESIDENTS	PREMIERS	FOREIGN MINISTERS
1938-39	İsmet İnönü	Refik Saydam	Şükrü Saracoğlu
1943	İsmet İnönü	Şükrü Saracoğlu	Numan Menemencioğlu
1944	İsmet İnönü	Şükrü Saracoğlu	Hasan Saka
1946	İsmet İnönü	Recep Peker	Hasan Saka
1947	İsmet İnönü	Hasan Saka	Necmettin Sadak
1949	İsmet İnönü	Şemseddin Günaltay	Necmettin Sadak
1950	Celâl Bayar	Adnan Menderes	Fuat Köprülü
1955	Celâl Bayar	Adnan Menderes	Adnan Menderes
1956	Celâl Bayar	Adnan Menderes	Fuat Köprülü
1957	Celâl Bayar	Adnan Menderes	Ethem Menderes
1958	Celâl Bayar	Adnan Menderes	Fatin Rüştü Zorlu
1960-61	Cemal Gürsel	Cemal Gürsel	Selim Sarper
1961	Cemal Gürsel	İsmet İnönü	Feridun Cemal Erkin
1965	Cemal Gürsel	Suat Hayri Ürgüplü	Hasan Işık
1965	Cemal Gürsel	Süleyman Demirel	İhsan Sabri Çağlayangil
1966	Cevdet Sunay	Süleyman Demirel	İhsan Sabri Çağlayangil
1971	Cevdet Sunay	Nihat Erim	Osman Olçay
1972	Cevdet Sunay	Nihat Erim-- Ferit Melen	Halük Bayülken
1973	Fahri Korutürk	Bülent Ecevit	Turan Güneş
1974	Fahri Korutürk	Sadi Irmak	Melih Esenbel

SELECTED BIBLIOGRAPHY ON TURKISH FOREIGN POLICY WITH EMPHASIS ON THE PERIOD, 1950-74

Ağaoğlu, Samet. *Sovyet Rusya İnparatorluğu* (Soviet Russian Empire). Istanbul, 1967.

"American Foreign Aid to Turkey for 1962." *Turkish Economic Review*, May/June 1963.

Andrei, D. Saharov. *Sovyet Rusya' da Düsünce Özgürlügü ve Barış İçinde Yanyana Yaşama* (Freedom of Thought and Peaceful Co-existence in the Soviet Union). Tr. Necdet Sander, Istanbul, 1969.

Aralov, Semen Ivanovic. *Bir Sovyet Diplomatnın Türkiye Hatıraları* (Turkish Memoirs of a Soviet Diplomat). Tr. Hasan Ali Ediz, Istanbul, 1967.

Arfa, Hassan. *The Kurds: An Historical and Political Study* London, 1966.

Armaoğlu, Fahir H. "Turkey and the United States: A New Alliance," *The Turkish Yearbook of International Relations*, 1965.

Armstrong, H. F. "Eisenhower's Right Flank," *Foreign Affairs*, 29, July 1951.

"Assembly Debates, Syrian Complaints Against Turkey; with news story," *United Nations Review* 4, December, 1957.

Ataov, Türkkaya. *Turkish Foreign Policy, 1939-1945*, Ankara, 1965.

Aziz, Aysel. "1964 Yılında Kıbrıs Buhranı ve Sovyetler Birliği," (Cyprus Crisis in 1964 and the Soviet Union), *Siyasal Bilgiler Fakültesi Dergisi*, September, 1969.

Aziz, Aysel. "Sovyetlerin Kıbrıs Tutumları," (Soviet Attitudes on Cyprus), *Siyasal Bilgiler Fakültesi Dergisi*, December 1969.

Ballis, William B. "Soviet-Turkish Relations During the Decade 1953-1963," *Institute for the Study of the USSR Bulletin*, 11. September 1964.

Batu, Hâmit. "La politique étrangère de la Turquie," *Turkish Yearbook of International Relations*, Ankara 1964.

Bayülken, Ümit Halûk. "Turkish Minorities in Greece," *Turkish Yearbook of International Relations*, Ankara 1963.

Bilsel, Cemil. "The Turkish Straits in the Light of Recent Turkish-Soviet Russian Correspondence," *American Journal of International Law*, October 1947.

Bishop, Donald G. (ed.). *Soviet Foreign Relations, Documents and Readings*, Syracuse, New York, 1952.

Black, Joseph E. and Kenneth W. Thompson (eds.). *Foreign Policies in a World of Change*, New York, 1963.

Burr, M. "Turkey and Bulgaria," *Fortnightly*, 176, August 1951. Reply, B.V. Koussev, *Fortnightly*, 176, October 1951.

Campbell, John C. *Defense of the Middle East; Problems of American Policy*, New York, 1958.

Campbell, John C. *The Middle East in the Muted Cold War*, Denver, Colorado, 1964-65.

"Capital Movements: Import of capital into Turkey; Capital exports from Turkey; Transfer of wealth to Turkey; Transfer of wealth abroad; Blocking of funds; Releasing of blocked funds (decree)," *Turkish Economic Review*, 4. September 1963.

"Correspondence between President Johnson and Prime Minister Inönü, June, 1964, as released by the White House, January 15, 1966 (text)," *Middle East Journal*, 20, Summer 1966.

Crouzet, François *Le Conflit de Chypre 1946-1959*, 2 vols. Brussels 1973.

The Cyprus Question, Chicago, 1965. [Institute of Greek-American Historical Studies].

The Cyprus Dilemma, New York (Institute for Mediterranean Affairs), 1969.
Dekmijian, R.H. "Soviet-Turkish Relations and Politics in the Armenian SSR," *Soviet Studies,* 19, April 1968.
Deshocquets, Claude. "Turkey and Global Strategy," *Military Review,* 41, June 1961. (tr. from *Revue de defense nationale,* 17, 1961).
Devereux, Robert. "Turkey and the Baghdad Pact (Question of Military and Political Value of the Pact to Turkey)," *SAIS Review,* 3, Autumn 1958.
Dışişleri Bakanlığı. *Türk-Sovyet İlişkileri,* Ankara, 1965-66.
Documents on International Affairs, London, 1936-1958.
Dodd, C.H. *Politics and Government in Turkey,* Berkeley, 1969.
Dranov, B. *Chernomorskie Prolivy-Mezhdunarodno-pravovoi rezhim* (The Black Sea Straits-International-legal regime), Moscow, 1948.
Davison, R. "The Turkish Republic: Fifty Years of Peace." *World Aff.,* 136, no. 2, (1973).
Edmonds, Martin and John Skitt. "Current Soviet Maritime Strategy and NATO," *International Affairs,* January 1969.
Dufour, M. "La Turquie et l'Union Sovietique." *Europe Sud-Est,* 3 (1972).
Ehrlich, Thomas, *Cyprus, 1958-1967.* London, 1974.
Eren, Nuri. "Middle East and Turkey in World Affairs," *Annals of the American Academy of Political Science,* 276, July 1951.
Erkin, F.C. "Turkey's Foreign Policy," *Academy of Political Science Proceedings,* 24, January 1952.
Erkin, Feridun Cemal. *Les Relations Turco-Soviétiques et la Question des Détroits,* Ankara, 1968. (Turkish version available).
Esmer, Ahmed Şükrü. "The Straits: Crux of World Politics," *Foreign Affairs,* Jan. 1947.
Esmer, Ahmed Şükrü. "Cyprus, Past and Present," *Turkish Yearbook of International Relations,* Ankara 1962.
Evans, Laurence. *U.S. Policy and the Partition of Turkey, 1914-1924.* Baltimore 1965.
Fernau, Friedrich-Wilhelm. "Nachbarschaft an Schwarzen Meer. Wendepunkte in den türkisch-sowjetischen Beziehungen," *Europa-Archiv,* September, 1967.
"Foreign capital in Turkey: Area distribution, countries of origin and industrial distribution of foreign capital in Turkey, 1951-64, and the effect of foreign capital on the country's economy." *Turkish Economic Review,* 7. September/October, 1966.
Friedman, J.R., *et. al. Alliance in International Politics,* Boston: 1970.
Gallman, Waldemar, Jr. *Iraq Under General Nuri,* Baltimore, Md., 1964.
Gilead, B. "Turkish-Egyptian Relations 1952-57," *Middle East Affairs,* 10, November, 1959.
Gönlübol, Mehmet. *Turkey in the U.S.: A Legal and Political Appraisal.* Ankara, 1960.
Gönlübol, Mehmet. and Halûk Ülman. "Türk Dış Politikasının Yirmi Yılı, 1945-1965," (The Twenty Years of Turkish Foreign Affairs), *Siyasal Bilgiler Fakültesi Dergisi,* March, 1966.
Grigoreyv, K. "Soviet-Turkish Relations," *International Affairs,* Moscow, April 1956.
Harris, George S. *The Origins of Communism in Turkey,* Stanford, California, 1967.
Harris, George S. *Troubled Alliance: Turkish-American Problems in Historical Perspective,* 1945-1971. Washington, D.C. 1972.
Hartmann, Hans Walter. *Die auswärtige Politik der Türkei, 1923-1940,* Zurich, 1941.
Heinze, Christian. "The Cyprus Conflict: The Western Peace System is Put to Test," *Turkish Yearbook of International Relations,* 1963.
Hotlinger, A. "The Cyprus Complex." *Swiss Rev. of World Aff.,* 22, no. 3 (June 1972).

Howard, Harry N. "Changes in Turkey," *Current History*, May 1965.
Howard, Harry N. "Development of U.S. Policy in the Near East, South Asia, and Africa During 1955," *U.S. Department of State Bulletin*, 34, March 26, 1956.
Howard, Harry N. "Germany, The Soviet Union and Turkey During World War II," *Departent of State Bulletin*, July 18, 1948.
Howard, Harry N. *The Partition of Turkey: A Diplomatic History, 1913-1923*. New York, 1966.
Howard, Harry N. "The Turkish Straits after World War II: Problems and Prospects," *Balkan Studies*, II, 1970.
Howard, Harry N. "The United States and the Question of the Turkish Straits," *Middle East Journal*, January 1947.
Howard, Harry N. "The United States and Turkey: American Policy in the Straits Question, 1914-1963," *Balkan Studies*, IV, 1963.
Hurewitz, J.C. *Diplomacy in the Near and Middle East: A Documentary Record, 1535-1914*, Vol. I, 1914-1956, Vol. II, Princeton, 1956.
Hurewitz, J.C. "Russia and the Turkish Straits," *World Politics*, July 1962.
Iatrides, John O. *Balkan Triangle: Birth and Decline of an Alliance Across Ideological Boundaries*, The Hague, 1968.
Jäschke, Gotthard. *Die Türkei in Den Jahren 1942-1951*, Wiesbaden, 1955.
Jäschke, Gotthard. *Die Türkei in Den Jahren 1952-1961*, Wiesbaden, 1965.
Karpat, Kemal H. "Ideology in Turkey After the Revolution of 1960," *Turkish Yearbook of International Relations*, 1965.
Karpat, Kemal H. "The International Relations of Turkey," (Review Article), *International Middle East Journal*, 2, 1972.
Karpat, Kemal (ed.). *Political and Social Thought in the Contemporary Middle East*, New York, 1968.
Karpat, Kemal H. "Recent Political Developments in Turkey and Their Social Background," *International Affairs*, July 1962.
Karpat, Kemal H. *Turkey's Politics. The Transition to a Multi-Party System*, Princeton, N.J. 1959.
Karpat, Kemal H. *Social Change and Politics in Turkey*, Leiden 1973.
Kazancıgil, A. "Die Türkei und die Entwicklung im *Ostlichen Mittelmeer*." *Europa Archiv*, 28, no. 12 (1973).
Kılıç, Altemur. *Turkey and the World*, Washington, D.C., 1959.
Krecker, Lothar, *Deutschland und die Türkei im Zweiten Weltkrieg*. Frankfort am Main: 1964.
Kürkçüoğlu, Omer E. "Recent Developments in Turkey's Middle East Policy," *Dıs Politika* (Foreign Policy), June 1971.
Kyriakides, Stanley. *Cyprus: Constitutionalism and Crisis Government*, Philadelphia, Pa., 1968.
Laqueur, Walter. *The Struggle for the Middle East: The Soviet Union in the Mediterranean, 1958-1968*, New York, 1968.
Lenczowski, George. *United States Interests in the Middle East*, Washington, D.C., 1968.
Leonidov, A. "Story of Turkish Diplomacy," *New Times*, Moscow, April 8, April 15, 1964.
Luke, Sir Harry. *Cyprus*, 2nd ed., London, 1965.
Mango, A.J.A. "Turkey and the Middle East," *Political Quarterly*, 28, April 15, 1957.
McGhee, G.C. "Private Enterprise in Turkish-American Relations," *U.S. Department of State Bulletin*, 27, October 13, 1952.
McGhee, George C. "Turkey Joins the West" *Foreign Affairs*, July 1954.
Miller, Linda B. *Cyprus. The Law and Politics of Civil Strife*. Cambridge, Mass., 1968.

Novel, E. "October 1973: Turkey Celebrates the 50th Anniversary of the Founding of the Republic." *NATO R.*, 21, no. 5 (1973).
O'Ballance, E. "Turkish Contribution (summary of Turkey's war potential; size, equipment, quality of armed forces)," *Army Quarterly*, 69, January 1955.
Olcay, Osman. "Turkey's Foreign Policy," *Dış Politika* (Foreign Policy), June 1971.
Okçün, A. Gündüz. *A Guide to Turkish Treaties*, Ankara, 1966.
Oran, Baskın. "Türkiye 'nin 'Kuzeydeki Büyük Komşu' Sorunu Nedir? Türk-Sovyet Ilişkileri, 1939-1970," (What is the Big Neighbor Problem in the North? Turkish Soviet Relations, 1939-1970), *Siyasal Bilgiler Fakültesi Dergisi*, March 1970.
Organization for European Economic Cooperation. *The work of the conference on financial assistance to Turkey and on Turkish debts: memorandum by the secretariat of OEEC; agreement on commercial debts owed by residents of Turkey*, August, 1959.
Peretz, Don. "Self-deception in American Foreign Policy: The Struggle in Turkey," *Progressive*, 24, August 1960.
Perlmann, M. "Turkey's Diplomatic Offensive," *Middle Eastern Affairs*, 6, March 1955.
Philalethes, M. "The Cyprus Problem in Historical Perspective." *Cyprus Today*, 9, no. 3 (Jl-S, 171).
Pipes, Richard E. "Muslims of Soviet Central Asia," *The Middle East Journal*, Spring and Summer 1955.
Pipinellis, P. "Greco-Turkish Feud Revived," *Foreign Affairs*, 37, January 1959.
Psomiades, Harry J. *The Eastern Question: The Last Phase. A Study of Greek-Turkish Diplomacy*, Salonika (Greece), 1968.
Ramazani, Rouhollah K. *The Northern Tier: Afghanistan, Iran and Turkey*, Princeton, 1966.
Robinson, Richard D. *The First Turkish Republic: A Case Study in National Development*, Cambridge, Mass., 1963.
Rohn, Peter H. "Turkish Treaties in Global Perspective," *Turkish Yearbook of International Relations*, 1965.
Routh, D.A. "The Montreux Convention Regarding the Regime of the Black Sea Straits," *Survey of International Affairs, 1936*, London, 1937.
Rustow, D.A. "The Foreign Policy of the Turkish Republic," *Foreign Policy in World Politics* (R.C. Macridis, ed., New York 1958).
Sadak, Necmeddin. "Turkey Faces the Soviets," *Foreign Affairs*, April 1949.
Sanjian, A.K. "Sanjak of Alexandretta (Hatay): Its Impact on Turkish-Syrian Relations (1939-56)," *Middle East Journal*, 10, Fall 1956.
Sar, Cem. "L'association entre la Communauté Economique Européenne et la Turquie," *Turkish Yearbook of International Affairs*, Ankara 1962.
Schram, S.R. "L'U.R.S.S. et la Chine Devant la Revolution Turque," *Orient*, Vol. 14, 1960.
Seyda, M. "Turkey's Foreign Trade, 1949-1958: distribution of commercial exchanges by monetary areas, trade balance, relative order," *Turkish Economic Review*, 1, February 1960.
Skinner, C. Wickham. "Test Case in Turkey: the histories of seven American manufacturing subsidiaries, all active in Turkey for five years or more, furnish examples of the hazards and rewards of foreign investment," *California Management Review*, 6, Spring 1964.
Soysal, Ismail. *Türkiyenin Dış Münasebetleriyle Ilgili Başlıca Siyasi Andlaşmalar*, Main International Treaties of Turkey, Ankara, 1965.
Spyridakis, C. *A Brief History of Cyprus*. Chicago, 1964.
Survey of International Affairs, 1951 through 1963, London, 1954-1965.

Tachau, Frank, and Ulman, A. Halûk "Dilemmas of Turkish Politics," *Turkish Yearbook of International Relations*, Ankara 1962.
Tachau, Frank. "The Face of Turkish Nationalism as Reflected in the Cyprus Dispute," *Middle East Journal*, Summer, 1959.
Tansky, Leo. *U.S. and U.S.S.R. Aid to Developing Countries: A Comparative Study of India, Turkey, and the U.A.R.*, New York, 1967.
Tarakcı, Akif. *Sovyetler Birliği 'nin Bugünkü Türkiye Politikas* (The Soviet Policy Towards Turkey Today) Ankara, 1969.
Tekiner, Süleyman. "Soviet-Turkish Relations and Kosygin's Trip to Turkey (Dec. 1966)," *Institute for the Study of the USSR Bulletin*, 14, March 1967.
Thomas, Lewis V., and Richard N. Frey. *The United States and Turkey and Iran*, Cambridge, Mass., 1951.
Thornburg, Max Weston, Graham Spry, and George Soule. *Turkey: An Economic Appraisal*, New York, 1949.
Trask, Roger R. "U.S. and Turkish Nationalism: investment and technical aid during the Ataturk era," *Business History Review*, 38, Spring 1964.
Trask, Roger R. *The United States Response to Turkish Nationalism and Reform, 1914-1939*, Minneapolis, 1971.
Tuncer, Selahattin. "U.S. Aid To Turkey: total aid to date exceeds one billion, 300 million dollars," *Turkish Economic Review*, 2, March 1961.
Türkeş, Alparslan. *Dış Politikamız ve Kıbrıs* (Our Foreign Policy and Cyprus), Istanbul, 1966.
"Turkey and the Cyprus Crisis," *World Today* 30, no. 8 (1974) 368-71.
"Turkey and U.S. Reaffirm Bonds of Friendship and Cooperation: Exchange of Greetings and Exchange of Toasts, April 3, 1967, with Joint Communique, C. Sunay, LBJ," *U.S. Department of State Bulletin*, 56, April 24, 1967.
"Turco-Egyptian Flirtation of Autumn 1954," *World Today*, 12, November 1956.
"Turkish Foreign Policy (background and recent trends: relations with the Arabs, Russia and the West)," *Egyptian Economic and Political Review*, 5, Feb/March 1959.
Rostow, F.V. "U.S. and Turkey, Partners in World Security; address," *U.S. Department of State Bulletin*, 58, April 29, 1968.
Ulman, A.H. and R.H. Dekmijian, "Changing Patterns in Turkey's Foreign Policy, 1959-67," *Orbis*, 11, Fall 1967.
Ulman, A.H., "Türk Dış Politikasına Yön Veren Etkenler (1923-1968)" (Conditioning Factors of Turkish Foreign Policy, 1923-1968), *Siyasal Bilgiler Fakültesi Dergisi*, 23 (1968).
Ulman, A. Halûk. "Türk ulusal savunması üzerine düşünceler," (Thoughts Concerning Turkish National Defense), *Siyasal Bilgiler Fakültesi Dergisi*, 21 (1967).
U.S. Department of State Bulletin Washington, D.C., 1946-1971.
Uyguner, Muzaffer. "Question of Foreign Capital: foreign investment in Turkey in 1964 amounted to 266 million liras," *Turkish Economic Review*, 7, May/June 1966.
Vali, Ferenc A. *Bridge Across the Bosporus: The Foreign Policy of Turkey*, Baltimore, 1971.
Vali, Ferenc A. *The Turkish Straits and NATO*, Stanford, 1971.
Vere-Hodge, Edward Reginald. *Turkish Foreign Policy, 1918-1948*, Ambilly-Annemasse, 1950.
Wadsworth, G. "Military Aid to Turkey," *U.S. Department of State Bulletin*, 22, June 26, 1950.
Weisband, Edward. *Turkish Foreign Policy, 1943-1945: Small State Diplomacy and Great Power Politics*. Princeton, N.J., 1973.

Xydis, Stephen G. *Cyprus: Conflict and Conciliation, 1954-58*, Columbus, Ohio, 1967.
Xydis, S.G. "A Note on Naomi Rosenbaum's Success in Foreign Policy: the British in Cyprus, 1878-1960." *Canadian Journal of Political Science*, 4, no. 3 (summer 1971).
Xydis, S.G. "New Light on the Big Three Crisis Over Turkey in 1945," *Middle East Journal*, 14, Fall 1960.
Xydis, S.G. *Cyprus, Reluctant Republic*.
Yegenoğlu, Özgür. *Orta Doğu Ülkeleri ile Ticari Ilişkilerimiz*, (Our Commercial Relations with Middle East Countries), Ankara, 1968.
Zorlu, F.R. "Turkish View of World Affairs; address, July 1, 1959," *Vital Speeches*, 25, September 1, 1959.

INDEX

Abdulhamit II (Sultan) 108
Acheson (Dean) Plan 163–164
Afghani, J. 110
Aid – Consortium to Turkey 214–216, 219
AKEL 193
Arabs 108–133
Ali, Mehmet 108
Aras, Tevfik Rüştü 82
Ataturk – Mustafa Kemal 4, 15, 16, 25, 52, 111, 210
Azam Paşa 115

Baghdad Pact 30, 55, 116
Balkan Defense Pact 89
Balkan Entente 88
Bandung Conference of 1955 30, 118
Basic Agreement 38–39
Bilateral Agreements 33–38
Bissios, Dimitri 204
Bourgiba, Habib 126

Çaglayangil, Ihsan Sabri 94
Cahun, Leon 113
Caramanlis, Constantin 204
Clerides, Glafcos or Glafkos 193, 200
Committee of Union and Progress 77, 110
Common Market 1
Congress of Eastern Peoples – 1920 75
Constitution (1961) 7
Crimean War (1853) 108
Cypriot National Guard 191
Cyprus Conflict 1954–56, 13 1967–74 91–92, – American Reaction 18, 163, 197

Defense Cooperation Agreement 65
Demirel, Suleyman 10, 64, 68, 127
Democratic Party 17, 22, 84, 212
Denktaş, Rauf 194

Ecevit, Bülent 69, 106, 197, 203
Eisenhower Doctrine 1, 55, 120
Enosis 136
EOKA–B 139, 193, 196
Erim, Nihat 10, 23, 25, 64, 68–69 (and opium production), 133
Erkin, Feridun Cemal 90
Export – Import Bank 5

First Grand National Assembly, 1920–22 16
"Flexible responses" theory of 43, 62–63

İnönü, Ismet 17, 19, 22, 40, 87
Ioannides, General 191, 194
Israel, 108–133
Işık, Hasan 94

Johnson, Pres. "letter" on "Cyprus" 59–60
Justice Party 22, 32, 64, 94, 97

Kamil, Mustafa 110
Keban Dam 111
Kırdar, Lutfi 86
Köprülü, Fuat 116, 137
Küçük, Fazıl 91

Lausanne Conference 81, 136
London Conference of 1955–56 140–141
London and Zurich Agreements 13, 59, 145, 150–151

Macmillan Plan 144, 147
Macomber, William B. 197
Makarios, Archbishop 14, 59, 186, 191-196, 204-5
Marshall Plan 13, 53
McNaughton, John 65
Menderes, Adnan 6, 41, 56, 84–85 (foreign policy of), 138
Military Facilities Agreement 35, 36
Mujahids 191
Modernization (as state principle) 4–5
Montreaux Convention 10, 13, 74, 82
Mousul – Hatay problem 112
Mutual Assistance Treaty 83, 212

National Salvation Party 11
National Unity Committee 14

Nicosia Treaties of 1960 13, 18

OECD 1
OEEC 211
Opium (as a problem of foreign relations) 67–70

Pachachi, Adnan 128
Pan-Islamism 108, 109–111
Pan-Turansim 77
Paris Treaty of 1856 168
People's Houses 78
Plaza, Galo 164–165
Provisional Turkish Administration 177
Public Debt Administration 52

Radcliffe (draft constitution) 145–146
Republican Party, People's 7, 22
Revolutionary Students Federation 63

Saadabad Pact 112
Sabbatai, Zevi 113
Sami, Bekir 81
Sampson, Nikos 71, 186, 196
Sarper, Selim 87, 138
Sisco, Joseph 197

State Planning Organization – Turkey 67, 214
Status of Forces Agreement 35

Tasca, Henry J. 198
Treaty of Friendship (with USSR) 2, 74, 81
Treaty of Nonaggression & Neutrality 81
Truman Doctrine 1–13, 33, 52
Turkish Labor Party 8, 61, 65
Turkish Workers' Party 21

United Arab Republic 121
UN Resolution on Cyprus, 1964 160–161
Ürgüplü, Suat Hayri 88, 94

Vambery, A. 113
Vance, Cyrus 71, 176

Warsaw Pact 89

Young Ottomans 108

Zorlu, Fatin Rüştü 86